# CROSSING THE LINE

*Violence and Sexual Assault in
Canada's National Sport*

Laura Robinson

M&S

**Canadian Cataloguing in Publication Data**

Robinson, Laura
    Crossing the line : violence and sexual assault in Canada's national sport

Includes bibliographical references.
ISBN 0-7710-7560-X

1. Hockey players – Sexual behavior.   2. Sexually abused teenagers.
3. Violence in sports.   I. Title.

GV847.R56 1998      796.962´62      C98-930123-0

Set in Bembo by M&S, Toronto

We acknowledge the financial support of the Government of Canada through the Book Publishing Industry Development Program for our publishing activities. We further acknowledge the support of the Canada Council for the Arts and the Ontario Arts Council for our publishing program.

Printed and bound in Canada

McClelland & Stewart Inc.
*The Canadian Publishers*
481 University Avenue
Toronto, Ontario
M5G 2E9

1 2 3 4 5      02 01 00 99 98

Crossing the Line

This book is dedicated to my late parents,
June Eleanor Robinson and Arthur Abraham Robinson

# Contents

# Acknowledgements

This book would not have been possible without the support and assistance of the following people: Anne Collins, the first editor to commission this story, and Barbara Moon for continuing to fight for it as a magazine piece from 1992 to 1995. Leslie Fruman, Sheila Pin, and Lyndon McIntyre at "the fifth estate" for their tireless work on the documentary "Thin Ice," and Susan Teskey, David Studor, and Michael Hughes for more CBC support. Special thanks to Alberto Manguel for insisting that this book be written in the first place. Thanks also to Grant Fleming, Terry McLeod, Carol McNeil, Kenneth Bell, and Garth Matiery, all of the CBC; Bill Currie of the *Chatham Daily News*; Eric Francis of the *Calgary Sun*; Allan Adams of the *Toronto Star*; Carl Nelson of the *Guelph Mercury*; Terry Craig and Vance Oliver, formerly of the *Saskatoon Star Phoenix*; David Brownridge, formerly of the *Swift Current Star*; Michele Landsberg of the *Toronto Star*; and the other journalists across Canada who generously shared files and clippings.

Thanks also to Susan Milne and her family, Sandi Kirby, Don Smith, Steven Ortiz, Don Sabo, Greg Malszecki, Jennifer Joyner, John McMurtry, Fred Mathews, Naomi Levine, Linda Campbell, Peggy Reeves Sanday, Marg McNeill, Allan Klein, Brian Pronger, Michelle Schreyer, Danielle Aubrey, Brian Bell, Glen McKay, Bruce Brown, Lloyd Graham, Ian McLean, Rick Newstead, Todd Ternovan, Murray Walter, Ron McDonald, Bryna Coppel-Park, John Campbell, Jill

Spelliscy, and Mary Lissel for their professional guidance and support. Thanks to Brenda, Joe, and Jessie Zeman, Karen Strong, Joanne Lajambe, Kelly Anne and Ken Carter-Erdman, and Dave Ellis for excellent accommodation and meals while this book was researched, and to Karen, Kelly Anne, Maria, Jeanette, Peter, Michael, Susan, and Ruth for skiing with me when I needed a break. Thank you to Syd Paul for telling me about Swift Current in the first place.

Special thanks to Mary MacNutt, Chris Winter, Bronwyn Drainie, Shirley and Paul Bruer, and Brian, Tim, and Jan Warrilow for listening to these stories, and to my agent, Jennifer Barclay, and especially my editor, Alex Schultz, for believing in this book. Most importantly, sincere thanks to the young people who were brave enough to talk about what happened to them in the hope of slowing the tide of abuse children and young adults continue to suffer.

---

# The Penalty Box

Canadian winters are long and cold. Ice forms in most of the country by late October and stays well into spring, and there is a time for all Canadians in the darkest of winter when we are sure spring will never arrive. We either live winter out or perish, and if there is any communal way to help endure, even celebrate, the season, it is through the game of hockey.

Many of us ski, both Nordic and alpine; curling is another popular activity; and millions ice-skate purely for pleasure, with no thought of stick or puck. But compared to hockey, these winter sports are intimate acts that connect individuals to the snow and ice. They are not seen as being distinctively Canadian, as a way in which this country is defined, both at home and abroad. Only hockey enjoys this status.

Travel across Canada in winter and two characteristics of the country will quickly become apparent. One is its vastness; Canada's geography is of such great variety, it is easy to forget it is all one country. The second characteristic is that after miles and miles of unbroken natural landscape, whenever a small town or city finally appears, you are guaranteed to find within that settlement at least one hockey arena. It could be Chicoutimi, Quebec, where along the sidewalks there are paths tunnelled through the snow, leading to the arena where the Saguenéens junior team plays. It could be Lion's Head, in the limestone landscape of Ontario's Bruce Peninsula, wracked by snowsqualls each year, and home of the Peninsula Panthers in the senior men's league. It could be the village of La Brett, tucked into the grandness of Saskatchewan's Qu'Appelle Valley, where at dusk the snow turns blue, and the sky even bluer, while at the arena the Eagles hone their skills. Or it could be any of the thousands of communities in between. Alongside the schools and churches and homes across the country, the hockey arena is an essential part of every town's life.

Hockey is a wonderful, traditionally Canadian game. This book does not try to persuade the reader that the sport itself is problematic, or that most coaches and players are, in fact, predators. But it does ask the reader to examine the male-only, violent, multimillion-dollar subculture of rep hockey (A, AA, and AAA), from ages eight to seventeen, and major-junior hockey, from ages sixteen to twenty (and by extension the NHL), and consider what has happened to a game so dear to so many people's hearts.

Young men are put in a precarious position in this subculture. Critics call its undemocratic practices feudal – certainly, they mimic other traditionally male models of hierarchy, such as churches, the military, and, more recently, gangs. Added to this subculture is the modern know-how of marketing experts, who reduce young men to commodities that are bought and sold on the whim of older men who stand to make money by signing or trading the right player. Promotional material from the Canadian Hockey League (CHL) speaks of products and packages when they refer to human beings.[1] And despite his youth, a player better get used to this treatment if he wants to stay in the system. Families, friends, home towns are not considered when a player is bought or sold.

No one has done any scientific studies to determine whether this system produces the best-quality athlete and human being. William

Houston's insightful series in the *Globe and Mail* during the winters of 1997 and 1998 certainly cast serious doubt on the wisdom of turning teenage boys into wholesale goods. Unfortunately, there is little hope for change. The CHL does not serve the needs of the players, but rather the appetite of an almost exclusively male-dominated market for the physical abilities of young men. Junior hockey would look quite different if it served the needs of Canadian youth.

It would also look quite different if it really did seek to produce the top players in the world. But as the 1997 Junior World Hockey Championships and the 1998 Winter Olympics clearly demonstrated, this is not the case. Canada sent what was supposed to be a fine junior team to the World Championships. While a few of the very best players were not released by their NHL franchises, it was thought there was enough depth within the junior ranks to field a gold-medal team. Besides, other countries were missing some of their best players. Certain European stars were penalized by their own federations for not attending training camps and choosing to play in the NHL instead, and they, too, were left off the roster.

While the Canadian Hockey Association (CHA) considered it was possible the team might not bring home the gold, a podium finish was taken for granted. But the team finished almost as far away from the podium as was possible, placing eighth out of ten teams. Their final loss was to Kazakhstan, a team that couldn't afford matching pants and socks, and skated on rusty blades.

The poor showing was a fluke, protested the guardians of the status quo in junior hockey. The team got off on the wrong foot and never recovered. Canada, they claimed, still produced the best hockey players in the world. Then the Nagano Olympics came along, and what was assumed would be a cakewalk for the Canadians turned into a sporting disaster. Canada lost to the Czech Republic in the game that decided who would meet the Russians to contest the gold medal, and then lost again to Finland for the bronze. The nation that defines itself by the game of hockey was out of the medals. What went wrong?

Canada was so convinced it had the best system to build young hockey players that there was no room for self-doubt, and no widening of the lens even to look at the kind of programs in place in other countries. But in fact Canada would do well to take a look at what is going on elsewhere. According to International Ice Hockey Federation statistics, while Canada has 3.5 times as many young people involved in organized hockey than does Sweden, Finland, Russia, the Czech Republic, and Slovakia *combined*, it is quickly losing pace with these same countries in terms of top players. In 1988, 83 per cent of the NHL first all-star team was Canadian, and 17 per cent was European. In 1997, the breakdown was 66 and 33 per cent respectively. The 1998 projected first all-star team is as follows: right wing, either Teemu Selanne, a Finn, or Jaromir Jagr, a Czech; centre, Peter Forsberg, a Swede; left wing, John LeClair, an American; defence, Sergei Zubov, a Russian, and Nicklas Lidstrom, a Swede; goal, either Martin Brodeur, a Canadian, or Dominik Hasek, a Czech.

The statistics that follow put this in even clearer perspective. Even though Canadians amounted to 61 per cent of the NHL in the 1996-97 season – while Europeans amounted to 20 per cent – only three Canadians under thirty years old placed among the top twenty NHL scorers, compared to five Europeans. In the 1997-98 season the disparity was even greater, with four Canadians under thirty in the top twenty, compared to seven Europeans.

The Stanley Cup can no longer be said to be the pinnacle of great hockey. NHL hockey is simply not up to the standard played in the elite leagues of Europe today. The Europeans are producing more talented athletes, and they don't see the need to draft and trade sixteen-year-old boys.

The Canadian system would be defensible if it were succeeding in other ways – if it were giving young players a terrific education, for instance, as the U.S. college hockey system claims to do. But a few people outside of the CHL would make those claims for Canadian junior hockey, where going to class and studying hard comes second – often a very distant second – to the team's life in the arena and on the road.

Perhaps we could excuse a system that wasn't turning out top hockey players or bright academics if it were instilling values that would help young men be better human beings, especially in their relationships with women, but nothing could be further from the truth. Instead, in the social context of junior hockey, young men see themselves treated as objects, and consequently readily objectify young women. Sports sociologists talk about the locker room as a "rape culture," a sex-segregated, male-dominated culture that displays a high degree of hostility to, and contempt for, women. Anthropologists have established that tribal societies with these characteristics have high frequencies of sexual violence, including rape, both individual and gang, and that in our society this can be seen amongst fraternity members, for instance, and members of male sports teams.[2]

In the rape culture of the hockey locker room, where females are referred to as "groupies," "puck bunnies," "pucks," and "dirties" among the players, there are also the "designated females": the rookies, the new kids, the more vulnerable boys, who have often, but certainly not always, escaped to junior hockey from abusive or neglectful homes. It is these boys, the most vulnerable and weak (like a woman, to use a common hockey insult), who are most at risk within the hockey subculture. When Sheldon Kennedy, the former Swift Current Broncos player who charged his coach, Graham James, with sexual abuse, talked about his relationship with his father, he said that as a fourteen-year-old, he couldn't leave home fast enough. When he later talked about his relationship with James, he added, "He treated me like I was his wife."

Claims hockey officials make about the game teaching teamwork, self-discipline, and goal-setting recede shamefully in the shadow of what was revealed in the 1996–97 hockey season. It will be remembered like no other, not for the last-minute goal that saved face for a nation, not for the superb finesse of the Great One, not for ancient rivalries between the Leafs and the Canadiens, but for the soul-wrenching honesty of young men, starting with Kennedy and another anonymous player, and their disclosures about Graham James.

In the wake of their revelations, many other players and boys who simply loved the game came forward to tell story after story of abuse. No one will ever be able to watch a hockey game in the same way again. Public relations men like Dave Harris of the Greyhounds in Sault Ste. Marie (who was fired after the 1996–97 season) will no longer find it easy to brush aside allegations of sexual abuse by players and coaches.

What hockey officials and the sports media have yet to recognize is the link between becoming a victim, like Sheldon Kennedy, and learning how to victimize in one's own relationships. Ninety per cent of male victimizers, in a 1992 study done by Winnipeg psychologist Mary Campbell for the city's Catholic Children's Aid Society, had first been victims of sexual abuse.[3] Dr. Fred Mathews of Central Toronto Youth Services, a leading expert on the subject, puts the percentage of victims who become victimizers at 30 per cent – but holds that the percentage is far less if effective therapy is received.[4] Both believe sexual abuse of boys is as common as sexual abuse of girls, and stress that for the victims of abuse the first step in stopping the cycle is to acknowledge their pain and its cause.

We do not know how deeply entrenched the sexual abuse of hockey players by men who control them really is, but Sheldon Kennedy's example allowed a steady stream of victims to come forward expecting to be heard in a safe and compassionate environment. One thing is for certain. The world of hockey with its hierarchical structure, where men decide which boys stay on the team and which ones will be sent home, where bodies are judged and discarded, where violent play is encouraged and even rewarded, where lifelong dreams can be granted or snuffed out, and where the players in turn perpetuate an abusive culture, is, without question, the perfect place for a sexual predator to hide.

This book seeks to answer the most paradoxical of questions. How can the game that defines Canada, that unifies the country in so many ways, that feeds young dreams or merely entertains in the darkest of winter days, also be responsible for the systematic dehumanization of young men and young women?

While damage is being done to the sexual, emotional, and psychological health of hockey players by abuse, and by the coercive, poisoned environment in which it takes place, players, especially major-junior stars, are at the same time accorded a godlike, untouchable status. These young men are prized for their physical prowess, their aggression, strength, and power, that wins games through ability and talent, and also brute force. In the traditional male world of hockey, they are masculinity personified, larger-than-life man-boys swooping into small towns and cities across Canada and the northern United States.

Many of the players, just like the fans, believe the PR about themselves. Since they first stepped out on the ice as little boys and showed their extraordinary talent, they have held the coveted status of male hero in a culture that worships sports heroes of only one sex. They receive what other boys can only dream of, and, like any other privileged male athlete, they become used to getting whatever they want.

It is not surprising, then, that along with sexual-assault charges against coaches and handlers have come charges against players. What should be surprising, though, to Canadians who believe in equality, is how little alarm this has caused the sports media and hockey officials. Certainly, until the abuse happened to a young man, who later made it into the NHL, the attitude was that the girls and women who came forward to police were troublemakers who thought that perhaps if they slept with hockey players they'd make it into the NHL, as a wife or full-time groupie. Meanwhile, the hockey establishment figured boys would be boys, and, if things got a bit messy, they could step in to patch it over. It is very telling indeed that the Players First Policy, announced in August 1997 by the CHL, provides a framework for counselling, investigations, and a 1-800 number players and CHL employees can call if they feel harassed, yet provides no services for girls who have been abused by players.

This book looks at how the many myths of the hockey world have been built up over the years, why they are so sacred, and who they really protect. It also looks at what needs to happen for hockey to achieve the wonderful potential it holds for Canadians.

Each chapter provides case studies to show how dysfunctions in hockey have occurred in different but closely related ways. Chapter One, "Memorial Cup Celebrations," and Chapter Two, "Young Gods," look at abuse of women by young hockey players and how a community can fail to recognize what is going on, even when the abuse occurs right under their noses. These chapters tell the story of Jarret

Reid, a promising athlete with the Sault Greyhounds, who was convicted on sexual and physical abuse charges when police interviewed his former girlfriends. According to the hockey fans in Sault Ste. Marie, their team could do no wrong, and one of the complainants in this case actually had to move away, so great was the pressure on her to shut up.

Chapter Three, "Analysing the Game," breaks the game down, not from a technical perspective, but from a socio-psychological one. It provides the reader with a new and more in-depth analysis than is provided by the hockey media, examining the culture of the locker room and the society that consumes the commodity of hockey.

Chapter Four, "Baptized a Hawk," looks at ritual and sexually abusive initiations of rookie players. The uses of the rituals, the coercive nature of initiations, the secrecy that surrounds them, and the subsequent deviant behaviour of many victimized hockey players is discussed. Interestingly, one of the stories about initiations among the Greyhounds is told by a member of the team who was a rookie when Jarret Reid was the assistant captain. Such patterns of abuse emerge throughout the book, tracing its cyclical nature.

Chapters Five, "When You Know You Just Have to Score," and Six, "The Empty Net: Part One," look at the disturbing phenomenon of hockey teams and gang sex, where several players have sexual intercourse with one female. These cases look at what happens when that female goes to the police with a sexual-assault charge. There is a striking similarity between what happens here and what happens in team initiations. Sexual activity is in a group, it is frequently humiliating for the often quite inexperienced young woman, violent, and highly voyeuristic. Intimacy and respect for women do not exist in these cases.

Chapters Seven, "The Empty Net: Part Two," and Eight, "Covering Up in Swift Current," address the case of coach Graham James, who sexually abused players for years and pleaded guilty in January 1997 after two players, one of them Sheldon Kennedy, came forward. These chapters go well beyond what was described in the media when the story broke, and look at how the practice of "not telling" and the aura of secrecy surrounding abuse allowed James to continue unabated for so many years. It gives evidence that some of James's charges learned from a young age to apply the tricks of his trade for their own ends.

Finally, Chapter Nine, "Changing the Line-up," seeks to find ways in which the game so dear to the hearts of so many Canadians can be reclaimed by them.

This book deals rather explicitly with sexual-assault cases. In almost every one of these instances there was disagreement about whether the alleged victim consented to the sexual activity. The issue of consent is at the heart of most sexual-assault cases that make it to court. Despite the frequency with which this crime is alleged, there is very often a grey area about what consent means and how one might prove it was not given, Guilt – and innocence – hinge on the Crown's ability to show, beyond a reasonable doubt, that consent was not given.

Since that is the case, we have made the decision to name in this book only those sexual assailants who were found guilty in a court of law. In every other case we have kept those accused of serious sexual assaults anonymous, like the equally anonymous victims. The exception to this is complainant Scott McLeod, in Chapter Four, who wanted us to use his real name. To the same end, other identifying details of the cases have sometimes been altered. In every case, however, direct quotes come from court records or from interviews I conducted, and the sources are noted. Despite these disguising shifts in detail, these stories are true – and very disturbing.

Junior hockey, and what we have recently learned about it, presents a complex scenario. Sexual abuse is not just physical; it affects the whole human being. Damage is done to the sexual, emotional, and psychological health of the victim, and also to other group members living in the same poisoned environment. Other athletes in this environment know something is wrong, even if they don't know what it is – and besides, who can risk challenging management when they decide your future?

But as complex as this may be, and while every individual places the line of ethical, honest behaviour at a slightly different place, all victims know when a perpetrator has crossed it. Furthermore, sexual abuse is a horrendous crime, not simply a slip-up in otherwise rigorously honest behaviour. Unfortunately, in sports, where many people in power encourage athletes to cross lines of honesty (if you can check illegally and get away with it, do it), ethical behaviour is often not highly valued. For example, one official, after hearing about sexual-assault charges against a national-team coach, said in astonishment, "I knew he was stealing team equipment and skimming off per diems, but I didn't think he sexually assaulted, too." I would argue that when those coaches cross the line they know exactly what they are doing.

Women athletes have always known when a hug or a kiss from a coach or other male in power goes from a congratulatory gesture to a self-serving grope or lingering-too-long kiss. Interestingly, when the CBC's "the fifth estate" produced "Thin Ice," an hour-long documentary on hockey and sexual abuse, with the exception of the reporter, Lyndon McIntyre, it was an all-female production.

Sport is rife with coaches who believe there is no ethical line for them. Dishing into athletes is one of the perks of the job. But there is also a line for those who are not directly involved with the athlete but are on the board of directors, for instance, and could use their position to advocate on behalf of young people. When such a person knows or suspects there has been less than exemplary behaviour towards a young person in sport, and doesn't try to assist that person or alert police, they too have crossed the line.

"I knew he liked the young girls," said one coach about another, "because he used to meet little hookers at the gates to the athletes' village at the Pan-Am Games, but I didn't really think of him as dishonest." He was referring to a coach charged with three counts of sexual assault and one of sexual exploitation (he was later acquitted). But until the charges were laid, he had never allowed himself to imagine what this coach might do to young female athletes. Doing so would have disturbed the boys' club they both enjoyed.

Vera Pezer, a sports psychologist who works at the University of Saskatchewan, believes there are only three possible ways to explain the failure of an adult in charge to recognize this poisoned environment, where certain athletes are awarded special treatment, additional attention, or put in an uncomfortable or compromised position, especially over a long period of time: "They are either amazingly stupid or naive, have a gross insensitivity to the lives of young people, or are in a state of denial." Whatever the reason, says Pezer, they should be relieved of their duties, as they are not able to do the job required.

There may be one more reason that abuse is allowed to occur in sport, and particularly in junior hockey. Because the players are literally turned into products, commodified as youthful masculinity – virility in the raw – there may be a number of men and women involved in the sport who, while not directly assaulting players, live vicariously through their borrowed youth and sexuality.

Many people have abandoned their own bodies. They keep their cars in better shape than their physical selves. There is very little physical relationship with the self, perhaps because the mass media tells us that only young, fit bodies are sexually desirable and active. We live in a time in North America when almost everything has been turned into a commodity. Youth is paramount, and, without question, youths and children are increasingly sexualized. There are great similarities between boys being drafted into the junior hockey ranks as early as fourteen and girls' beauty contests, where parents tart up their young daughters and display them on runways.

Adults responsible for the well-being of young players, who would never themselves sexually abuse a young person, may allow the abuse to occur, not because they are unaware of it, but because they, like so many of us, see the athlete as a masculine commodity that serves them, despite their protests that they love the boys as their sons. If they really cared for their charges, they would have allowed themselves to consider the risk to which the young men are often so obviously exposed.

In this equation, it is important to remember that direct sexual abuse and the abuse of a person's sexuality are not the same. Sex is the physical manifestation of sexuality. As sports sociologist Michael Messner of the University of Southern California put it in a speech entitled "Studying Up on Sex," sexuality is "the social organization and deployment of desire – and the attendant social construction of modern identities . . . in a matrix of domination."

A perfect example of what Messner is referring to is the 1992 *Maclean's* story about Canada's silver medal in men's hockey at the Albertville Olympics. The magazine put a photograph of the goalie for the men's team on the cover – a shot that embraced the mythology of hockey teams as powerful armies, able to conquer at will. They pointed to the team's success as proof of "Canada's virility on skates." One wonders what they thought the national women's team was doing one month later when it won the world championship for the second straight time. The corollary of this is a *Toronto Star* sports-section headline after a home-team loss: "MAPLE LEAFS IMPOTENT."

The ideal of male virility is so entrenched in hockey that it is unquestioned in Canada's national magazine and the country's largest newspaper. Similarly, junior-hockey organizers conceive of male sexuality along lines that satisfy the men who have invested in it, and players lose a great deal of control over how they are sexually and socially constructed when they are bought and sold by adults. Is it surprising, then, that sexual-assault charges have been laid against several junior players over the past years? Their confusion about their sexuality and that of females is inevitable when it is controlled by others. This in no way excuses any sexual assault committed by junior players against girls and young women, but it explains why they act in such a violent, coercive manner without empathy or compassion.

Generations of young men have played hockey in less than healthy environments, where emotionally mature values like honesty, respect, and integrity have had great difficulty surviving. These young men have an untouchable status as hockey players, while those in charge go to great lengths to deny and ignore signals of abuse within the team and by the team.

For the young hockey player it is difficult enough in this environment to find the maturity to deal, often unassisted, with the emotional and physical risks outlined above, but he must also negotiate the intimidating matrix of leagues, tiers, and age groups that form organized hockey today.

At the bottom of the hockey hierarchy are pick-up, house-league, and school teams. Many of these teams are not registered with the CHA. For instance, if a group of teachers wants to rent ice-time and play hockey twice a week – either by themselves or with their children or students – they are free to do so. It is not necessary to register as a team with the CHA. However, if they want to play in a CHA or CHA-member-sanctioned tournament, then they would have to register, and would be counted in CHA statistics. Much of hockey at all age levels in Canada is played in this unstructured, recreational, and often spontaneous way. There is almost always a non-checking rule, and various ages and both sexes are starting to play together.

Hockey players registered in minor hockey are categorized by their age, sex, and ability, and by the location in which they live and the population of the area. They belong to regional organizations which in turn are under provincial organizations that belong to the CHA.

There is a vast and confusing scheme of teams, tiers, leagues, and levels, not to mention all the rules and exceptions to the rules that can apply in a boy's hockey career. For instance, in Ontario, under the Ontario Hockey Association (OHA), a junior-B team, which is two tiers below major junior, can recruit players in a variety of ways. Junior-B players are normally between the ages of seventeen and twenty-one, but each team can also recruit four minor-age players who are sixteen or under. The team can also sign "affiliate" players of any age from their local minor-hockey league if so many regular players have been injured or are missing that vacancies in the roster must be filled in order for the team to compete properly. Added to this is the rule that allows seven "imports" to play, which means players from outside the team's designated geographic "zone" are also eligible to play for the team.

Young hockey hopefuls, facing a selection process such as this, have little chance of controlling their own futures in the sport, and probably have little understanding of how to begin to navigate a path that will take them closer to their dreams of playing in the NHL. The relationship between coach and player is, consequently, critical. The player has no choice but to depend on his coach entirely. Even if he plays his heart out, he still knows that he can always be replaced; there are plenty of excuses available to justify trading him off into the shadows. The only way a player stands a chance to impress the coach is to become an irreplaceable part of the team.

In the CHL, there are fewer exceptions to the rules, but the rules that do exist favour coaches and franchise owners almost exclusively. Each June the CHL holds its draft, where major-junior teams choose the next crop of players. Each league – Quebec, Ontario, and the West – has its own regulations that stipulate who qualifies for the draft. In the Ontario Hockey League (OHL), the 1998 draft takes players born in 1981. Many would say that a seventeen-year-old may not be mature enough to leave home and play on a team up to a thousand kilometres away, but even younger boys can be recruited. Each team can also select two players born in 1982 or younger, as long as they pick them in the first rounds of the draft.

Graham James arranged Sheldon Kennedy's eventual arrival in Swift Current when he saw him play as a fourteen-year-old in a Winnipeg hockey school. Kennedy grew up in Elkhorn, Manitoba, a farming community outside of Brandon. Swift Current was hundreds of kilometres away, but, under the present system, Kennedy's move was the norm.

It is into this morass that every talented twelve-year-old hockey player peers. Why would we assume that the best person to steer him through this confusion is his coach?

CHAPTER ONE

---

# Memorial Cup Celebrations
## *Jarret Reid and the Sault Greyhounds*

It's Memorial Cup night. The town of Sault Ste. Marie has been buzzing with excitement ever since their boys, the Greyhounds, won the OHL championship. Despite the cold and rainy weather, the fans keep coming, pouring into the parking lot at Sault Ste. Marie's Memorial Arena. Inside the foyer Barry Lassard is playing rhythm guitar with his band. He had started playing in a band when he wasn't working his shift at Algoma Steel, but after thirty-seven years with the company he's now retired from the maintenance department there and is free to perform with his band at a wide variety of community functions.

His father, Ceese Lassard, worked for Algoma too, but what he's really remembered for is his hockey playing skills. He was a member of the team from the Sault that in 1924 won the Allan Cup, the premier senior men's award in amateur hockey. "My father was asked to go pro with Detroit," Lassard comments between sets in the arena's foyer, "but he ended up on the farm team and played in the Central

American Division they had then. He came back to the Sault and worked for Algoma until he died."

Hard work and hockey are themes that surface time and time again in the Sault. Nothing comes easy in the North. Ask the Esposito brothers, Tony and Phil; they're from the Sault. So are Ivan Boldirev, Jerry Korab, Lou Nanne, Matt Ravlich, Gene Ubriaco, Ron Francis, and Rob Zettler, all NHL players. Also from the Sault is Jarret Reid.

Reid, who grew up just outside of town, started playing hockey almost as soon as he could walk. He flew up the ranks of the Sault's minor-hockey system. By age seventeen he was chosen by the Greyhounds as their first pick in the OHL draft. In his first two seasons the five-foot-eleven, 180-pound athlete scored more than ninety goals. He led the team in scoring, with fifty-three goals in his second year alone, including twenty power-play goals, enough to impress coaches who invited him to the Canadian National Junior Team Selection Camp. The Hartford Whalers were interested, too, and selected him in the sixth round at the NHL draft, 143rd overall.

Reid travelled to Hartford for the 1992 camp, and came home with a cheque for two thousand dollars, his reward for being the best-conditioned athlete in attendance. By the 1992–93 season, he was assistant captain of the Hounds, and an outstanding student at St. Mary's High School in the Sault. Unlike many junior hockey players, Reid excelled in his studies. He was a good-looking, popular young man, both in school and with his neighbours in Havilland Bay, outside of the Sault. One neighbour described him as "a truly gentle spirit." Upon graduation from high school, he enrolled part-time at Algoma College, the town's university-accredited school. He was probably the best-known member of the team in the community and volunteered his time to causes like Big Brothers, the United Way, and Sault College. In the souvenir magazine at the 1993 Memorial Cup, the college took out a quarter-page advertisement. In it, Reid, dressed in his hockey uniform, is leading a young boy, also dressed to play, up a set of stairs. The caption reads, "Follow Your Dreams, One Step at a Time."

Roberta Reid, Jarret's mother, still has a letter written by a boy who received help from her son during a difficult period. In fact, Reid has dozens of letters of reference from teachers and employers, as well as notes from friends and kids who wrote to express their appreciation of his conscientious attention and help.

Detective John Campbell of the Sault City Police coached Reid in his last year of rep midget hockey. "He's a great kid . . . 98 per cent of the time," Campbell says, "but the other 2 per cent of the time is very problematic."

Campbell had been called to the Plumber Hospital in the Sault on January 14, 1993, to interview a sexual-assault victim. He realized Reid's former girlfriend, Susan Smith, was in Emergency for a similar reason. "I stumbled into the case. It made it really hard on me to start investigating a former player for sexual assault. I didn't sleep for three days. I wanted him to go farther than I did. I wanted him to play in the NHL."

Campbell was a local boy who played for the Hounds when he was Reid's age. He went on to play in the American League, but never made it into the NHL. "To have one of your players make it to the pros gives a coach such incredible satisfaction. You always hope for it, but don't expect it. I've had season's tickets for the Hounds for years; I'm their number-one fan. But first I'm a police officer, and I take that responsibility very seriously. I don't lay charges unless I think I can get a conviction."

Susan Smith had come home from seeing *Forever Young* at the movie theatre with a date.[1] It was midnight, she remembered later, and she immediately went to bed because she had an exam the next morning at Algoma College, where she was enrolled in the nursing program.

She quickly fell asleep, but awoke at around two in the morning to the sound of her apartment-door buzzer. When she answered it, Jarret Reid replied over the intercom.

Reid told her he and his teammate were locked out of their billeting-parents' homes and had nowhere to go. Could they come up? Smith had to think about the request. She went back to her bedroom, put on a housecoat, and returned to the intercom. She told them to come up, and started gathering blankets and pillows, stacking them in the living room.

The players arrived and, according to her testimony at a preliminary hearing eleven months later, Smith told them she was "really tired" and had a class in the morning and was going to bed. "I talked to them a bit about little things, like what they had done that night and where they were. That was fine, and then I excused myself." The players had been to the Water Tower Inn, a local hotel, restaurant, and bar that is very supportive of the team. "I went back into my bedroom and I locked the door. . . . I didn't want anyone in my room," Smith said.

Reid and his teammate weren't quite as tired. They decided to watch *Silence of the Lambs* on video, but Smith said she could hear it in her room and went back out to the living room and requested that they turn it down. Before she did this, however, instead of putting on her housecoat, she put on a pair of jogging pants.

Smith made small talk again, told them they could help themselves to anything in the fridge, excused herself once more, went back to bed, and once again locked the door behind her. She hadn't had time to go back to sleep when she heard someone trying to open her door. She opened it approximately ten inches and saw Reid on the other side. She remembered Reid saying that his friend wanted to go over to another teammate's house, but Reid didn't want to go, because he didn't know the billeting parents very well. According to Smith, Reid asked her if he could "stay here with you."

Smith testified that she replied, "Jarret, no. I want you to go." Then, she said, he grabbed her arm – not hard, but he didn't let go, and said, "Oh, come on, Susan, please, just let me stay here. . . . Please let me stay." She continued to say no. Finally, she said, he replied, " 'Fine,' in a snarky kind of way," and walked away from her bedroom door, which she promptly locked.

Susan heard shuffling, and a door shutting. She lay in bed a little bit longer, and realized they had left her place without turning off the television. She was angry by this time, as thoughts of her early-morning exam came back. She walked back into the living room to turn off the TV, and said she found "Jarret . . . on the couch . . . and it appeared to me that he had his zipper down on his pants and his hands were in front of him on his lap.

"What are you doing here?" she said she asked him, and he replied, "I didn't really think you wanted me to leave, Susan."

She turned off or turned down the TV – she can't remember precisely which – and said, "Well, you're here now. Your blankets are there. You can go to sleep there. There, they're already there for you."

As she started to walk back to her bedroom, she said Reid "grabbed me by the arm and pulled me onto his lap and he started kissing at my neck. He started pawing at my breasts."

She said she kept saying, "No . . . Jarret, please. This is not – I don't want this to happen."

She got up and sat on another couch. She said they talked about "stupid things. I was really confused. I was scared that he was there, and I got up and I said, 'I'm going to bed. . . . Your stuff is here. You can go to sleep there.'

"I decided that if I could run to my bedroom and get behind my bedroom door, if I could lock it, I knew that I would be okay behind there. Jarret ran with me at the same time and got to the door at the same time. He then shut the door. . . . I was frantic trying to open the door, and I said, 'What's wrong with the door?' and he said, 'I locked it.'"

Smith testified that Reid said, "Susan, please, just let me sleep in your bed. . . . I'll sleep on my side of the bed and you sleep on your side of the bed. I promise you that I won't touch you. Nothing's going to happen.'"

She said she was afraid. "Just the look in his eye really frightened me and I knew that, you know, he had other things on his mind in the first place. I really believe that."

In the cross-examination with Reid's lawyer, Frank Caputo, who has since become an Ontario General Division judge, Smith repeated how she felt. "I was afraid that he was going to try and do sexual things to me that he had started to, attempted to do, on the couch, and I really did not want it to happen. . . . I tried to open the door, to get the door open, because I didn't want to be in a closed room with him."

She tried to humour him, telling him if he wanted to sleep in her bed, he could, and she would sleep in the living room. But he grabbed hold of her wrists and tried to pull her on top of him on the bed. She said he told her, "You're not going anywhere, Susan."

Susan, who prided herself on her high level of fitness, said she fought him as long as she could, but eventually her arms gave out, and he pulled her onto the bed, locked his legs around her, and grabbed her breasts.

Susan said she fought, and managed to flip him on his back. She told him she wanted him to stop it, that what was happening was "stupid." Despite her strength, she couldn't last in this position and Reid flipped her on her back and straddled her, held her wrists over her head, and tried to use his teeth to pull her shirt over her head, telling her "he just wanted to bite [her]," and bit her breast.

Then, she said, he tried to pull her jogging pants off and asked her, "Susan, just let me rip your clothes . . . please, just let me rip your pants off. What are they? They're just lycra pants. They can't be very expensive. I'll take you shopping tomorrow, and I'll even go with you."

She said she fought him and told him, "You're not doing that." She managed to get free and told him, "That's enough, please. Let's stop it. I'm sleeping on the living-room floor," at which point, she left the bedroom and tried to sleep on the cushions and blankets in the living room. Reid said nothing.

Ten minutes later, she said, Reid came out of the bedroom, pulled the blankets over her head, crawled in beside her and put his hands down her pants. "He touched my clitoris. I pulled his hand away. He then started rubbing my back. He tried to grab my breasts again," Smith testified.

She quoted herself as saying to him, "Jarret, I can't fight you any more." In the hearing she added, "I was exhausted. It was, what time, three o'clock in the morning? I was just physically drained and tired from what happened, fighting with him in the bedroom."

She said he replied, "I like it when you're tired, Susan," and proceeded to flip her onto her back, hoisting one of her legs up to her chest so he could hold it there with his chest, and with her head cocked against the coffee table, held her hands above it.

She said she asked him, "Jarret, what are you going to do? What are you going to do, rape me? I'm saying no to you. What are you going to do, rape me?" She said Reid replied, "Do I really have to take it that far?" and pulled her pants down around her thighs. He pressed his penis against her, she said, and tried to penetrate her, but she moved out of the way so he couldn't.

He then penetrated her with his fingers, but she pulled his hand away. She said he commented, "Oh, what do you mean you don't want me? . . . I can't believe you're saying no to me," and pressed his erect penis against her leg.

Smith said she started to cry, and said, "Jarret, I just want you to go," and grabbed his penis and pushed him off.

At that point, she said, he got up, rolled his eyes, went back to the bedroom to get dressed, leaving her lying on the floor. After he had gone she rose and from a window watched him walking up a lonely Sault Ste. Marie road as she cried and pulled her pants back up. She testified, "I got up and I went into my room and I curled up and I went to sleep. And I was thinking . . . what am I going to do? I honestly thought, Okay, if I press charges or if I call someone, for one thing, are they going to believe me? For another thing, look who Jarret is. For other things, I didn't want all of this, all of what's happened, in the media. I knew what was going to take place. I was figuring that he didn't penetrate me with his penis. I didn't think that there'd be evidence that anybody was going to believe. . . . I went to sleep. I was awakened by my girlfriend Yvonne, who called me in the morning."

Smith missed her exam the next day. In total, three friends called, and later arrived at her apartment between two-thirty and three that afternoon. Her neck, back, and especially her buttocks were very sore, and she had a scratch on her hip. Her shins were bruised as well, but mainly she felt "really awful – I was shocked. I didn't know exactly how I was feeling. I was numb."

One of her friends called her own mother, who worked at the Women in Crisis Centre in the Sault. After that, Susan called her older sister, who also came over. The women talked it over and decided to go to the sexual-assault unit at the hospital. It was here that Detective John Campbell inadvertently became aware of the case. It would be the first of many charges brought against Reid by former girlfriends.

The people of Sault Ste. Marie learned about it soon after, when Reid was formally charged with sexual assault on January 14, 1993.

But much would happen between the time charges were laid and June, when the case was to go to trial.

Reid's team started its climb to the top of the Emms Division in the OHL, which also included the Detroit Junior Red Wings, the London Knights, the Owen Sound Platers, the Niagara Falls Thunder, the Kitchener Rangers, the Guelph Storm, and the Windsor Spitfires. It was now or never for the Hounds. During the season, they'd played in lacklustre fashion, winning, and then losing, never having the consistency they knew would be necessary to make it into the playoffs. Yet they had fifteen players still on the team from the year before, when they won the OHL championship and qualified for the Memorial Cup, which had been held that year in Seattle. For most of them, it would be their last season. The team would practically have to start anew in the 1993–94 season.

The Hounds would have to win almost every one of their last eight games in the regular season if they were going to catch Detroit, who were leading in the division. They went 7–0–1 and tied the Junior Red Wings in the standings, but ended up claiming the division title because they had recorded more regular-season wins. Many of those wins were compliments of Jarret Reid. He led the team in regular-season scoring, with thirty-six goals and ninety-six points.

An ecstatic team moved on to the Super Series, which would determine the OHL champions. They surprised everyone by eliminating the heavily favoured Peterborough Petes in just four games, which also allowed them to host the Memorial Cup, as it was scheduled to be played in the East this season.

It seemed all 81,000 citizens of the Sault were supporting the team. From May 14 to the championship game on Sunday, May 23, the town celebrated hockey with festivities, special events, and playoff games between the championship teams from the various leagues of the CHL. Twenty-five thousand came out for the championship parade. Signs were erected everywhere wishing the team the best of luck. Memorial Cup fever took over where winter had left off, and the players, especially those who would be leaving, were getting a little sentimental. Coaches Ted Nolan, Bill Hughes, and Dan Flynn, had become Teddy, Billy, and Danny. Rick Kowalsky quoted general manager Sherry Basin when he referred to the team: "Sherry always says, 'If you want to be a good person, surround yourself with good people,' and that's what this team is all about."

Coach Ted Nolan had come through the Greyhound ranks himself as a player, and later played for the Detroit Red Wings and the Pittsburgh Penguins. He grew up in the First Nations community of Garden River just outside of town, and when his professional career was over, he came home to coach the home team. They were "his boys."

"I coach the way I was brought up," said Nolan before the first Memorial Cup game got under way. "I value closeness, togetherness, strong family values. No one on the team is a star. If a guy gets on a pedestal, we pull him down as fast as we can."

The race for the Memorial Cup is an emotional and physical journey for these young men, but it's also a ritual. Most of the players at the championship shaved the sides of their heads, military-style, from the top of their ears down. As if to compensate for this lack of hair, they attempted to grow goatees. On faces that had just started to sprout hair a few years earlier, it was a valiant attempt at an outward show of maturity.

The Sault, along with their adoring fans, sailed through the preliminary rounds. Their OHL rivals, the Peterborough Petes (who, as the second-place team in their league, could participate because the first-place team, the Hounds, were hosting the playoffs), were there, along with Quebec Major Junior Hockey League's Laval Titans, and the Western Hockey League's Swift Current Broncos. For the semifinal the host broadcaster, TSN, decided to give viewers an athlete's perspective and had Reid doing colour commentary. In the end nothing could stop the Hounds, and the final game would be played against their old rivals, the Peterborough Petes. This time, TSN's preamble for the game would also feature Reid, with the cameras covering him from the moment his car drove up to the arena until he stepped out on the ice.

The owners and board of directors of the Hounds couldn't have been more proud. At the time, John Reynolds was chairman of the team and one of fifteen directors. Just a few years before, in 1989, when the franchise was losing money, it was almost sold to Detroit.

"But if you're from the Sault, you're a fighter," says Reynolds, "and we raised one million dollars, which is an unheard-of amount of money to pay for a junior team, and we kept the Greyhounds. [A junior team has] been here since the First World War, and no one could imagine the Sault without their hockey team. I guess you could say the winter would be awfully long without the Hounds."

Reynolds was also manager of human resources for Algoma Steel. "We sat down with the unions, banks, and government, and didn't leave the room until we found a solution," says Reynolds, referring now to the company's fight to stay in business. "It's a struggle, but we're staying here, just like the team. Hockey's been a catalyst in keeping spirits up in this town. For nine dollars, people can have a regular night out. We don't talk about 'fans.' This is a love affair."

The mall by the arena, which housed many of the community-outreach programs supported by the Hounds, reflected Reynolds's optimism. It was all done up in the team colours – grey, red, and white – and everyone was having a Memorial Cup sale.

But when the Hounds were mentioned in a women's clothing store in the mall, the owner replied without the enthusiasm so obvious in everyone else's voice: "Oh really, well, I hear they're doing quite well." Her information about the status of the Hounds sounded second-hand.

And when the subject of Jarret Reid came up, her face darkened. There was silence. And then she said, "The girl who charged him used to work here. It was a very scary situation. He used to stalk her, just stand outside the store and wait until she finished. He's a dangerous human being. She's not here any more, though," she continued. "The town turned against her. It was very difficult for her to stay in the Sault. She's in Vancouver until the trial."

Back in the arena, the final game was about to start. Barry Lassard's band was going full tilt as an over-capacity crowd jammed in. NHL star Ron Francis, a Sault native, followed a red carpet onto the ice. Behind him was Miss Auto Body Shop, a young blonde woman wearing a tiara. One assumed the local business was a team sponsor, though it wasn't completely clear why she was there. The only other female obviously involved in the Cup was the young woman in the media room in between periods, dispensing liquid cheese onto nachos for reporters.

The first period was fast and furious. At the end, the Hounds led 2−0. During the second period the love affair Reynolds spoke of became torrid. The Petes scored, and the hometown crowd expressed its undying allegiance to its team with ear-shattering chants and great waves of grey, red, and white. By the end of the second period, the score had not changed.

In the last period the score rose to 4−2. Reid and the rest of the Hounds played like a true winning team. The hockey was hard, fast, and physical, and the collective heat of this passion created a mist that rose from the ice. The rink became ethereal, a Canadian Camelot. These were northern knights fighting for the Sault, where people don't just get up and leave when things get tough.

The clock showed one minute left of play. The fans were like an evangelical congregation, swooning over twenty-eight saviours on skates. The tension was unbearable. The puck moved quickly from player to player, but no one could break away with it. Ten seconds to go. Eight seconds. The boys in grey, red, and white started to throw their sticks in the air. Off flew the helmets and gloves. Five seconds. Twenty-two more players started to pour over the boards. Three seconds. Coach Nolan and the rest of the staff hopped the boards. The buzzer sounded. Winter was over. The boys had brought the Cup home.

The little guy does win. The guy who doesn't get up and leave, shut down the steel plant, and take the team to Detroit. There hadn't been much cause for celebration around here lately, but now there was, because there *was* a god, and he wore skates, and played for the Hounds.

Family, friends, and the media flooded onto the ice. Everyone had a deadline for their story and it was past ten o'clock already. Once the Cup had been presented and the team had skated its victory lap, the players and coach Nolan cordially gave impromptu interviews amongst the confusion of the media. Most of the fans were filtering out of the exits, but there remained a distinct cluster of young women – distinct because they were very pretty, and because the amount of make-up they wore made them look much older than they probably were. They had moved down to the seats by the ice, next to the ramp that would take the players into the dressing rooms. They sat, watched the players, and waited. On the ramp itself was another group of young women, just as pretty, but less heavily made up. They waited as well, each trying to catch a player's eye. Every so often they looked disconcertedly at the girls in the stands.

One group, the one on the ramp, had privileges. They were allowed into the halls that would lead these young men into the locker room, where the hockey players would soon transform themselves from sweaty athletes to showered-and-shaved dream dates. The young women on the ramp were the girlfriends, and each one had waited all winter for her boyfriend to finish with his hockey love affair. Finally, at the end of this game, his attention could return to her.

The girls in the stands would have done anything to trade places with the ones on the ramp. They, like everyone else in the Sault, wanted to be part of the success, of the celebration.

As the wait continued, the girls on the ramp began to glare at the ones in the stands. They knew they were replaceable, just like their boyfriends, who could get traded halfway through a season if the men who owned them decided there was a better body somewhere else.

On the ramp there was one girl who didn't seem preoccupied with what was going on on the ice. She wasn't a girlfriend at all, it turned out; her family used to provide a billet for one of the Petes' players when he played for the Windsor Spitfires.

So what did she think of all this?

"You can tell those girls right away," she said in a seasoned voice. " 'Pick me!' It's everywhere. Oh my God, after a game, you wouldn't believe it. It's like they think they're heroes – look at all the girls they've slept with.

"We used to get phone calls all the time for our player," she continued. " 'You were asking for me?' girls would say. He'd meet them at parties. There's such a double standard. It's so hard to control sixteen- to twenty-one-year-olds. It's part of their hockey ego. Ninety per cent of the team may be okay, but there's three on every team who have no morals. You know they get most of the attention, and they set the standard. Most of the guys have steady girlfriends, and you think, if only they knew."

After the Hounds' celebrations that night, Jarret Reid visited Melanie Anderson, another former girlfriend. He stayed the night. One month later, after the police had investigated Susan Smith's charge against him, Reid was charged with twenty-one more criminal offences, including five sexual assaults, two break-and-enters, nine bodily assaults, one uttering a death threat, two mischief charges, and two breaches of a bail order. It was on the strength of Melanie Anderson's evidence that police brought charges against him.

Anderson had been Reid's second real girlfriend. They both attended St. Mary's College, the local Catholic high school, where they met in Grade Nine. But it was in the fall of Grade Twelve, in 1990, that they began to spend more time with each other. In February 1991, they started steadily dating.

Their birthdays were on the same date in March, they attended the same English class, and eventually shared the same locker at school. Anderson told a preliminary hearing on December 13, 1993, that, "in the beginning I was in love with him. As the relationship progressed we started fighting a lot more and we had our problems. I think a lot of it stemmed from jealousy . . . that's when everything began, because of the jealousy of other men or other boys that I knew."

Despite several break-ups, they'd always get back together, and they continued to date while Anderson went to Lake State University in Michigan and Reid went to Algoma until November 1992.

Anderson says she tried to get him to go for help. "He wasn't very good at controlling his anger and his jealousy," Anderson stated at Reid's preliminary hearing, "and that's what was very difficult for me. . . . All I wanted, and he knew this, and I told him this, was that he would get help and that was it."

The first assault came five months after they started dating. The couple were to go to hear a band play with Anderson's parents, but they got into an argument. They decided not to join her parents, and instead Reid went home and Anderson met some girlfriends at the Good Times Bar at the Ramada Inn. She had no sooner ordered a beer and lit a cigarette than Reid walked up behind her and asked if he could talk to her. He often became very confrontational when he wanted to talk, so she went outside to avoid making a scene.

They got into his car, and as Reid starting driving out of the parking lot, he began to cry. "Why? Why are you doing this to me? Why are you smoking? Why do you want to smoke?" Anderson said Reid yelled at her through his tears. Then, she said he started to drive up the Great Northern Road, away from the city, and told her, "'Tonight I'm going to kill you. Tonight you're going to die.'"

He kept repeating those phrases, according to Anderson, and she started to cry, too. He drove the car behind Bawating High School, off Second Line, and pulled alongside the garages at the back. He was hitting the steering wheel with his hands and yelling, and then he turned to Anderson and started punching her in the head and kicking her. "He was wearing cowboy boots, jeans, and a white shirt. And he was kicking me and he was punching me very hard," Anderson told the hearing. "That was the hardest he'd ever hit me. . . . At one point he pulled down my pants and he bit me on my thigh, and I didn't know why, but he did. And then he told me to get out of the car, and I said I didn't want to get out. He kept saying, 'Get out, get out.' I said, 'I can't.' So he came around to my side of the car, and he opened the door, and he said, 'Get out,' and I said, 'I can't,' and so he pulled me out of the car."

Anderson said Reid seized her hair and pulled her out of the car and onto the ground. He then dragged her by the hair across the ground to the rear of the garages.

"Then he stood me up in front of the garage," Anderson continued, "and he just looked at me. He was standing in front of me, and then he kicked me in the side of the leg, inside, on the right side by my knee, and I went down on the ground. I fell and I thought my leg was broken."

He ordered her to get up, but he had kicked her knee as if it were a football, and she couldn't. "I can't. I think my leg's broken," Anderson said she replied. He pulled her up by the shirt and kicked the same leg in the same spot.

A dazed Anderson fell to the ground once more. He told her she was going to die and dragged her by her shirt across the ground to a patch of grass behind the school. Reid lay her on her back and started to choke her. "He was kind of over top of me, and he had his hands around my neck," she said. "It was very hard. I couldn't breathe, and he was choking me and . . . the last thing actually I remember is . . . laying there, and I had my eyes closed, and I remember thinking that I was going to die, and I remember looking around and thinking, what kind of a place is this to die, and then the other thing I thought was, I'm in love with this guy and if I die today, this is how I died, you know. And then I remember passing out. I don't know how long."

Anderson estimated it took her a full minute to regain consciousness, and as she did, she saw that Reid had walked to his car. "When I opened my eyes and I was still there, I was glad, and then I heard the door shut on his car. And he put it in reverse like he was going to leave, but then he came back and he walked over to me, and then he said, 'Come on, I'm going to take you home,' and I said, 'I can't walk.' And so he helped me to the car."

Anderson said Reid helped fix her shirt and hair, and they both wiped her face off as he kept saying "we'd have to fix myself up before we went home so my parents wouldn't know anything. And then we drove around for a bit, just till I calmed down, because I couldn't stop crying. We talked for a little bit and then he parked the car at my house, and I went in and I went to my room. That was it."

She said she told no one of the beating, despite the lumps on her head and discomfort for the next three days. It was the first of a number of attacks that stretched over many months. Reid would buy her gifts while he was away on hockey road trips, but then, upon returning home, accuse her of having "cheated" on him while he was away. He would then beat and rape her so she would learn that he was the only man in her life, and tell her this treatment was all she was good for.

Not all the assaults took place in secluded areas at night. Anderson was once on her way to her creative-writing class at school and was carrying a book of poems she had written. Reid stopped her in the school hallway and asked if he could talk to her. They went for a walk, and he brought up the subject of old boyfriends again. He seemed calm, and they went to sit in his car to talk about it. But Reid became agitated. Anderson said nothing and just stared at the floor. There was nothing to say; any boyfriends she'd had were in the past, and she had remained faithful to Reid.

Reid became more angry, demanding answers. Anderson told him, "I'm not saying anything any more. I'm not answering these questions any more." At that point, she says, he punched her in the head. She covered her face, and he continued to punch her, causing bumps that would last for days. He grabbed her book and started ripping out the pages. Anderson's poetry was important to her, and she told him to give the book back, but Reid wouldn't, unless she answered his questions.

He got out of the car with the book, and Anderson followed him, carrying the rest of her textbooks. By this time she had missed her class, but as she caught up to him, she tried to take the book back, and a struggle ensued that scattered her other books. Reid pushed her to the ground and kicked her twice in the ribs with his black shoes, part of his school uniform.

Anderson was in a great deal of pain, but she was angry. It took her a while to get up, and she had to crawl under cars to retrieve her textbooks. She stood up and chased after Reid, who had run into the school. They ran down the hallways screaming at each other, but teachers just closed their doors to the noise. It was the first time Anderson had ever fought back. She picked up a garbage can and threw it in Reid's direction.

Reid had gone to their locker, and when Anderson reached it, she grabbed his duffel bag and told him he would get it back when he returned her book. He refused and walked away. She grabbed the lock and threw it at him, hitting him in the elbow. Reid started to cry, and ran out the school's front doors towards his car. Anderson pursued him across the school's front lawn and managed to keep him from closing the car door.

Reid opened the door instead and started punching Anderson again, this time in the chest and shoulder area, causing serious bruising. She moved away, and he slammed the door. Reid, who was still crying, drove the car in reverse, but Anderson jumped on the hood and banged on the windshield. He opened the door, gave her the book, and drove away.

No teacher, including the principal of St. Mary's, Harvey Barsanti, who later wrote a strong letter of recommendation for Reid, intervened, despite the fact that Reid threw Anderson to the ground and assaulted her on school property. The argument in the hallway was disturbing enough for teachers to close their doors, and Reid left the school by the front entrance, with Anderson running after him, during class time. None of this, apparently, was cause for alarm.

Bob Denham, who taught both Reid and Anderson, testified he was "very pleased with the way [Reid] handled himself. I thought he was a role model [for other students]. . . . We used the term 'St. Mary's man,' and at the time I gave that unequivocally to him. . . . I found him to be very generous with the things that he did." Denham also testified that Reid had never exhibited any "aggressive behaviour amongst his peers."

Other assaults occurred in front of teammates or while they were in the next room. At times they had to hold Reid back from attacking Anderson, or create interference so he couldn't drag her outside and beat her up. None reported him to police or to the sexual-assault centre.

When Anderson appeared at school after the Christmas holidays, she had a black eye; that Anderson was an occasional cigarette-smoker had provoked Reid to teach her another lesson over the holidays.

"He took one of the cigarettes out of the package, and I was . . . sitting on the bed at this time, and he took the cigarette and he started to shove it down my throat for me to eat it," Anderson later told the court at Reid's hearing. "He was holding my face with one hand, and in the other hand he was holding the cigarette, and he was pushing it down my throat and . . . he cut my gums with his fingers, because I remember the tobacco getting in there and it stung."

Anderson's gums were bleeding, and she started to cough up parts of the cigarette. At that point, Reid started punching her. She tried to cover her face, but he landed a hit to the eye. She told him she'd probably have a black eye, at which point he stopped. It had already begun to swell and discolour.

They decided to go to her friend's house and make up a story. The three of them decided they would say she'd been in a snowball fight and was hit in the eye. Reid also told her, once again, he didn't want to break up.

One of the most terrifying incidents occurred on March 25, 1992, when Reid called Anderson from the Memorial Arena downtown. She was home alone, cleaning the house. They got into an argument – she couldn't recall what about – and when they hung up it was unresolved. About five minutes after getting off the phone, Anderson says, "I was starting to vacuum in my living room, and . . . there's a big front window and you can see the whole front yard, and . . . I saw his car parked . . . and I saw him walking up the driveway. So I kind of panicked, and I turned off the vacuum cleaner, and I locked the front door and the garage door and the patio door. . . .

"I ran downstairs into my basement, and I went into the coldroom, and I remember going in the corner . . . and sitting on the floor in the corner and piling boxes over me. . . . I was very scared, very scared. . . . I was shaking, because it was really cold, and I had the lights off and everything."

Anderson heard Reid banging on the front door and yelling at her to open the door. "He was screaming and, and then I started praying, and I remember saying, just saying every prayer I knew. And then . . . I heard somebody running through the house, screaming my name."

Eventually, she says, Reid stopped, but Anderson was afraid he was going to trap her. She waited another fifteen or twenty minutes. When she finally went upstairs, she saw that the front door was split wide open, right down the middle.

Anderson ran to her girlfriend's house. On the way out, she noticed that the window through which she had seen Reid was also broken. Once at her friend's house, she phoned her father and asked him to pick her up on the way home from work. As he drove her home, she told him that "Jarret had broken in and kicked in the front window and I was hiding in the coldroom."

When they arrived at the house, Reid was across the street at Anderson's aunt's house. Her father confronted Reid about the break-in, but Reid told him the door was already like that when he arrived and he had gone to get Anderson's aunt.

Anderson sat down on the porch swing. Reid sat beside her and asked, "What happened here?"

She replied, "You know perfectly well what happened here."

He retorted, "I didn't do this."

The more they talked about it, the more he denied it. But Anderson's father joined them in the discussion and questioned Reid again. "I'm giving you the chance now, Jarret, to admit," Anderson remembers her father saying. "Tell us if you did this or not."

Reid replied, "I didn't do it."

"Well, I'm calling the police," Anderson's father responded. "I just want you to know that."

Reid told him that would be fine, and he left.

A detective arrived to assess the damage and asked whether they would be laying charges. Anderson refused to do so, because the NHL draft was coming up and she didn't want to jeopardize Reid's chances. "I was concerned that . . . if the charges did go through then it would affect his draft."

In the next few weeks Reid and Anderson broke up several times. Many of the break-ups were accompanied by a beating and rape by Reid, who left several bruises and bumps on Anderson and threatened to destroy, or did destroy, items of her clothing as he tore them off her. During one incident, when they were in her parents' truck, Reid raped and attempted to sodomize Anderson. "I kept saying no, and cried throughout the ordeal, but eventually realized he didn't seem to care that I was crying or whatever," she said. "So then I just figured that, I don't know if it was a smart thing to do, but . . . I thought to myself that I was going to turn the situation around. . . . I started insulting him and I became very arrogant and I was saying, 'Are you finished yet? Are you done using me? Are you done?' . . . And then he got angry and . . . he tried to turn me around and he said that he was going to give it to me up the ass, and he turned me around. . . . I was screaming and crying."

Eventually Reid stopped before he completely penetrated her. He pulled his pants up, said it was over, that he didn't want anything to do with Anderson any more, got out of the truck, and walked to his billeting parents' house.

It was while Jarret Reid was terrorizing Melanie Anderson that the Crown brought its charge of sexual assault against Reid on behalf of Susan Smith. Detective John Campbell, in the process of investigating Smith's allegations against Reid, was asked by the Crown to interview his other known girlfriends. After many months of assault by Reid, Anderson was finally given the opportunity to tell her story of abuse.

After Reid had been charged again by the Crown, this time with assault of Anderson, he continued to stalk her. He came to her house one night and insisted on coming in. When he found out her parents and older sister weren't home, he walked in and sat down on the living-room couch. He told Anderson, "I want to fuck you," and she replied, "That's not going to happen. . . . You have a charge laid on you. . . . You don't need this. Why are you doing this?"

Reid replied, "I don't give a shit about that," and Anderson responded that if anything happened she would call the police.

Reid's answer was short and fast: "You would never call the police. You would never tell anybody," at which point he started to take off his pants. Anderson started to cry, and kept telling him she "wasn't going to." He started taking off her pants, as she tried to hold on to them. He told her not to worry – he'd take it slow as he entered her.

Anderson couldn't stop crying, as Reid told her again he was doing it slow. When he finished, he tried to comfort her: "Well, I didn't hurt you, did I?"

If Reid was in great emotional pain during this time – as his second lawyer, Michael-Anne McDonald, and his mother, Roberta Reid, later portrayed him – it didn't hurt his hockey game. The team was idling in third place in the Emms Division during the regular season, with Reid leading with sixty assists, and ninety-six points. After he was charged with the first sexual assault, it was business as usual on the team, and he continued to rack up the points. The team soon started a winning streak that would eventually take them to the top. As the Greyhounds triumphed in the Emms Division, went on to win the OHL championship, and prepared for the Memorial Cup, Reid never let them down. If teammates like Ralph Intranuovo were at all disturbed by Reid's behaviour, they didn't show it on the ice. After all, as captain Rick Kowalsky said, the team was like family. And as coach Nolan put it, what they were doing wasn't work, it was "intense fun." Just a bunch of boys having fun.

Smith and Anderson's lives, on the other hand, had changed dramatically. Detective John Campbell believes Smith was "run out of town" because she had accused Reid of assault, and was forced to move to Vancouver until the trial resumed. On the Easter weekend, while still in the Sault, she'd gone out with her friends to the Eastgate Mall, but so intense was the public scrutiny of her, her mother made arrangements for her to join her brother in British Columbia. Before she left, though, Reid contacted her – which contravened the terms of his bail agreement – and pressed her to drop the charges. Smith believed he meant he would seek psychological counselling if she dropped the case, something she was willing to consider, but in the end Reid made no attempt to get help for his problems, and Smith left with the charges still standing.

# CHAPTER TWO

## Young Gods

### *A Convicted Felon Makes the All-Star Team*

Jarret Reid was found not guilty of the alleged assault of Susan Smith. "She fell apart on the stand" when the case went to trial, says investigating officer John Campbell. "Like a lot of sexual-assault complainants, she was a lot stronger in the preliminary hearing, but the two-year wait for the case to be tried took its toll on her."

When it came to Anderson's allegations against Reid, the case never even went to trial.

Reid pleaded guilty to several extremely violent and brutal crimes of rape, sexual assault, and assault causing bodily harm. He had also tried forcibly to sodomize Anderson, but through plea-bargaining was able to prevent this particular detail from appearing on the record. Yet Reid's lawyer, Michael-Anne McDonald, stated that in a professional examination a forensic psychiatrist found no "unusual pathologies" in Reid's psychological make-up. She argued that Reid was a young man of above-average intelligence who got swept away with his love of Anderson. That was all.

How can both the psychological profile presented by McDonald and that of the convicted offender revealed in court testimony live within one person? This apparent contradiction is, in Reid's case, extreme, but the causes of Reid's behaviour are at work on every player in the system. Reid is in fact not an isolated case, just a very clear example of what can go wrong.

Dr. Stanley Yaren, director of forensic psychiatry for the Province of Manitoba at Winnipeg's Health Sciences Centre, has assessed sex offenders for the past twenty-one years. "It is common," says Yaren in his office in Winnipeg, "that psychiatrists will make comments like [McDonald's] about sex offenders because we have a narrow understanding of mental disorders and illnesses.

"When we examine for these things, we are looking for pathologies like schizophrenia or manic depression, illnesses that might rob a person of their choice of behaviour. If someone has one of these severe psychotic illnesses, they really do believe a voice has told them to kill or harm someone. But what we find with most sex offenders is that these diseases of the mind are absent."

Yaren says there are plenty of categories of sex offender – pedophiles, for instance, or exhibitionists or sexual sadists – who may have personality disorders but who still know that what they are doing is wrong.

"A personality disorder is not a diagnosis that a psychiatrist thinks of as causing an individual to be unable to make choices," says Yaren. "Someone can be a pedophile, know it's improper, illegal, and immoral, and still choose to gratify his own sexual desires. They know in the social context it's not appropriate to act on it; they still have the ability to make choices. Most sex offenders fall into this group."

Two doctors found Reid to be free of any serious mental disease, such as schizophrenia or manic depression, that would prevent him from controlling his actions. But he did appear to have a serious personality disorder in order to display uncontrollable anger on so many occasions and inflict repeated sexual and common assault on Anderson despite her attempts either to fight him off or plead with him to stop.

Yaren says this is typical of men (who commit the vast majority of sexual assaults) who seem unable to put themselves in someone else's position. They lack all traces of empathy, and their need for immediate gratification overshadows the victim's resistance and well-being. "Such an inflated sense of your own power, the belief that you are irresistibly attractive to women," continues Yaren, "that you have every right to impose your will on them, because they really mean 'yes' when they say 'no,' indicates a highly narcissistic individual.

"She may say 'no,' but the guy can't imagine any woman would be able to think that way about him, so he constructs his own rationalizations, typically vocalized as 'The bitch wanted it.' The ability to rationalize behaviour, especially in an intelligent human being, will lead to all kinds of antisocial, violent behaviour, but it doesn't mean the individual can't choose otherwise. Their choice is to be violent."

Don Smith agrees. He was not only the referee-in-chief for Hockey Manitoba, but is also a twelve-year veteran in counselling and rehabilitation of sex offenders and victims. (In February 1997, after it was revealed that Graham James coached for several years in Manitoba, Hockey Manitoba named Smith the province's player advocate. The organization believed James's behaviour most likely had a history that started long before he reached Swift Current, and hoped that victims of any abuse in hockey would feel free to call Smith for counselling and support.)

Like Stanley Yaren, Smith believes that sex offenders are not, for the most part, diseased individuals, but rather are almost always men who, through a series of social and psychological experiences and rationalizations, have learned to lie to themselves about their behaviour until it becomes, in their view, normal.

"We've developed within our work in Corrections Canada," says Smith, who counsels offenders in prisons, "theories that try to explain the connection between thoughts and actions. We believe if we can modify the thought process, then the action committed by the offender can also be modified. In order to do that, it's important to understand one more component in the thought process. We talk about the rational emotive theory, the relationship between emotions, feelings, thoughts, and actions."

This theory, says Smith, shows sexual assault is a behaviour, not a sickness, as many people would like to believe. Offenders can choose to control this behaviour under the right rehabilitative circumstances, but only if they accept that their behaviour is wrong and truly want to change it. So if it's possible to "cure" a sex offender, it follows that, somewhere along the line, the offender first has to learn the behaviour of sexual assault.

Smith says that offenders learn their behaviour in a variety of ways. "For instance," explains Smith, "let's start with the Y chromosome in men, and the levels of testosterone and serotonin they have. There is a greater potential for sexual aggression in men because of these factors, but let's not underestimate the word 'potential.' Most men don't sexually assault, but they still have this biological make-up, and that's because men either learn to act out their aggression in negative ways or learn to control it and channel it in healthy directions."

It is in the culture of the family, says Smith, that boys first learn how to deal with aggression, well before sexual aggression is a component of their own behaviour. If a boy is the witness of abuse, and especially if he is the victim of abuse, the chances are high that he will become a sex offender. In fact, according to a 1992 study done at the Marymound Family Resource Centre in Winnipeg,[1] funded by Health and Welfare Canada, which shows this relationship between young male sex offenders and family violence, 88 per cent of offenders had been victims of sexual abuse before they started offending.

In this scenario, it is easy to see that patterns of physical and sexual abuse appear normal to young offenders, especially as responses to feelings of frustration and aggression. And because violence and sexual aggression are interpreted as positive signs of masculinity, a boy comes to see aggressive behaviour as desirable; it is what a real man must do to exert power. Girls tend to internalize the behaviour and find themselves in relationships later in life where they continue to be abused, though a significant number (but not nearly as high as males) also become abusive adults.

Added to this predisposition to abuse acquired by many boys during childhood are the equally important social and cultural influences at work on all men. We live in a world where images of women as sex objects to be dominated by men bombard us daily. "Just watch a rock video channel for a while," Smith comments. "It gives the same messages as what is officially seen as pornography, and pornography plays a big part in the lives of sex offenders."

But factor in the male-ego-boosting world of hockey to this equation, he adds, and the picture gets even worse. Getting young men to see girls and young women as equal partners, deserving respect and dignity – in other words, to get them to de-objectify females – is next to impossible.

"I don't think there's anything in hockey that teaches appropriate sexual behaviour," states Smith. "Junior hockey players are treated as if they're special, they have entitlement to whatever they want, they have fans, and groupies. . . . Sure, they have an emotional life, but emotions are channelled into aggression. There's no sensitivity out there, no belief in equality, and that includes how they feel about their teammates."

Junior players constantly talk about their loyalty to each other, but it is a conflicted loyalty. "They know there are scouts in the stands looking for the most promising player," explains Smith. "Your first loyalty has to be to yourself if you have to shine in front of a scout."

Early on, says Smith, junior players learn an inflated self-worth and, consequently, a lack of empathy for others. "You have to go back when the boy is younger. The parents most often instil these values. They figure if their son makes it into the NHL, he's worth millions and they'll get some of it. Or they transfer their own dreams, especially the fathers. . . . The son will achieve what the father was unable to do. It's all vicarious, and it's all external forces on the young man. Real self-esteem and confidence have to come from within."

The world of junior hockey is a place where teenage boys learn they are the young gods of a national religion, where their strength, aggression, and physical prowess are coveted skills that older men willingly buy, sell, and trade.

It was impossible during the Memorial Cup in Sault Ste. Marie not to be reminded that the Greyhounds were everyone's sweetheart. Joining in the adulation were the businesses and individuals who erected signs cheering their team on. People wore the team colours and applauded every move the local boys made on the ice. As PR man Dave Harris said, no matter where a player went, everyone knew he was a Greyhound. And as Melanie Anderson told Reid the night of the Cup victory, there were always plenty of girls willing to entertain him. The same can be said for the rest of the players on the fifty-one other teams in the league.

The residents of the Sault, and of all the other towns where major-junior hockey is played, may be sincere in their love of their teams. After all, they provide an escape to a fantasy world that is all about winning, and allow them to get as close as possible to future NHL players. The arena is the hub of excitement all winter long for sports fans. There are no other so-called stars who fly into rural Canada and set the place on fire with their puck-handling and skating skills. This alone makes the players larger than life in many people's eyes. On top of this, life in rural Canada has always been hard. There is nothing wrong with a little respite from the pressing business of crops, herds, mines, lumber camps, smelters, and snowstorms. But the game is about much more than providing an escape for the fans, especially when you consider the role of the players.

In the 1993 Memorial Cup souvenir guide, Jim Cressman, who writes for the *London Free Press,* wrote, "The CHL has entered into a more aggressive marketing campaign although [Ed] Chynoweth [the league president] says the leagues and teams could still do more to promote their No. 1 commodity, the players. 'We're more pro than ever before. We have an identity, but we have to do a bigger job on the star syndrome,'" Chynoweth says, meaning they should put more effort into making stars of certain players. One tactic to achieve this is the establishment of a vast number of awards for the players.

At the Cup's awards banquet, each of the three leagues within the CHL had nominated a player of the year who would be competing for the CHL's top award. Each player was the subject of a two-page article with plenty of photos published in the Molson-Cooper Memorial Cup Magazine, a glossy 160-page souvenir of Memorial Cup week. As well, there is the Karcher Award for community service, the Transamerica Life Plus-Minus Award, the Molson Coach of the Year Award, the Cooper Goalie of the Year Award, the Toshiba Rookie of the Year Award, the Valvoline Top Draft Prospect of the Year Award, the Chrysler Defenceman of the Year Award, the Canadian Airlines International Executive of the Year Award, the Canon

Camera Most Sportsmanlike Player of the Year Award, the Canadian Airlines International Scholastic Player of the Year Award, and the Tip Top Tailor Trophy to the team with the best record. Before the nominees for these awards arrived in the Sault, they'd already won similar division and league awards.

The awards are sponsored by large corporations, so the CHL can get access to plenty of corporate cash to keep the industry alive, while the corporations benefit by associating themselves with the mythology of young virility the players represent. But the actual commodity, the players, are only boys and young men, without the life experiences that would help them put in perspective all the adulation from those enjoying the vicarious thrill of their prowess.

When treated like this, how do young Canadian male hockey players learn the prerequisites of appropriate sexual behaviour, the values of intimacy, the ability to empathize or to listen to other people's needs, sometimes putting them ahead of their own? How do these commodities of maleness learn to be nurturing human beings, and develop the ability to see others without seeing them through hockey's distorting lens? Finally, how could junior hockey – a place where millions of dollars are spent promoting young men while completely ignoring talented young Canadian women – possibly teach young men to have respect for women? It is within the confines of this world that Jarret Reid abused Melanie Anderson.

There were strong indications that Reid learned his abusive behaviour at home. Crown attorney Rod Guthrie recognized it in his acceptance of what he described as an extremely lenient sentence, telling Justice Pardu, "I was of the view, based on evidence, and also the evidence that we have of the individual counts showing the controlling nature of it all, . . . that he himself as a young man was a victim of violence."

However, both Reid and his lawyer, Michael-Anne McDonald, denied it, and argued it was Reid's broken heart, public humiliation, loss of a hockey career, and deep regret that should be considered when deciding for a shortened sentence. In his Statement by the Accused, Reid said, "I just think that, you know, being in love at the tender age of 17 with somebody you're probably ill-matched for is very difficult, and I am deeply sorry for my actions through this relationship. I lacked the strength and maturity to not only recognize the unhealthiness of the relationship but to end it as well.

"I think there's no acceptable excuse for the inappropriate behaviour between young people who think they're in love."

Nowhere in his entire statement did Reid refer to any abuse in his past, or even to his abuse of Anderson. In fact, when he spoke of "inappropriate behaviour between young people," it was as if Reid considered Anderson at least in part responsible for his actions.

Michael-Anne McDonald said in reply to Guthrie's contention that Reid had been abused as a child that when Reid referred to "the cycle he knew he had to break," he wasn't talking about a cycle of family violence at all, but rather the cycle of jealousy and passion that he and Anderson had in equal amounts for each other. She argued:

[Jarret Reid] recognizes full well that he is responsible for his conduct and that no one but himself bears that responsibility, and he endeavoured to relate that to Your Honour. . . . But it does put his conduct in context of a great love affair of two young people who are 17 when they start and are 18 when these offences arise. That a young man who has been his parents' pride and joy and who has been focused and goal-oriented, and is achieving his goals, loses sight of that family and those goals over his love for this young girl . . . this young man has come to recognize his responsibility and his need to avoid such relationships and to avoid such obsessive love that it causes criminal acts to occur.

While Reid and his lawyer denied that Reid may have come from a violent home, and never used phrases such as "sexual abuser," or "physical abuse" in their statements, preferring the term "inappropriate response," they did mention how devastating the whole affair had been to Reid's hockey career and his family.

"The pain, stress, and humiliation I've caused my family and my friends is of great concern to me," Reid told Justice Pardu. "There's many hockey fans and kids who looked up to me as a role model and I let them down and I'm truly sorry for that.

"I believe I've learned a great deal from the mistakes that I made while I was a teenager. I've made sacrifices all my life in fulfilling a dream of one day becoming a professional hockey player and that dream is now gone and I'll have to pay for the rest of my life for the mistakes I made at that age."

McDonald emphasized Reid's loss in the world of hockey in her submission on sentence:

> Time mattered more than anything else before because in terms of the NHL if you weren't there when you were 20, if you weren't there when you were 21, you weren't there when you were 22, you weren't going to be there. Mr. Reid has recognized that he is not there now and he is not going to be there because his opportunity has passed. . . . He has already been deterred by emotional, social and economic penalties which have devastated not only himself but his whole family who had given up a great deal to support him in his chosen career.

Without question, McDonald painted Reid as a young man who was hopelessly in love, to the point that he lost control. It was love, not a learned behaviour of violence, that made him do this. The result of his inability to control his romantic impulse was the loss of his first real love: a career in the NHL. Surely Justice Pardu could see what a terrible setback he had suffered?

Melanie Anderson was not present in court when the time for sentencing eventually arrived. The length of time the case took to get to court had exhausted her. First, at Reid's request, given the number of charges against him, the preliminary hearing had been adjourned for six months. Then, with a great deal of legal manoeuvring, he managed to have his trial put off. This allowed Reid to fit in two more seasons of hockey, one in the United States, and one in Belleville. But the new date set for the trial conflicted with Anderson's school year, and she missed writing an exam when the trial began in June 1995. This trial was stopped when it was only half over and delayed until the fall.

Anderson did not re-enroll at university in the fall of 1995, because she anticipated the stress of the continuing trial would be too great.

Just before the case was to go to court, Reid contacted Anderson at work, which contravened his bail order. He would have had to face this additional charge if McDonald hadn't had the quashing of it added to the plea bargain. Not surprisingly it was an emotional setback for Anderson, who had already forfeited a semester of university in order to deal with the case. She didn't appear at his sentencing, and was in no shape to make a victim-impact statement to the court. In the end, Reid pleaded guilty to three charges of sexual assault, three assaults, one assault causing bodily harm, and one break and enter.

Finally, while Reid and McDonald tried to provoke sympathy because Reid lost the dream of playing professional hockey, no one mentioned that it is a dream only boys are allowed to have in the first place. It is a privilege Reid could aim for simply because he was male. Could there be a connection between a culture that denies girls opportunities to be physically strong, powerful, and have "intense fun," to quote coach Nolan, in a structure similar to the CHL, and one that has epidemic amounts of violence against women in the population at large?

Former Montreal Canadiens goalie and lawyer Ken Dryden talked about the way in which hockey players have things smoothed over for them in the CBC's "fifth estate" documentary "Thin Ice," which first aired in the fall of 1996:

"Somebody who is a star at twenty-three was a star at seven, was a star at ten, and twelve, and fourteen, and every year along their path up to twenty-three. I mean, you have a sense about yourself that you can do whatever it is you want to do, whenever you want to do it, and there are no consequences. You will get out of the consequences yourself or somebody else will get you out of them. You want to understand that twenty-two-year-old hockey player, understand the thirty-five-year-old rock star, understand the fifty-year-old politician or the fifty-year-old businessman: the same thing, that same sense of impunity. Any problem I've got, I've got a whole company of fixers here."

When Jarret Reid was charged with the first count of sexual assault in January 1993, the Greyhounds had twenty-seven other players they could have sent out to the Swiss Chalet restaurant in town on behalf of Big Brothers to sign autographs. They chose to send Reid. When the program for the Memorial Cup was put together, Sault College didn't have to have a photograph of Reid leading a young boy up a set of stairs, but they chose the player facing a sexual-assault charge. When TSN had the idea for a junior player to do colour commentary for the semi-final game, they had two entire teams to choose from. They chose Reid. When they decided to focus their cameras on one of the fifty-six players before the final game, they chose the one player who faced sexual-assault charges. Just as Reid chose to be violent, these three powerful organizations chose to support him.

Dennis Mills, a Toronto Member of Parliament, and father of Reid's teammate Craig Mills (who now plays for the Chicago Blackhawks) when he played for the Belleville Bulls, wrote a letter of recommendation for Reid which was presented to Justice Pardu. "I knew there was some kind of trouble that Jarret was in, but I didn't think it was very serious. I didn't think he'd been charged," says Mills, who obviously hadn't read the Belleville newspapers or *The Hockey News*. "I found Jarret to be caring, approachable, and hard working." Mills now chairs a Commons Committee on hockey. Former Greyhounds assistant coach Danny Flynn also wrote a letter of recommendation in his new capacity as head coach of the St. Francis Xavier University hockey team.

In practice, coach Nolan's claim that "no one on the team is a star," and "if a guy gets on a pedestal, we pull him down as fast as we can," has a hollow ring. Perhaps it was easier for him, and the rest of the Greyhounds' staff, to see their relationship with Reid strictly in terms of hockey and not concern themselves with his life beyond the game. But if Nolan were to claim that, then he would be arguing against the holistic First Nations philosophy on which he says his coaching style is based, where the spiritual, physical, emotional, and cultural aspects of a person are equally important.

The CHL has its own version of what constitutes a whole-person athlete. The Canadian Hockey Association, the national governing body to which the CHL belongs, was represented in the 1993 Memorial Cup guidebook by the president of the association, Murray Costello. He wrote: "The CHL, to its genuine credit, is paying ever more attention to providing educational opportunities so the players are *fully prepared for the challenges that lie ahead, both on the ice and off* [my emphasis]."

One wonders what kind of education the CHL was providing the rest of the players when Reid was intentionally showcased after he was charged. One can only speculate as to how much the team had known about Reid's personal life and how it put him at risk. Players and their girlfriends witnessed some of the attacks. Others witnessed an attack that came in broad daylight in front of a busy high school. In the wake of these attacks, Melanie Anderson's personality changed from outgoing and sociable to isolated and fearful. But no one intervened, either on behalf of Anderson or on behalf of Reid.

Sports psychologist Vera Pezer's explanation (on pages 10-11) about how Graham James got away with abusing athletes as long as he did applies here as well. Either the Greyhounds' staff was terribly naive, they were grossly insensitive to the personal problems of their players, or they were simply denying the high risk Reid represented.

Coach Nolan described the Greyhounds as a family, and described himself as a man who believed in family values. Other officials in the game frequently use the same term when they defend the moral fortitude of the "hockey family." It is a term often bandied about, but it can mean just about anything. What exactly are hockey's family values, and what do they teach young men about honesty, integrity, self-respect, and respect for others? As we shall see, the circumstances in which young hockey players find themselves in junior hockey are alarmingly similar to circumstances described in studies of young sex offenders. Violence, a history of abuse within the family, the availability of pornography, a belief in the close adherence to traditional gender roles, and disruption of attachments (moving frequently into new, unfamiliar environments) are just a few of the attributes these two groups share. If the player can be considered part of a "hockey family," it is plainly dysfunctional. (While the studies of sex offenders can't be described here in any detail, they are listed in the Bibliography for interested readers.) The point is, the values ingrained in hockey demand rigorous and objective analysis.

While a coach is certainly not the only man in charge, the symbolic parent of any junior hockey team will always be male. Hockey, in fact, is filled with father figures. But what kind of a father?

Without exception, junior-hockey coaches, including Graham James, come from within, not outside, the hockey world. Not all have played at every level – house league, minor leagues, major junior, and the NHL – as Nolan has, but most have NHL or major-junior playing experience. All coaches, whether former pro players or not, have been living and breathing hockey since boyhood. They are technically of a high calibre. The job is far too competitive for even mediocre coaches to survive for any great length of time. The owners of the teams need winners, and coaches are directly responsible for the team's success. But how does a career in pro sport prepare a coach to guide an impressionable boy through the difficult adolescent years?

While at the University of California, Berkeley, Dr. Steven Ortiz spent four years studying the marriages of forty-eight professional sportsmen, including NHL hockey players.[2] He defines the marriages as "institutionalized adultery." Wives are discouraged by management from travelling with their husbands, and if they do go to a game, they are instructed not to stay in the same hotels or visit the same bars, because it is here the players meet their girlfriends.

Ortiz classifies the status of the wife on a road trip as "second-class" or "non-person." The wife must "know her place," or jeopardize her husband's standing on the team. Any player whose wife doesn't follow the traditional role risks being seen as "pussy-whipped" by his teammates, and the respect of the rest of the team means everything. The relationship between the men becomes so strong, and is considered so important, it perpetuates male dominance; relative to them, women are nothing. "The men will put down their own wives in the inner sanctum of the locker room," says Ortiz. "They'll call them hags or worse, say they're terrible in bed, anything to show their dominance."

Ortiz believes the team is the most important family in the players' lives, but, like their relationships with their wives, it is fraught with problems. Not all professional male athletes are highly promiscuous and dishonest, but so many are that manipulation and dishonesty become the norm. The silence of the rest of the teammates guarantees that the players get away with whatever they want – much like a spoiled child.

Don Smith's observations back up Ortiz's study. After being involved with hockey for most of his life, as a player, coach, referee, official, and parent, he's still amazed at the lack of emotional maturity amongst the men involved in the game. "Male emotional development, especially the development of intimacy, lags far behind that of women," comments Smith. "Male bonding occurs through the team – that's their version of showing emotion – but in fact, there's no such thing as emotional intimacy for them.

"It's not that they can't do it, it's that they won't learn how, because it challenges everything they've ever learned about being a man. For instance, I co-coach my son's team. He's five years old. Through my work, and generally . . . I coach from a balanced perspective, seeing the dynamics that involve a whole child.

"But my [coaching] partner is the stereotypical win-at-all-costs coach. There's no emotion except anger. These kids are five years old. What does that teach them?"

While house-league hockey, where Smith coaches, may have room for men like him, or even women, major-junior hockey is completely controlled by tradition-bound men. There are no women on the CHL board of directors, or on the executive committee. The only female staff member of the Greyhounds is the office manager.

When Jarret Reid was released after serving three months of his nine-month sentence, it was one of hockey's father figures who stepped back into his life.

Reid was released on parole from prison in December 1995, and he immediately joined his former assistant-coach from the Greyhounds, Danny Flynn, at St. Francis Xavier University in Antigonish. Like all players who play semi-pro or professional hockey and then join the CIAU (Canadian Interuniversity Athletic Union), Reid sat out his first year at St. Francis Xavier, but he was made centre for the team, the X-men, by Flynn for the 1996–97 season.

The X-men had a great year, finishing second in the Atlantic Division of the CIAU, and seventh overall across the country. Reid scored an amazing twenty-four goals and twenty assists in twenty-seven games, and totalled only twelve penalty minutes. In the CIAU playoffs, he scored another three goals and one assist. He was back on track.

For the first time ever, universities in Canada and the United States each put together a hockey all-star team. While Canada has tradition-ally been *the* country for the sport, the Americans have been placing more and more university players in the ranks of the NHL. A Canadian win in hockey at any level is no longer a sure bet, so this country's officials wanted to field the best team possible. Players were chosen in four different ways. First of all, the three coaches for Canada's all-star team, Daryl Young of Dalhousie University, Myles Muylaert of the University of Guelph, and Tim Bothwell of the University of Calgary drew up a list of players. Coaches from the various universities were allowed to nominate players, the CHA had their own list, and the NHL was invited to observe and nominate university players.

Jarret Reid made it onto Flynn's and Young's lists and was on the team as a centre. Reid was released from school for one week to attend the CIAU training camp in Windsor, Ontario, in preparation for the all-star game in Detroit on April 4. Players from across the country had to get used to playing together, as opposed to against one another.

"We crossed in the team bus," says Daryl Young from his Dalhousie office. "U.S. Immigration came on and asked for the names of the players and where we were going. They asked certain players more questions. But they didn't ask Jarret anything.

"He was a really good team player. If his play on the ice is any indi-cation, then he's under control. He was in really good shape, worked very hard for us, and has lots of skill. Off the ice he was very quiet and reserved. He's a powerful player, and did *so* well for us. He assisted Kevin Powell on the third goal when we were tied with the U.S. in overtime. It was a short-handed goal. A great effort."

Young was aware that some kind of sexual-assault charges had been laid against Reid. "I wasn't sure what ones were dropped and what ones he was convicted on," he says. But Young believed Reid had done his time and was intent on rebuilding his life. He says he wasn't aware that it was against American law for a convicted sex offender to cross into the United States.

"I had no idea we were breaking an American law," says Young, who oversaw the logistics of getting the team to the game at Detroit's Joe Louis Arena. Danny Flynn said through St. Francis Xavier's Vice-President of Advancement, Anne Camozzi, that he had no idea Reid was not allowed to cross the border.

That none of the coaches and officials involved in the game would know that newly released criminals are not welcome in the United States is difficult to imagine. Professional hockey player Bob Probert made this American law quite famous when he crossed the border while playing for the Detroit Red Wings. Probert, who also started his career with the Sault Greyhounds, in 1983, was notorious for his possession-of-cocaine and drunk-driving convictions. The NHL continually went to great lengths to get him over the border to play for his American team. It made for several front-page articles about players, drugs, and the law. Did Young, Muylaert, Bothwell, Flynn, and St. Francis Xavier's athletic director, Dr. John McFarlane, who also knew about Reid's background, think American laws applied to drug offenders, but not to rapists?

The coaches may plead ignorance of the law, but Reid certainly can't. All Canadians on probation are warned by their probation officers of the possible consequences if they try to cross the American border. Clarence Falconer, Reid's probation officer in Antigonish, confirmed that Reid was fully aware of what he was doing. U.S. Immigration is very firm on the procedure. The United States does not allow entry until at least three years after probation has ceased, and Reid was still in his first year of a two-year probation.

Norman Byron, Acting Deputy District Director for Immigration in Detroit, says his department does not believe in going light on sex offenders who want to enter the United States. "If we catch him doing it again, we will take action against him. There could be criminal proceedings, and if anyone aided and abetted, like the coaches, they could be held liable next time they try to cross.

"This doesn't speak very well of the teams," continues Byron. "If people found out this guy was with their children, would they want him around? I call them 'our little junior professionals – little monsters with contracts.' They're just like pro athletes with criminal records – the stars of the team. The rules don't apply to you, sonny.

"Athletics is a big money-maker," he concludes. "These people will do anything and everything to protect them."

Norman Bryon has heard just about every excuse in the book. He tends to operate to the letter of the law, and appreciates it when others do, too. "I'll tell you the athlete who understood this. It was [baseball Hall of Famer] Ferguson Jenkins. What a ball player! But he had an old, old marijuana-possession charge. It was nothing. But every time, he went through the proper channels. Now, he had class. I don't want to talk about these athletes now."

When contacted, CIAU executive director Mark Lowry said he had no idea Reid was a sex offender or that he had illegally crossed the border. He also said he would have to discuss the procedure on this with CIAU president Liz Hoffman before commenting. Hoffman did not return the phone call placed to her, and Lowry did not return calls. Meanwhile, at St. Francis Xavier, all calls for Danny Flynn were referred either to the athletic director, John McFarlane, or dean of men, Rick Benson. "If you want to talk about the team, how they're doing, scores, etc., I can help you," says McFarlane. "Otherwise I have no comment."

Rick Benson is very involved in the university's sexual-assault-prevention program. "I have a personal commitment to this area," he says from his home in Antigonish. "I have no tolerance for assaults of any kind."

Interestingly, at his sentencing in 1995, Reid had promised Justice Pardu that he would speak out against violence against women. But none of the women's centres in either Sault Ste. Marie or Antigonish has been contacted by Reid, and neither have the high schools or senior public schools in Antigonish. The women's caucus on campus received no request from Reid to speak on violence against women, and didn't know he was a sex offender until the fall of 1996. "Clarence Falconer [Reid's probation officer] told me Jarret had been rehabilitated," says Jen Bezanson of the women's caucus, "but I think women on campus should have been told from the start."

Anne Camozzi also confirms the university's commitment to a safe environment. "We abhor and completely disagree with violence of any kind," says Camozzi. "Violence won't be tolerated. We were told from the start by Mr. Flynn that Jarret was actively committed to rehabilitation. It's been a top priority, and his coach has had ongoing discussions with us and Jarret that this will continue. He was allowed to leave practices early to attend [anger-management] sessions with counsellors and his probation officer."

Two days later Camozzi calls back. "I am still confirming the university's commitment to zero tolerance, but if you want some other information, perhaps you should call Antigonish RCMP."

The RCMP in Antigonish confirmed that on April 21, 1997, three weeks after the all-star game in Detroit, Reid was charged with three new counts of assault and two breaches of parole. His new girlfriend at St. Francis Xavier had reported him to the police. On September 11, 1997, Reid pleaded guilty to one count of assault – Crown Attorney Ron McDonald rolled all three counts into one – and one count of breach of recognizance when he contacted the complainant after the assault charges had been laid. Just two weeks later, Reid, having got himself a new lawyer, decided to change his plea to not guilty and awaited trial once more.

Reid would be joining teammate Andrew Power, according to the RCMP. During the season Power was charged with two counts of sexual assault – one on September 26, 1996, the other on January 26, 1997, the same day he scored a goal and an assist in a 6–2 win over the Acadia Axemen.

Jarret Reid's story raises plenty of questions, including whether a convict while still serving parole has the right to continue his education and hockey career when the rights of women to continue their education and lives in a safe environment may be affected.

McFarlane is a man of few words on the subject. "I didn't give it much thought," he says at the start of the 1997–98 school year. "If you want to know about the Reid case, you have to talk to . . . our public-relations lady."

Crown attorney David Fairbanks prosecuted Reid. The three separate assault charges were rolled into one, and breach of recognizance was also added after Reid, true to form, contacted the complainant after the charges were laid. As he investigated Reid's past, Fairbanks found out about the previous offences, but was equally disturbed by information he received about St. Francis Xavier University, the CHA, and the Canadian Olympic Association.

In the 1996-97 academic year, when Reid became eligible to play for the St. Francis Xavier Xmen, university officials gave him their prestigious Athletic Leadership Award. This is an award that recognizes leadership both on and off the playing field. Anne Camozzi says the university will not reveal the amount of money it gave to Reid, but did confirm they knew before they gave him the award that he was a convicted sex offender. (Neither will the university reveal how many males versus females have been given athletic leadership awards, but it does say at least 30 per cent of the awards – but not necessarily 30 per cent of the money attached to them – must go to female students. As well, the university, which has no women's varsity hockey team, will not disclose its budget for its men's hockey or give a breakdown of its funding of male versus female sports in general.)

In the 1997-98 season, after Reid was charged with committing the new assaults, the Canadian Olympic Association (COA) awarded him a Petro-Canada Athletic Leadership Scholarship. The athlete must supply two letters of recommendation to the COA, one from their university or school, and the other most often from their sport-governing body. It was Flynn and assistant athletic director Joe McDonald who wrote the school's letters. Jamie McDonald and Glynnis Peters of the CHA – the staff who are responsible for recommending athletes for the award – both say they can't find a copy of the letter recommending Reid and can't remember who signed it, though Murray Costello, the president of the CHA, says he was aware of Reid's criminal past. Jim Murray of the COA, who gave his stamp of approval to Reid's scholarship, says he can't locate the letter either.

Camozzi would not comment when asked why neither Flynn nor McDonald alerted the CHA and the COA after Reid's third set of charges and retracted all letters of recommendation. They had from April to December 1997, when Reid received the scholarship, to do so.

On February 3, 1998, Reid formally withdrew from St. Francis Xavier. As of that week he would be spending the next five months in jail at the Pictou County Correctional Centre, with an additional two years on probation. "Some leader he is," says Fairbanks. "He was still on parole when he received those awards. What would it take *not* to be a leader in their eyes? Murder?"

# CHAPTER THREE

# Analysing the Game

## *The Culture of the Hockey Arena, Inside and Out*

After every important hockey game, and between periods, experts analyse styles of play, penalties, defence, offence, injuries, salaries, and a host of other elements. Don Cherry, on "Coach's Corner," goes further. He will often give an opinion on the level of aggression in hockey, on social issues related to hockey, and on the game beyond the confines of the NHL. For instance, in 1993, during a "Hockey Night in Canada" broadcast, he plugged the Sault Greyhounds and said he believed Ted Nolan's boys had what it took to win the Memorial Cup. Cherry has always had a soft spot for junior hockey, and each Memorial Cup week he interrupts his NHL analysis with a commentary on the junior championship and praise for particular players and coaches.

Cherry likes to throw commentaries in during "Coach's Corner" about other aspects of hockey. In October 1996, after "the fifth estate" broadcast its extensive documentary on hazing and sexual assault in junior hockey, he denounced it as "*National Enquirer*–style journalism," referring to the reporter on the piece, Lyndon McIntyre, as "Linda."

While Cherry's remarks are always provocative, they are based on his personal and immediate reactions to the world of hockey. There is no true in-depth analysis of the culture of hockey, by Cherry or the rest of the sports media.

It is not surprising that Don Cherry and the president of the CHL, David Branch, publicly denounced "the fifth estate"'s "Thin Ice." Hockey, and the sports media, live in a world where reality rarely intrudes. Cherry looked straight at the camera and told parents, "Moms and dads, I know what you're thinking: Should we let him go to the OHL and things like that?" Cherry told them junior hockey was "100 per cent safe." Two months later, Graham James pleaded guilty to sexually assaulting Sheldon Kennedy when he played for the Swift Current Broncos, and following Kennedy's example, scores of young men came forward to complain about sexual abuse.

How can someone so close to the game be so far off the mark? In many ways what has happened in hockey is like the revelations of the abuse suffered by boys while in the care of religious institutions. Both are what Steven Ortiz calls "total institutions."

"Monasteries, mental institutions, cults, and professional sports teams fall into this category," Ortiz says. "They are enclosed, cut off from society, and have a very exclusive feel about them. The locker-room culture of sport is a good example. The rest of us would see a lot of what goes on in there as inappropriate behaviour. Women are denigrated, talked about only as objects, and men are afraid to say anything about intimacy with women, because it wouldn't be manly. So their behaviour becomes normalized. Consequently, in order for people to be accepted by the team, they rationalize abnormal behaviour."

Ortiz believes the team constitutes a "mobile total institution," because of the highly transient nature of professional sport. Thus, with the player's life in a constant state of flux, with the team often on the road and the constant danger of being traded or injured, the arena and the locker room are among the few stable elements in his existence. This enhances the sense that the arena is a bastion.

That hockey is like a religion in Canada can hardly be in dispute. Those who run the sport speak openly in these terms. As the Western world became more secularized, the sports stadium or arena replicated the church as a place of male communion and worship. One God has become many.

But what happens when the world outside of church or hockey clashes with these total institutions? It has taken people from outside both the hockey establishment and church institutions to raise the issue of sexuality and sexual abuse within them. As Ortiz points out, the total institution never willingly allows discussion about issues that have the potential to rob those in power within the institution of their positions. Both hockey and organized religion have denied the role sexuality plays in people's lives and the subsequent potential for abuse. They would prefer to ignore sexuality altogether, yet stereotypical gender roles define them. In many ways, they operate in a paradoxical situation: what they so vehemently deny is in fact a powerful part of their culture.

According to Sandi Kirby, sports sociologist at the University of Winnipeg, "Total institutions, if they are strong enough, can ignore all the major issues of our time, including human rights, globalization, workers' rights, free enterprise, the rise of liberal democracy, and the rise of the ethic of care in sport. It is only when complaints reach the public and are too serious or too numerous to be 'buried' that total institutions are forced to examine their fundamental practices and values."

In these traditional constraints, Jarret Reid's actions are very predictable. It was often when he'd had enough of his girlfriend, when he decided she had been soiled by going out with other men, when he felt her jeans were too suggestive, when she smoked – in other words, when she was a slut in his eyes – that he abused her. Several times after he broke up with her, he told her that he would use her for one thing now, and proceeded to rape her.

While the belief in entrenched gender roles obviously comes from traditional views of women, the rationalization Reid used to justify his violence originated in his own mind. Don Smith refers to the mental process that rationalizes inappropriate behaviour as cognitive distortion. "Their emotional needs are met through power and control," explains Smith. "They have low self-esteem, brought on by feelings about the self from external forces. The cognitive distortion process overcomes the conscience which says 'this is wrong,' and replaces it with an internal disinhibitor so the fantasy can be acted upon. Internal disinhibitors give permission to act inappropriately. That's why we know there's nothing spontaneous about what they are going to do. Sex offences are premeditated and rationalized in the offender's mind. As well, alcohol is an example of an external disinhibitor."

It should come as no surprise that alcohol played a significant role in the sexual assaults discussed in this book. In fact, the only offences examined here that didn't involve considerable amounts of alcohol were the ones perpetrated by Graham James.

The signs of the dysfunctional hockey family couldn't be more clear. Why, then, couldn't those in positions to do something about it see what was happening? Perhaps, just like the offender who uses the process of cognitive distortion to ignore his conscience, those in power employ the same process to reassure themselves that the hockey family lives in a happy, healthy home.

There is no question that Reid and other players are prized for an athletic prowess that encompasses strength, power, aggression, and violence, often taken to be the hallmarks of masculinity. But it is completely denied by those in charge that encouraging these characteristics reinforces this idea of aggressive male sexuality. Owners can talk about hockey being "masculine" or the media refer to a team's "virility," but when asked if that means it's about male sexuality, they look horrified.

This traditional model of male sexuality automatically defines female sexuality as passive. It is a cruel irony that aggressive, self-centred sexual behaviour is the antithesis of what women respond to sexually. Part of the rehabilitation of sex offenders is to teach them what women like and respond to. "From birth, males are taught they are superior," Don Smith comments. "It's very easy for them to view themselves as sexually powerful, but how does this style of sex translate into pleasure for women? It doesn't.

"These kinds of men, and they're not all sex offenders, but rather men who have translated their masculinity as power and control, get off on dominating women, and sexually fulfilling themselves. A healthy sexuality includes men doing things that excite women. A man with a more mature sense of self and sexuality will get turned on when the woman he's with gets turned on. We literally teach offenders how to turn women on.

"Part of this healthy equation has to do with understanding and internalizing intimacy. We say that sex alone is great, but sex with intimacy is wonderful. Education is part of my responsibilities as Manitoba's player advocate, and I'm going to be talking to the older players about this very point."

In October 1997, however, Smith's position with Hockey Manitoba was terminated. René Gregory, chair of the Harassment and Abuse Committee in Manitoba, said, "We are going with the CHA's Players First program." When asked if Hockey Manitoba will be implementing any educational program similar to that recommended by Smith, Gregory replies, "I don't know that we're going to delve that deeply."

But just scratching the surface demonstrates the need for programs as envisioned by Smith. In the pressbox at the Memorial Cup in the Sault, former Greyhounds player Shawn Simpson, now a scout with the Washington Capitals, defended a woman's right to have sex with four players at once, as it appears one teenager did with members of the Capitals. She later charged the players with gang rape. He stated, "You can't tell her how to live her sexual fantasy."

Simpson is right. People's fantasies are their own. But, if it's a fantasy acted out by willing participants, when it's over the relationship the participants had before the encounter should remain the same. But, as Simpson admits, that's not the case in hockey. "Girls can't win in this game," he says. "If they say 'no,' unless they're really pretty and could be a real girlfriend, the guy tells the rest of the team not to bother. If she says 'yes,' you get laid, and tell the rest of the guys she's easy so they can have sex, too. Then she's a slut, and no one would ever have her as a girlfriend."

While the reputations of young women who don't necessarily act like "good girls" are ruined in the small towns where junior hockey is played (whether or not the sex was consensual), the players' reputation is, if anything, enhanced. Don Smith believes sexual-harassment education must be framed in terms of female sexuality, respect, and intimacy. But no one has ever really asked women what they want from hockey. And if they did, it's not likely the answer would be "Better sex." There would be demands for more ice-time, women's pro leagues, career contracts, television coverage, World Cup events, respect, equity, and an end to the gratuitous violence that mars the sport now.

But, these egalitarian values don't mirror the culture that has built both the exclusively male arena and the social environment around it.

Along with the rise of the sports stadium and arena were profound economic changes.

As Canada shifted from an agricultural base to an industrial one, to the high-tech economy and free-market system that is forming now, the foundations of small towns have been severely shaken. The shutting down and "downsizing" of resource-based industries like Algoma Steel and St. Mary's Paper in Sault Ste. Marie are only two examples of the profound change that has come from outside the community. Every time a giant like Algoma Steel is downsized, the ripple effect causes dozens of secondary businesses in the community to suffer or close altogether.

In Swift Current, Saskatchewan, home of the highly successful Broncos, the downtown core is all but boarded up. Businesses that survived the Depression, droughts, two generations of young men fighting world wars, and the vagaries of the grain markets, couldn't survive the onslaught of American big business. For men who have defined so much of their worth by their ability to provide for their families, unemployment threatens their very identity.

The mall on the outskirts of town, anchored by the traditional Co-op store at one end, houses the American giant, Wal-Mart, at the other. Most of the people wandering aimlessly around in the middle of the day, drinking perpetual cups of coffee in the food court, are working-age men.

Meanwhile, the status of women has also changed. Many of the men who find themselves killing time in malls and arenas have wives who have left them, or returned to school, or make more money than they do. They may have to answer to a woman boss, may be ticketed by a female police officer, or may be represented by a female MP. They hear about women and girls winning court decisions over their right to ice-time or to play on boys' teams. Being a man, for many of them, used to mean having control, mastery, and power, but this definition of masculinity is rapidly losing ground.

Forces outside of work and the home have changed too. The relationship people have with sports, recreation, and their bodies has been all but destroyed by the sport-and-entertainment industry, which teaches us to live the wonderful experiences of sport through the actions of others instead of discovering the potential of our own body, mind, and spirit. A sports fan will yell, "We won!" when a team on television triumphs. But he has had no part in the effort, and the entire vicarious experience is over with a flick of the remote control. In reality, the viewer is not involved at all.

That's not the relationship we used to have with sport. An advertisement for a speed-skating match in the 1920s may trumpet the many great Canadian skaters on the rivers of Toronto, but in print almost as large it will also tell the spectators to bring along their own skates for skating to "a full orchestra" after the event. As late as the 1960s, after University of Toronto varsity hockey games, there would be pleasure skating to music. Many countries still engage in this kind of holistic sporting activity. During the 1994 Lillehammer Olympics in Norway, for instance, thousands of Nordic skiing fans skied into the woods to watch their heroes fly around the trails. Hundreds set up camp in the woods, skiing and keeping bonfires going day and night. The passive sports fan is a new, and chiefly North American, phenomenon.

We have always cheered on our favourite hockey teams – before the advent of TV, everyone huddled around the radio waiting for Foster Hewitt's voice to carry "Hockey Night in Canada" into homes across the nation – but there has never been the kind of emotional dependency on professional male sport that there is today.

Sports and physical activity are not supposed to be about passively watching superstars. They are about the exhilaration of meeting a fresh winter day face-on, and sharpening the edge of one's soul against a piece of smooth and unforgiving ice.

Outdoor community rinks were once commonplace, and women's hockey teams flourished until after the Second World War. But as hockey became more professional and elitist, more ice-time was given to boys and men, and, more specifically, to those who showed the potential to make it into the NHL. Hockey gradually shifted from community ponds, sloughs, and rinks, to indoor arenas, where fewer recreational skaters had access, and talented, male, hockey players were favoured.

Major-junior teams such as the Swift Current Broncos, the Sault Greyhounds, and the Regina Pats now cut deals with municipalities that allow their players priority access to ice. Don Cherry's new major-junior team, the Bulldogs, will benefit, partly at the taxpayers' expense, from a deal with the City of Mississauga, which is investing 24.5 million dollars in an arena that will have as its main tenant Cherry's team. And in the meantime, budget cutbacks for municipally funded and maintained outdoor rinks have since caused many of them to be shut down, as has a warming trend that has created uncertain weather conditions in parts of Canada. The result is that community hockey and recreational skating have been reduced to a pleasant memory for many Canadians. Furthermore, Mississauga's arena, like so many others, is located in an area inaccessible by foot. Children can't simply throw their skates over their shoulders and walk to the rink. An adult must drive them.

The media coverage of hockey has also changed, from radio broadcasts to highly commercial entertainment productions for television directed at a passive male audience.

American sociologist Dr. Leola Johnston of the University of Minnesota maintains it wasn't until television introduced carefully selected instant slow-motion replays that the men watching at home could convince themselves they were somehow connected to the athlete on the screen.[1] She studied the phenomenon of the male sports fan's loyalty to a particular football player who won the favour of the sports marketers in the late 1960s and '70s. His name was O.J. Simpson.

"Slow-mo allowed the men on the couches at home to imagine themselves as O.J.," says Johnston. "They became him, and he became them." When sport is watched just once at its normal speed, it is too fast for people to include themselves in the picture. But when replayed slowly several times, the audience is more likely to internalize the picture in front of them, Johnston believes. It becomes super-real. That's what made Simpson so acceptable to the television audience. He was a black man slowed down to their speed. Eventually, she says, as his image became "owned" by a white constituency, he too became "white."

The same thing happened in all other televised sport. The male athlete became a far more physical presence in living rooms and rec rooms across North America. The act of imagination required by radio took a back seat to the super-real images for consumption on television. The next step, believing that somehow you, the viewer, are the athlete, or have a relationship to him, is not very difficult.

A 1992 study from the United States showed that when the Washington Redskins *won* a football game, a hospital in Northern Virginia, where there was great support for the team, saw an increase in the number of battered women being brought into Emergency.[2] The sociologists and criminologists who conducted the study believe that "one of the central rationales for the enjoyment of aggression in sports is that it allows the spectator to share in the power process displayed in the contest. . . . In our study some aspect of the power of the winning team may be transferred to its adherents, giving them the sense that they are able to inflict violence when they choose, particularly against a weaker partner."

What this and other studies show is that the activity on the ice or playing field appears to be internalized by a certain kind of male fan as his own activity and triumph. So convinced are they of their role in the victory that they act out their new heightened position through violence, which is their way of establishing power.

And so, while one part of the equation that constructs masculinity has been turned upside-down by a global economy and a move towards equality for women, the other side has worked twice as hard at providing constant affirmation of male strength and aggression in the face of such challenges. This is just one of the many unspoken jobs for which the young men who play the game from October to May are responsible.

CHAPTER FOUR

# Baptized a Hawk
## *Initiations in Junior Hockey*

Scott McLeod celebrated his sixteenth birthday in October 1993, the day before the Tilbury Hawks' team party. He was also celebrating making the cut as a goalie on the junior C team. After all, he'd played hockey all his life in the small southern Ontario town of Tilbury and, for him, being selected by the team was a highlight of the year.

His mother and father, Mary and Paul McLeod, dropped him off at the Chatham home where the party was being held, told him to have a great time, and drove the thirty kilometres back home to Tilbury. They had been told the team's owners, coaches, and general managers would be in attendance. But at seven the next morning, Mary woke to a ringing phone. It was Scott, calling from a store in Stoney Point, five kilometres from Tilbury. He'd been walking for hours in the rain and was cold. Could she pick him up? When she found him, he was shivering and soaking wet.

From that morning on, Scott was never the same. His marks in school started to decline, and he stayed in his room whenever he

65

could. He talked about quitting hockey. "I noticed he wasn't himself after that," says Mary. "I asked another mother if she'd noticed a change in her son. He had told her about two things that happened that night: his penis had been tied to a string, and he had been told to masturbate in front of others."

The McLeods couldn't believe their ears. They asked Scott to tell them what had happened, but he said everything was fine. Still, he seemed to find no joy in anything he did. As time went on, they couldn't stand to see their son decline any further. Paul sat Scott down and pleaded with him to tell him what the matter was. When Scott finished telling his story, his father sat back in shock.

It started the second Scott walked in the front door. The large house, located on a prestigious street on the outskirts of Chatham, belonged to Dennis Lebert, one of the owners of the Tilbury Hawks and a well-respected ear doctor in the town. Someone gave Scott a beer. He had never drunk alcohol before, but wanting to appear as if he knew what he was doing, he took a few sips. That didn't seem to suffice. Someone put a funnel in his mouth, and poured beer down. They did it again. In no time, Scott was feeling woozy.

"They were persistent in giving us alcohol. Lots of beer. We might look like a wimp if we turned it down. They turned it into a game. They were getting us drunk on purpose, and led us into the garage," said Scott later.

Team members were sitting in the rec room, which was adjacent to the garage. There was a porn video on the TV. The players were constantly urged to drink and pressured to masturbate while the porn movie played. Then they were called into the garage, two at a time. When Scott passed through the door, even in his drunken state he was shocked.

A semicircle of chairs had been set up, said Scott, and the coaches, owners, managers, trainer, and senior players on the team were sitting in them. More beer was stacked by the walls. There was a strange set-up of a pail attached to a string, and a hockey stick supported across the backs of two chairs. "There was evil in that room," Scott said, upon reflection. "You could just feel it."

Scott and another boy were ordered to strip. He didn't know what to do. The owners, Scott said, "sat right up in front, not ten feet away, and they were cheering. The other players were outside the room. We didn't know what was going on until we got in there. Everyone was pretty afraid."

Scott did as he was told. These were the men who could make or break his hockey career. They tied the string to his penis, and then suspended the pail over the hockey stick. Out came the pucks. They started to throw them into the pail. As the weight increased, it pulled heavily on the string. It hurt, but Scott endured until the string pulled off.

Just when Scott thought it was over, there was another game to play. In fact, the evening had just begun. The captain of the team was told to put on a surgical glove. Then he was given two marshmallows and told to insert one in Scott's rectum, one in his teammate's. The rules of the contest were announced. Whoever squeezed the marshmallow out first, without using his hands, won. The other guy had to eat both marshmallows.

This was followed by another contest. A plastic Molson cup was filled to the brim with beer. The boys were told they were going to have to do push-ups. The cups were positioned on the floor so their genitals would dip into them after each push-up. Whoever did the fewest push-ups had to drink both beers.

Still the evening wasn't over. They were blindfolded and told to lie face-up on the floor with their tongues out. A grown man pulled his pants down and sat on their faces. "I don't know if they did it to bond the team," said Scott. "I asked all the time. No moral person would do that."

When the last game ended, Scott managed to escape with a teammate. They said they had to run outside and throw up. Instead, they grabbed the keys to his friend's truck and ran away. It was cold, dark, and raining. They'd been drinking, but made it to the teammate's house safely. Scott decided he needed time by himself to try to fathom what had just gone on. He also wanted to walk off the effects of the alcohol. It was best, he thought, to go the rest of the way home on foot. Finally, as the cold from the rain penetrated into his bones and it felt like the alcohol was wearing off, he called his mother from a lonely pay phone.

To this day, the McLeod family cannot understand what kind of a mind would think up such rituals and how on earth they would help create team spirit. "My son said he was scared," says Mary. "It's their dream to play junior hockey. Those men hold power and authority. Parents want their sons to go on, no matter what. But those parents who didn't stand up for their sons aren't parents. I don't understand how they could let that go. Those people are sick."

"Scott's doing better now, though I don't believe he's over this. Who knows how long it takes to recover from such a thing?" says Paul McLeod. "It's taken him a long time to forgive. He's always loved hockey – came through the minor leagues.

"We trusted those men. They're businessmen. The kids were scared. They said to themselves, 'If I leave, they won't want me in hockey.' Some people thought the boys could just leave, but they couldn't. I thought he would be in good hands. One boy was only fifteen. People have put it in the back closet."

The McLeods decided to approach the Tilbury Hawks' management about the initiations. They got nowhere. They invited over the parents they had first spoken to about the initiation and discussed options. But after contacting the other families, only one other believed their son. The rest told the boys they weren't going to be very good hockey players if they complained about these petty little things. "We felt very alone. The other couple supported us, but wouldn't get involved," says Mary.

Bob Day, a retired OPP officer in Windsor, heard the stories via the small-town hockey grapevine. He contacted the McLeods to offer support, and Scott decided he would make a statement to the Chatham OPP. "I'm not happy the whole thing happened, but I'm glad my son handled it the way he did," says Paul. "I wanted to be supportive, try to get him through it. The only thing I would have done differently: when I found out about it, I was shocked, and I didn't go immediately to the police. It was after the fact. Initially, there are so many things you think about. The biggest concern is for your own child. I knew how much my son wanted to play hockey. The issue was clouded, and you deal with it the best way you can.

"I haven't had a whole lot of experience in hockey," he continues. "I played baseball, but there was not a tremendous involvement in sport. I was naive. I said to myself, Don't panic. Try to come up with a solution that's going to hurt my son the least. So I talked to people I trusted. People should be aware of what's gone on in the past, and may continue in the future.

"Scott wanted to quit hockey. I probably should have gone to the police from the start. If you don't, you kind of contribute to the problem."

For Scott, once he and his parents decided the police should be involved, the issue became quite clear. "I lived through hell," he says, "but I believe what I did made me a better person. The others were scared and confused, they didn't want to make enemies, and they still don't. Most are still playing hockey – junior C and B. They still have dreams; they're just into selling themselves. I couldn't do that. The whole morality of it is unbelievable.

"I'd never go back and give up what I did. Counselling has helped me a lot. Thank God there's people around like the police, the Crown attorney, and counsellors. If it wasn't for my parents, I don't know where I'd be."

Todd Ternovan of the Chatham OPP led the three-month investigation. On February 28, 1994, thirteen suspects – including one minor – were charged under the Criminal Code, with the total number of charges reaching 135.

Shortly after the charges were laid, one of the complainants, Vanden Wright, and the minor who had charges laid against him, died in separate traffic accidents. Few close to the case believe they were in fact accidents at all, but rather acts of desperation that would not have occurred had they not been a part of the ordeal.

The rest of the accused were barred from contact with any of the victims, except "at hockey arenas for the purpose of playing scheduled hockey games and hockey practices only." The game continued for the owners, managers, coaches, and senior players.

Paul McLeod decided he wanted to know how these men could allow such disgusting things to happen to boys. He went to the arena and confronted one of the managers. He says the man just looked at him and replied, "You're lucky he's only in junior C. It's worse in A and B." Paul walked away in disgust.

The preliminary hearing got under way that winter and spring of 1994. Frank Montello, the lead lawyer for the Tilbury Hawks, argued an initiation isn't a sexual assault. The rookies were not forced to do anything; they gave consent. But while Montello was grilling Scott McLeod about what went on that night, perhaps the most telling stories were told in the benches filled by the accused and their wives.

The accused took up three solid rows at the front of the courtroom. For the most part, the owners, coaches, and managers were in their forties, though one was over fifty and another twenty-one. There was a uniformity in their appearance: short-cropped hair bristling with grey, reddened faces, and short, thick necks. The seams on their suits appeared to strain to contain their bulk, the collars on their shirts looked similarly challenged trying to encircle their necks. There was nothing about the older men in the three rows that suggested any of them played hockey or participated in any other kind of physical exercise. Each day their wives filed in quietly, dutifully taking seats behind their husbands.

But when Scott started to describe what the men did to him, the first three rows perked up. Grins and smiles emerged. The younger men amongst them slid forward in their seats. "During the preliminary hearing some of them actually started to laugh," says Mary McLeod. "I couldn't believe it." The wives sat stonefaced and silent.

Despite feeling that he wasn't being taken seriously, Scott pursued the matter. "I look at them for what they are. Sometimes they try to intimidate me. They snicker, too. I'm enemies with the guys [other players] who tried to cover it up. People outside of hockey took sides. I feel blackballed. Not many teams called me up to play after this. I don't feel I've been given a fair shot."

The hearings went on for weeks. The transcripts ran to a thousand pages. Players who felt they still had a chance in the system testified they were too drunk to remember who did what to whom and said they had given consent. Finally, on June 28, presiding judge Mary Marshman finished hearing all the evidence. That same day lawyers for the accused and Crown attorney Paul Bailey met to discuss a plea bargain. The most important issue, says Bill Currie of the *Chatham Daily News*, who covered the hearing, was of credibility. "By Scott's own admission, he had drunk a lot of beer," says Currie. "The other players who ended up being hostile witnesses had drunk at least as much. Who exactly was in the room at the time of the assaults, and who carried them out, is a difficult question. At parties, movement is fluid, people go in and out of spaces. It's difficult to prove beyond a reasonable doubt when alcohol is involved."

The Crown agreed to drop all charges against the owners, managers, and coaches, and to proceed against the twenty-one-year-old captain of the Hawks, Ed Fiala, and forty-four-year-old Paul Everaert, the team's trainer. The two men pleaded guilty on one charge each of performing an indecent act. They received a combined fine of six thousand dollars and each got two years' probation. In addition, they were ordered to stay away from arenas and could not work as a coach, manager, trainer, or owner for three years.

No one – except the ten men who had the charges against them dropped – liked the deal, but as Bailey says, "Proving sexual assault is always difficult. We ended up with several hostile witnesses, guys who kept saying, 'I don't remember.' All of a sudden a court in Ontario is saying what they take for granted is wrong. This hazing business can take on a life of its own. No one questions it. They say, 'I want to play hockey. I want to move up.' It's a quasi-military organization."

"I'm happy I went to court, that I didn't let go," says Scott, "though I'm not too happy about the end result. There were only two convictions, and they were the least guilty."

Another teammate's parents felt the same way. But though they were supportive of the McLeods, they didn't want to come forward in public. "Our son doesn't play hockey any more, he's moved on to college and tried to put this whole thing behind him," says his mother.

"We are thoroughly disgusted with the court system," she goes on to say. "I have no faith in it. We went along with everything the Crown asked us to do, but only got two convictions out of it.

"I'm equally disgusted with the Ontario Hockey Association. They knew what happened and didn't bother getting involved. The whole thing is unfortunate, and as usual the victims weren't treated fairly. Hopefully none of this will happen again."

The McLeods feel the same way about the OHA. At first the organization appeared concerned, but it did "absolutely nothing" to help the boys. The team was allowed a leave of absence from the OHA while the case went through the justice system, but no disciplinary action was taken.

Scott spent his last year of high school playing for his school team. "My peers don't bring the subject up with me," said Scott at the time. "It was tough to go to school." And what does he think about the OHA? "They were just part of . . . the cover-up. They never contacted me, didn't help at all."

Brent Ladds, who has been president of the OHA since 1981, didn't return phone calls to be interviewed for this book. In 1994, while testifying at the preliminary hearing, Ladds stated that when the Hawks party occurred the OHA had a regulation addressing initiations. Item J23 in the OHA's "Constitution Regulations and Rules of Competition Manual" reads as follows: "Any player, team official, executive member of a team, club or association having been party to or having had knowledge of any degrading hazing or initiation rite shall be automatically suspended for a period of not less than one year from playing or holding office with any team, club or association affiliated with the OHA or the CHA."[1]

Paul Bailey asked Ladds if the regulation was "simply ignored and not enforced, or is that something that the Ontario Hockey Association believes in and enforces?"

Ladds replied, "I think it's important to understand that throughout all, all of this, this is the first occurrence that we've had where a violation came to our attention. So there are no real precedents to, to evaluate what our position would be in varying circumstances. This was the only occasion that we had a chance to evaluate some type of submission with respect to hazing."

When asked by the Hawks' lawyer, Frank Montello, about an incident on September 26, 1992, at the Ramada Inn in Cleveland, Ladds said he did not recall a request from the Cleveland Junior Hockey Association for $3,200 in damages after a hazing party involving the Belle River Canadiens, another junior C team from southern Ontario. Montello was trying to show that the Hawks were by no means the first team to initiate new players, that the practice was commonplace and could not be considered assault. But Ladds could not remember Gord Petrie of Cleveland contacting anyone at the OHA or the CHA about the incident. Counsel for the defence produced a copy of an invoice for repairs sent to the CHA after the initiation. "I'm going to have to suggest to you I don't recall seeing that letter or hearing about that incident," Ladds said under oath.

But Said Maleki, owner of the Cleveland Airport Ramada, certainly remembers the incident and the bill. "They made a disaster of five of our rooms," says Maleki from Cleveland. "They aren't human, they're not even animals. A pig is a dirty animal, but I don't think a pig would do that. We found three hundred to four hundred beer cans in five rooms. Some of the toilets had beer cans jammed into them to the point that they were in the pipes. We had to burst a pipe to get them out. They broke toilet tanks as well, and then spray-painted . . . the walls, carpeting, mirrors, bedspreads, mattresses, and casings for the beds.

"They wrote totally obscene words on the mattresses and drew disgusting drawings on the bedspreads," continues Maleki. "There were indications that they had young women in there. Our housekeeping staff wanted nothing to do with these rooms. They stunk for two months because the spray paint was oil-based.

"Hockey players should be banned from any hotel in this industry," says Maleki, "and that includes their so-called chaperones. If anything, they're worse. In our case, they all went drinking in the bars in the Flats district in Cleveland and left the players to drink in the rooms. They didn't return until two-thirty a.m. By then, I had security guards in, and the police had been to the hotel three times. They were only authorized five to a room, and had six to seven in each room, and there were minors drinking in there. When I spoke to some of the players, they told me the chaperones and coaches would take money to keep quiet so the players could do things on the side. One said to me, 'I gave the coach two hundred dollars not to open his mouth.' Well, if they ever damage property here again, or threaten me in any way, I'll press charges."

Maleki sent letters and bills to officials at U.S.A. Hockey, and the Windsor association, asking them to forward them to the CHA. In the end, no one would take responsibility for the team's actions. Today, all the players, coaches, and managers of the Canadiens are banned for life at 1,600 hotels in the United States and Canada after Maleki reported the team to the American Hotel Association.

Despite the fuss kicked up by Maleki with both the American and Canadian hockey associations, and the damage done by an OHA team, Ladds maintained during the Tilbury hearing that he had no recollection of *any* other initiation in the OHA.

"We got involved in the Tilbury case because we heard rumours at the rinks. We got involved before the police or anyone else," says Ladds when pressed at the OHA's annual general meeting in June 1997. "We took some action based on it being out of Tilbury. Probably it was a board meeting, January, mid-February, before I ever heard from Mr. McLeod. I never heard from the kid, just his dad. His dad had phoned because he'd heard things at the rink." (This version of events is not supported by the McLeod family.)

The OHA board met, but at the time they were still just hearing rumours, and it wouldn't be until 1997 that the CHA had any sexual harassment or abuse policy the OHA could have referred to. "We formed a committee and said, We want to meet with these people," continues Ladds. "Let's see if there's any substance to the rumour. We met within ten days . . . in Chatham and reviewed the situation with them [the accused], and felt, based on our discussion with them, they had failed in providing proper adult supervision. In one particular situation the trainer is an adult, and he should have known better."

They suspended the trainer, Paul Everaert, and trusted that what the rest of the men told them was true. "They just gave us the facts," says Ladds about the team management. "The people who ran the hockey club are good people, very good people. As a matter of fact, apparently this hazing ritual had gone on for a couple years, and apparently their concern was the guys [the players] this year were trying to do more than the guys last year. They were really good people in the community, and they had a concern about the escalation of what was going on, and more so that younger kids were in there drinking and may get in a car and go on the road and drive home.

"So they had a meeting with the parents, and said, 'Now here's what's happening: they're going to have their little rookie party.' But Dennis Lebert said, 'They can use my home, and we'll have a few people there to make sure everything is [okay]. But we want the kids to stay because, in case they drink, we don't want anyone going home. You should be aware that there's going to be alcohol there, so if you're concerned about your son having a few beers, make us aware of that.'"

Ladds says the parents consented to the party, knowing there would be beer and a sleepover, but thinks perhaps the Tilbury Hawks had "failed in that maybe they didn't realize what these kids had in mind that night, and they should have stepped in, and secondly, with a couple of people there in an adult supervisory role, they would have been of assistance."

He says he believes that the men who were charged by police weren't present at the party. "Jimmy Debenham was there as a manager, and the trainer. I think all they perceived was that some kids were going to get their heads shaved, and there was going to be some beer drunk. They had some lunch there for the kids, and everyone was going to stay because there was going to be some drinking. My understanding from them that was the outside perimeters of what was going to happen."

Even though most of the adults charged weren't present, according to Ladds they were named "because in their role as a hockey club it's still an activity that takes place in their operation. They become principals."

When asked if he thinks that Scott McLeod was lying under oath, that they really weren't there, Ladds starts to back up. "While I'm going off the top of my head – you know what I mean, I haven't read the files yesterday – my understanding is certainly that [one of them] was not there. . . . But notwithstanding it all, I mean, it's their hockey club, and I can understand them being named in a suit."

But the action taken in Tilbury was not a civil suit; the accused were charged under the Criminal Code. Scott and Paul McLeod wonder if Ladds is even talking about the same team and initiation.

"I remember who was at that party," says Scott McLeod of Ladds's claim that the owners and the majority of the other men charged by police weren't there that night. "I told the truth on the stand."

Despite the fact that initiations occur in male organizations, Ladds hasn't thought about why they exist. "I don't know where they come from, probably somewhere way back. . . . But they're not just in hockey, they're in service clubs. In some cases it's not a source of humiliation. If a hockey club says we're going to have an initiation and we're going to shave all the rookies' heads, well, personally I wouldn't find that degrading. It's fine. If that's what they're going to do, then go ahead and do it. Probably the next year when the rookies came in, I'd make sure I did it to them because that's how I became a charter member of this organization. I think in it's pure sense, it's innocent.

"The concern," continues Ladds, "is when people get carried away and take liberties that really aren't part of the whole agenda. When you get into the sexual stuff, there's no place for it. It's not common sense. Certainly, I wouldn't want to be running a hockey club that didn't have a policy that safeguarded against it.

"But in this modern day and age when you look back, somebody getting their head shaved might find it offensive. But back when we played hockey, we didn't give another thought to it."

While the OHA spent a considerable amount of time talking to the accused, they didn't feel it was necessary to talk to the players or their parents. "I spoke to Brent Ladds once," says Paul McLeod. "Scott saw him on TV, and it appeared that Ladds was downplaying the whole incident. That really made him upset, so I thought I better phone [Ladds] and explain to him, for the sake of the kids it happened to, don't say anything, especially don't downplay what happened."

McLeod phoned the Cambridge, Ontario, office of the OHA and was told that Ladds was very busy preparing for a late-night meeting. "I remember saying, 'That's fine, I'll wait up for his call,' " says McLeod, "because I thought it was very important to talk to him."

At two in the morning, McLeod finally went to bed. There had been no return phone call. "I called the next day and was told he wasn't in the office, so I tried one more time the day after. The secretary told me he was really too busy to speak to me."

McLeod did his best to remain calm. "I told her he could either talk to me now, or talk to my lawyer. He was on the phone immediately. All I wanted to tell him was to have some sensitivity about the subject and not downplay it on TV. It wasn't just my son I was thinking about; there were ten other kids who went through that initiation. He was a typical politician and skirted the issue. I never heard from him again."

The McLeods did, however, hear from Dr. George Phyls, chief psychologist with the London Board of Education, whom the OHA had contacted. Phyls established the school board's policies on sexual harassment, and wrote to the families on behalf of the OHA about this subject in April 1994. He asked them to contact him if they had any questions or comments about the psychological health of their sons. This was a full six months after the initiation had taken place, but despite their misgivings about this very late show of concern, the McLeods called Phyls.

"When he finally called me back and asked me if I thought Scott needed counselling, I told him that Todd Ternovan of the OPP had asked us months before if he did, and he had been seeing someone already. As far as I can recall, that was the end of the conversation. The only thing I can remember from that call is thinking, What a waste of time."

"That case occurred quite some time ago," says Phyls, who has since retired from the board. "As I recall I sent a letter to all the parents of the boys on the team. I told them I would be in touch with them, and could provide counselling services, or facilitate counselling services from someone else for them. Mainly, I listened. Quite a few had already made arrangements. My major task was to listen to ten families. Most parents were very responsible."

Phyls quoted from notes taken during conversations with the families. " 'My son didn't readily participate,' " reads Phyls. " 'He didn't realize, when he wanted to be part of the hockey club, that this was going to be part of it.'

"'We're coping with the situation,' is what another family said. 'Most of us [families], or all of us.' Only one family was on the side of the team, according to my notes. 'My son is not a victim,' my notes say on this one. 'I feel the owners have really been shafted. The court appears to be making too much out of these things.'"

Phyls was particularly disturbed by the two deaths that occurred shortly after the initiation. "People saw them as suicides. I didn't even know [one of the boys] had died when I spoke with the first family. One of the things they were very concerned with was what was going to happen to the rest of the kids. What would the trial do to them? Who was going to help the kids? I think this was an incredible thing that happened in that community.

"Where does it all come from? It's part of a macho image, and how they view women. Some of these guys don't have a role to play, so this was something that gave them lots of power, in a macabre sense. They could use any kind of technique to denigrate the players, but they had to keep elaborating, and go further. There's a secret conspiracy of silence. If they thought any of this would get out, they never would have done it."

Phyls maintains he filed a report on his findings with the OHA. Ladds, however, was unable to produce that report, and instead, after several requests for the report, sent the minutes of a workshop led by Phyls at the OHA's annual general meeting. Phyls told those attending his workshop that 1994 had been designated "International Year of the Family" by the United Nations and talked about "the importance of the family unit in the life of young hockey players," adding that "the concept of a supportive family should be extended to hockey teams, and that it was important for each individual to play at his best with the common goal of doing well."

Phyls said the OHA sometimes had difficulty grasping his point, "and to deal with this situation teams must find a way to convince new players that they have something meaningful to contribute and that they are an integral part of the team." Phyls proceeded to discuss the Tilbury initiation, though the OHA minutes from the workshop don't mention the team by name. "He informed the workshop that some parents had accused the OHA of not doing enough right after the incident, pointing out that he himself had not been requested to come on the scene until about five months later," read the OHA minutes. Phyls outlined how regressive initiations are, and that they should no longer be tolerated, and asked the question: "What have we learned and where are we going?" In addition, he said the concept of certain traditions in hockey had to be revisited, and "just because some custom had been followed for years didn't mean it had to be continued.

"For young people to develop self-esteem and good character, it was important that the volunteers set an example of behavioural responsibility, and that the players themselves demonstrate respect for their peers. This would come about from dialogue, doing, sharing, and modelling," the minutes read.

There is no evidence that the OHA has acted on Phyls's recommendations.

In 1997, as Scott McLeod finishes writing his first-year exams at the University of Windsor, he's reflective of what it all means. From the start he said he only came forward to try to prevent sexual abuse from happening in the future. "As bad as it was, I think I made the best of it. All these fallen father-figures. The whole objective of hockey is to produce good young people. These father-figures just didn't care about that. I look back at my teammates, and it's unbelievable they would have engaged in this. It's not an environment you should bring kids up in.

"After the abuse happened, I turned to substance abuse. I was drinking, not totally out of control, but when the thoughts came creeping back into my mind, I needed something to numb the pain. I think it's important for people to realize this sort of thing can happen to kids after the abuse occurs. I don't have to do that any more. I played hockey at university this year, and played with my friends, and I've never had so much fun in my life. This summer I'm pumping gas full-time, and playing lots of baseball, and then I'll go back to school in the fall.

"If I hadn't come forward, those guys would still be out there. I'm sure there'd be another generation of kids screwed up. I use the analogy of a new crop being harvested. They'd get their hands on them too."

Paul McLeod adds that the family doesn't believe anyone on the team cared about the kids. "Jim Debenham is a scout for the OHA now. I remember so clearly when he told me Scott better get used to this if he wanted to play. He couldn't see why we were upset. The next time I saw him was after we got the release from the team for Scott and he was playing for Essex. He walked into the arena and came over to me and said, 'We're going to sue you.' This was before we had gone to the police, and I said, 'Go ahead, I hope you do.' In the back of my mind I knew it would be one way that everything would come out. They try to intimidate you, and it may have worked with some other families, but we knew what the truth was, and the only thing to be afraid of is that it can happen again. If it fades into the sunset, it'll start once more. That's why we stood up."

Meanwhile, the three owners have believed from the start that the media coverage of the case was biased. They threatened to sue the *Chatham Daily News* and court reporter Bill Currie, who covered the story extensively, but no legal action was taken. The sports department of the paper hardly covered the story at all. In the sports editor's office there is a plaque that was presented to the paper by the OHA for excellence in hockey coverage. The sports editor, Mike Bennett, agrees with the team owners that reaction to the initiation was overblown. He'd heard about the incident well before the McLeods went to the police, but didn't believe any assaults had occurred. "This sort of stuff has gone on forever," he says. "It's just in the past five years it's got really sexual. But they didn't put the marshmallow right inside, just between the cheeks."

One of them maintains that "it was just a rookie party. There were no victims, and no under-age people drinking. That's just a rumour. The Crown lays charges despite the fact there was nothing sexual about the activity, no indecent acts, and no negative effect on anybody else."

An observer close to the case believes they're still smarting. "These were all well-off businessmen in town," he says, "and then the cops come along and charge them with all kinds of sexual-assault charges. Doesn't look good on them."

Crown attorney Paul Bailey says his experience with the players was not like Phyls's, who said only one family felt their son had not been victimized. "I had two witnesses who would co-operate, and the rest were hostile. It's very frustrating dynamics, but very similar to a family where a victim, for whatever reason, doesn't want to participate in prosecution. You have circumstances where one sister won't testify against a father who sexually assaulted her or lend support for the other sister who is charging him. She hangs her own sister out to dry because she doesn't want to be unearthing the family secrets.

"Those dynamics were working here. Most of the players didn't want to do anything except bury it. It was a 'closed family incest case.' To say hockey has any real family values is absolutely absurd. I wouldn't let a daughter go out with one of these guys. If they think it's normal to do what they do to each other, what do you think their attitude is towards girls and sexuality? I see a lot of disgusting cases in this job, but this is really sick."

The OHA says the Hawks' initiation was an isolated incident. They say hazing is against the spirit of good sportsmanship that the OHA embraces. But that's not what Bill Lang believes. At fourteen years of age, Lang decided he'd try out for the Markham Waxers, a junior B team. Junior B and C hockey don't have the age minimums that major-junior hockey has. He was successful, and became the youngest member of the team. But making the team at such a young age didn't seem to be good enough. Certain members started to pick on him, just irritating little antics to remind him of his rookie status. Lang walked away from their pranks, but he could sense something sinister behind the stunts. One night during a bus ride to a game in Milton, senior players again turned their attention to the fourteen-year-old.

"It was a power thing with the team. They had to teach the rookies who was in charge," says Lang, who went on to play four years of junior hockey, then professionally in the United States, and later for the University of New Brunswick. "For some reason the coach wasn't on the bus on this particular trip, and the trainer was seventy years old. He didn't do a thing.

"A group of six or seven players came up and pulled me to the back of the bus. They told me I had to masturbate in front of them.

They ripped the shirt off me. I told them I wasn't going to do it. They insisted. This went on for quite some time, and thank God we got to the arena.

"It was as if nothing had happened on the bus. They acted like everything was normal. I was terrified, because I had thought my father was going to be at the game and I would be able to go home with him, but he was unable to attend."

The game was the first one his father had ever missed. "I tried my hardest to get to Milton," says Bill Lang, Sr., "but work at the office came up that I absolutely couldn't neglect. I asked someone who worked with me, who was on the team, to make sure Billy was okay. He was on the bus when the incident happened, but didn't intervene. He confirmed what they tried to do to my son the next morning."

The trainer testified later that Lang looked as if he was suffering from a concussion before he re-entered the bus after the game and was too agitated to eat anything when they stopped for fast food. During the ride home, the players turned on Lang again. "On the way home, I sat with the trainer. They came to get me again, and I wrapped my arms and legs around the seat. There was no way I was going to let them get me. The ringleader really manhandled me, but I didn't let go."

When Lang got home he immediately told his father what had happened. Seven rookie players had been singled out. The others, all sixteen years old, did what they were told, and masturbated in front of the senior players while fully naked. One also ran naked into the fast-food restaurant.

The next day Bill Lang, Sr., called the owner and the coach and threatened to press criminal charges if the team did not address the issue. His son was not going to play until those responsible for the assault were removed from the team. The following day the players were gone, but the Langs decided they should still go to the police. They could not believe teammates would be anything but respectful of one another.

Bill Lang went back to the team, but the Lang family had under-estimated the backlash their protest would provoke. The players had only been suspended from the team, not banned from the arenas. "One of the players who had been suspended by the team sat with his father behind me at Billy's next game and verbally harassed me," says Bill's mother, Debbie, who attended the game with her husband. "They said things like, 'The old man [her husband] can't satisfy you. Come up here and get it from a real man.' I was three months' pregnant. We had to have a police escort out of the arena that night. . . . It's left a scar."

Soon Lang had left the team for good. Now twenty-four, he continues to love and play hockey, but still has bad memories about his adolescent start in the more elite levels and has nothing but criticism for the OHA's role during his time with the Waxers. "The OHA did nothing. They should have stepped in and either suspended these guys [from the league] or taken away their playing privileges. The lack of action on their part was disgusting."

Bill Lang, Sr., confirms that there appears to be a real need to watch out for abusive sexual behaviour in hockey. "Believe me, I've seen and heard a lot with two sons in the CHL [their son Chad plays for the Peterborough Petes]. So many of those players need to watch each other having sex. I remember being in a parking lot while a girl did the deed to a player in a car while fifteen to twenty players and their girlfriends watched them. It's all pretty sick."

Not surprisingly, then, when Bill left home two years later at sixteen to play in the OHL, Debbie Lang was still "very frightened. I don't trust anyone with my sons," she says. "Billy told me, 'Mom, no matter what they did to me, I wouldn't play with myself.' That's what they wanted him to do while they watched. Can you imagine? Anything can happen out there. But I trusted my son. He'd already been exploited, so he knew what to watch out for, how to seek help, and fight his way out if he had to."

A trial ensued in September 1988. Justice Robert Osborne of the Newmarket Provincial Court commended Lang for coming forward and being honest and courageous. "Billy wanted to go to court and look the guilty parties right in the eye," says Debbie Lang. Only one player was found guilty and given an absolute discharge.

When questioned recently, Brent Ladds couldn't remember the Waxers, but eventually it came back. "Oh yes, the Markham Waxers. I forgot about that one. They were trying to be proactive in that one, releasing the players involved. I'm not so sure that was a good punishment for what took place in this particular incident. I think the players involved got off rather lightly. But at the time no one seemed overly concerned about it." Ladds still believes no charges were laid, even though the case was covered in the *Toronto Star* and the *Hockey News*. An article in the *Star* in September 1988 is headlined, "JUDGE FINDS HOCKEY PLAYER GUILTY IN HAZING RITUAL."

The Langs have no time for the OHA. "They're one big old-boys' club, covering up for one another," says Bill Lang, Sr. "I don't see the need for any kind of an initiation whatsoever. Why do they have to even shave heads? It's intrusive and humiliating. What's all this about? Certainly it has nothing to do with hockey.

"The OHA didn't want to face what was happening, so they pretended nothing had. If people only knew what was really going on, these hockey organizations wouldn't be worth so much money. It's all about money and power. They don't care at all about the kids."

When Rob Boyko of the University of Guelph Gryphons refused to participate in a rookie initiation on January 28, 1996, it set off a chain of events that turned into a nightmare.

The hazing started before a Super Bowl party the senior players had planned in the locker room for the rookies. Each player had "drafted" a rookie (often called their "bitch") for the week. Adam Pender, a veteran on the team, drafted Boyko. "You're my guy," he said over the phone, and told Boyko he better show up to the locker room for the party.

A rookie who is drafted by a senior player is expected "to share a lot. They like to watch you do things for them and tell the rookie when it's his turn to do something," says Michael Lannon, Boyko's lawyer.

"It was posted on the blackboard the week before the party that the rookies were to attend," Lannon continues. "But there were also plenty of innuendoes. The rookies were told to bring condoms, booze, and wear loose-fitting clothes, because they wouldn't be wearing them long. There was talk of screwing a three-legged cat, or a groupie. When guys know that seventeen-year-old girls get gang-banged, and all the team does is keep chanting, 'Do it, do it, do it,' a cat's not out of the realm of possibility.

"Rob was very nervous. Somehow he'd escaped the worst of initiations when he played major-junior hockey, and didn't expect it in a university. He was very reluctant to go, but was pressured, so in the end he went, but didn't bring the booze. He didn't feel well and didn't want to drink anyway. He was training.

"When the captain and assistant captain opened the door of the locker room to let him in, he saw the other rookies lying naked on the floor. There was no way he was going in there. They were furious with him for showing up late and not bringing any booze, and started to swear at him. He left, but not before they told him not to bother to show up for practice the next day."

Boyko left a note at coach Myles Muylaert's office, tried to get in touch with him the next day, and called him three or four times the next night. Boyko didn't show up for practice the next day, but he did find out there had been a meeting between the captains – whom Boyko felt had extraordinary power – and Muylaert. He was suspended until he apologized to the team. Boyko refused to apologize.

"It starts way back in minor hockey," says Ron Boyko, Rob's father, a coach at the minor level. "There's such great pressure to make it at the triple-A level. I remember one mother telling me about her little boy getting grabbed by the arm by a coach in the dressing room because the coach didn't feel he played well enough. You don't do that to anyone, but especially not little children. She complained, and was told, if she wanted her son to go anywhere, never to mention what goes on in the dressing room. I love the game, but I don't like the power people have over the game."

Rob quit school and hockey. The Boykos and their lawyer, Michael Lannon, believe the University of Guelph handled the case badly. No serious reprimand was given and no apology made. "It wasn't so much the hazing, which he didn't participate in, but the fact that it happened in university," says Lannon. As of spring 1997, Rob is working several part-time jobs and weighing his options for the future. Meanwhile, he has a $2-million-dollar lawsuit against the university.

While certain people in the hockey world believe Boyko over-reacted to the incident, he appears to be in good company. Ken Dryden spoke to "the fifth estate"'s Lyndon McIntyre in their "Thin Ice" documentary. Months after the documentary aired, Dryden became the president of the Toronto Maple Leafs. "At a certain point it's abuse," Dryden told McIntyre. "I mean, it's assault, it's abuse, it is straight humiliation. It is taking ritual and tradition as licence to do things you would never do to anybody else, anywhere, anytime else, in your life. And that's simply not right."

Like Rob Boyko, Ken Dryden was always very much aware of the potentially devastating effects of initiations and hazing rituals. The mere threat was intimidating. "I was always afraid it was going to happen. I was always sure that when that next year came around and the voices in the dressing room would start to gather and start to say, "I think we should get . . . I think we should get . . ., that my name would come up. And I would sit in my place in that room and I would just cringe. . . . I always thought of it as an immense, immense risk. 'If I go through the other side of it, I'm going to feel so humiliated by it that I can't take it. I'm going to go, I'm going to leave. I'll leave hockey.'"

To those outside of hockey, the effects of initiation are similarly obvious. "The fifth estate" also interviewed Val Ridley, who at the time was seventeen years old and had been intimate with more than one player on the Peterborough Petes in her home town. She told McIntyre about the changes she saw in rookies. "The rookies always come in really shy, really quiet. And then once the veterans get a hold of them and they have their initiations, that's it. It's like a total different person."

The changes that occur in players because of initiations don't seem apparent to those in charge of hockey, or, if they are, they are seen as positive. The CHL until very recently was not troubled by their existence. David Branch, president of the CHL, denounced "the fifth estate" documentary partly on these grounds, while Jim Donlevy, the educational consultant for the Western Hockey League, states simply that brutal initiations don't happen any more because they've been banned. Perhaps Donlevy is unaware of the initiation of an Alberta junior player who was stripped naked and locked in the washroom of the team's bus. While the bus sped along a winter highway at night, the player, while attempting to force his way back into the bus, fell out the emergency exit. He was found with broken bones and unconscious by the side of the highway. His family is now suing the Alberta Amateur Hockey Association. In December 1997, parents and at least one player launched a formal complaint with the OHA about a similar initiation that occurred on the bus of the Kingsville Comets, a junior-C team outside of Windsor, Ontario. The coach, Richard Ropchin, was present at the time and later said, "I think hazing is too strong a word for something the kids may have done."

Donlevy has only praise for the CHL and WHL: "I wouldn't be in the sport if I thought otherwise, and am proud to be associated with the league. I don't think I'm naive; I think I know honesty and integrity."

Recent initiations may have escaped Donlevy's attention because the victims are too embarrassed or humiliated to talk. Unfortunately, their silence is conveniently misinterpreted. Initiation may well be successful in bonding a player to a team, not because the relationship gives him great pleasure, but because the forced alliance of the initiation joins victim and perpetrator as co-conspirators; they share a "dirty little secret."

Abuse may not always be overtly sexual, but players are frequently asked to perform humiliating physical stunts that are potentially harmful, and in every case the entire relationship is psychologically and emotionally abusive. Jud Richards, formerly of the Sault Greyhounds, was also interviewed in "Thin Ice." When he went to a Hounds' initiation party, he did so with great trepidation. He remembers driving there with two other rookies. All three felt sick before they even entered the room the team had booked in a hotel.

They were ordered to take all their clothes off, and made to drink out of a punch bowl that contained, "different alcohols . . . gross things, I'm not sure exactly what. Possibly spit and maybe urine, I'm not sure," Richards told McIntyre.

Naomi Levine, a lawyer and harassment consultant in Winnipeg who now works a great deal in sports, says the form the initiations take proves there's much more at work than moulding a good hockey team. "Of course these coaches and players will claim there was nothing sexual about what they did. But then why did the players have to take off their clothes? If the initiation isn't a sexual assault," asks Levine, "why, in certain initiations, is the penis or the anus such a focal point?"

Greg Malszecki, a sports historian at York University, argues that there is a deep connection between "the erotic and the combative" in sports. He refers to the sexualized violent language of sport, which he calls "man talk." Modern sport is filled with man talk, argues Malszecki. Just look at how words such as "penetration," "attacked," "obliterated," "impotent," and dozens of others are used in the sporting world.

Malszecki's analysis of language applies very nicely to Ed Chynoweth's choice of words. Chynoweth has been president of both the WHL and the CHL and is now part-owner, governor, and general manager of the major-junior franchise the Edmonton Ice. In the 1993 Memorial Cup souvenir book, he is quoted as saying, when referring to the drafting of European players to the junior leagues, "The International Ice Hockey Federation has expressed a concern to the CAHA. *The whole concept is not to rape the European federations* [my emphasis]."

Sport offers the "father" a way of initiating the "son" into this masculine language, says Malszecki. "Sport complements the relations between father and son by generalizing the social responsibility for making a 'man' out of a 'boy' by having other men test to see whether the job is being done satisfactorily," he says. "We can understand how the initiation rites of bringing a male child into adulthood through tests of endurance would shatter the bonds of childhood and any connection to the soft, gentle, and nurturing world of mother, sister, aunt, and female playmates. In the world of men and male supremacy, such tenderness is a betrayal of a man's life work."

Malszecki defines this culture that is obsessed with obedience and maleness as "homo-social" and believes its roots are in warrior society, which has shaped modern Western culture. "For a man, the attention of any man is more important than the attention of women. The only relationship that really matters is one between a minimum of two men. The role of women is to nourish the man emotionally so he can withstand the dysfunctional relationship he has with men. Not only are women out of the loop, but they end up contributing a great deal of labour to sustain such relationships because the dysfunctions men have with each other are never-ending."

Other academics emphasize the relationship between secrecy, ritual, and an extremely gendered culture in which the roles of both male and female participants are highly scripted, with disproportionate power in the hands of men. In *Secret Ritual and Manhood in Victorian America*, Mark Carnes, a professor of history at Columbia University in New York, looks at fraternal orders like the Freemasons, the Odd Fellows, the KKK, and hundreds of other secret societies that flourished during the Victorian era in North America to show how American society encouraged male-only ritual organizations to thrive.[2]

These organizations contributed to the framework of twentieth-century masculinity, and by the early 1900s, lodges outnumbered churches in large American cities. Even most ministers belonged to an order, the rise of which Carnes directly links to a male reaction to women's growing authority in the home and church.

While lodges and orders are remnants of the past, hockey organizations operate in a manner similar to these Victorian societies. Its organizations fought girls in the courts when they started making it on to boys' teams in the 1970s. Hockey officials successfully lobbied the Ontario Conservative government in 1981 to amend the Human Rights Code by adding Section 19(2), which withheld the rights provided under the Code from girls and women in sport and recreation. In 1985, Justine Blainey's case against the Ontario Hockey Association reached the Supreme Court of Canada and the Human Rights Commission before the OHA was forced to allow her to remain on the boys' team she and her brother played for.

The lodge has been replaced by more public gathering places, such as stadiums, arenas, gyms, bars, and strip joints. While membership may be open to more people, much of what happens in the crannies and corners – in locker rooms, garages, rec rooms, training camps, and motel rooms – is still very secret and genderized. Except for the fact that the rituals of this subculture have taken a sadistic turn today, little has changed since the Victorian era.

Like today's rookie, an initiate in Victorian times was seen as "immature or unmasculine," writes Carnes. The second stage of the journey occurs when the "angry father figures" kill or nearly kill him in a theatrical performance, after which he is reborn a man, and may join the family of men who have saved him from a life of femininity. "Emotional orientations by maternal nurture would give way to the sterner lessons of ancient patriarchs, venerable kings, or savage chieftains," says Carnes, and adds that the initiate "was reconciled to the fathers of the tribe."

When comparing the fraternal orders and hockey teams, Carnes wonders why the team needs to initiate at the end of the twentieth century, when men have had time to accept women as equals. "It's interesting that making the team isn't enough," he says. "It's not like these boys are the small bookworms in their class. They're already hockey players. So what does the initiation prove?

"They need to brainwash themselves that they require a masculine adult association. That would explain why initiations surface in hockey now," he says. "They still need to see the adult male role as very specialized, laden with machismo, and the initiation is the way to guard against any normal maternal imprinting. There is a great deal of hypermasculinity that tries to overturn the child-rearing done by women."

Carnes isn't surprised none of the people in hockey think of initiations as homosexual acts. He points out that even early this century, a man could have anal intercourse with another man and not think of himself as homosexual as long as he did the penetrating. "What's happening with these hockey players doesn't seem much different," he says.

While Malszecki has examined the history of language and male-only rites, and Carnes has looked at institutions, Alan Klein, a professor of anthropology at Northeastern University in Boston, has looked at the modern way in which sport and masculinity intersect, with his most recent study taking place among competitive body-builders in Los Angeles.[3]

"They were all hustling on the side," says Klein, meaning the amateur bodybuilders were male prostitutes in the gay community. "It's very interesting, because these guys identified themselves as straight, yet they hadn't had straight sex in four years. They were very conflicted sexually, which led to a string of other problems."

Klein says the allegedly straight bodybuilders turned to prostitution in order to subsidize their habit of bodybuilding. Like most prostitutes, they saw it as a way in which they could make desperately needed money in a short period of time. "The straight guys built up psychological defense mechanisms – homophobia, gay-bashing, they'd only perform oral sex, no anal, they'd swear during sex and show no enjoyment – lots of things that would allow them to think they were straight."

"We see a great decline in hustling once bodybuilders go pro," says Klein. His observations aren't unlike those of Scott McLeod, who said his own teammates "still had dreams. They're just selling themselves, I couldn't do that." The dreams, of course, were to make it into the pros, just like the bodybuilders. Former Manitoba player advocate Don Smith says junior hockey is about the "commodity of maleness." In this context, Chynoweth's comments about the boys being the CHL's number-one commodity, and about "raping" the Europeans by taking their best players, are most fitting.

Hockey teams are very similar to platoon units. In fact, plenty of coaches still coach in a military manner; they like to create a "My way or the highway" bootcamp atmosphere. Organized Canadian sport is derived from the British all-boy private-school system. When the British first immigrated to Canada they brought with them a model of sport that stressed the playing field as the preparatory ground for battle. It's not for nothing that it has been said, the battle of Waterloo was won in the playing fields of Eton.

Like the military, the world of hockey depends on the authority of those in charge. The organization is critically weakened if the rank and file feel free to question what they are called upon to do. A junior hockey team at the beginning of a new season needs to become a unit, and the individuals within it bound as soon as possible into a seamless whole. Initiations are considered the shortest route to this kind of cohesion. When players are induced to break sexual taboos, they have crossed a line together and shed inhibitions that would otherwise place limits on what they are willing to do for the sake of the team. In this way they become part of a well-oiled machine without the friction of each other's conscience.

Before revelations about sexual abuse in hockey shook Canada in 1997, in January 1995 we were treated to videotapes on national TV of the Canadian army's Airborne Regiment. The acts depicted included smearing rookies with excrement and feigned sodomy.

The *Toronto Star* reported, on January 14, 1997, that Shidane Arone, the Somali teenaged boy who was tortured to death by members of the Airborne while the regiment was in Somalia, may also have been sexually assaulted by them. Olad Abdulle Mohamud told the Somalian Canadian Association that, while he was being treated in the Canadian Forces hospital in Belet Huen, he could hear Arone's cries from the camp: "Guys, don't undress me. I am male. Stop it. Keep your penis from me, I am male." Olad also said he saw the Airborne beat Arone, "then they started climbing on him from the rear like a woman."

As in hockey, the military mind, and the military's supporters, will not accept that these incidents are evidence of fundamental problems with the institution. While the seemingly bizarre and extreme acts of the Airborne – both in Canada and in Somalia – grabbed headlines around the world, a Canadian investigation into sexual abuse in the military got almost no press at all. The week before the Somalia inquiry released its report on killings by the Airborne and the subsequent military cover-up, the *Globe and Mail*, on June 28, 1997, printed a short article closely related to the Airborne story entitled, "Released Documents Reveal Cases of Cadet Sexual Abuse." From 1993 to 1995, cadets had reported more than 150 cases of sexual abuse. For the most part, the abuse was at the hands of other cadets, but the abuse was also by instructors and those in positions of authority. The military says it has worked to address the issue of abuse, has introduced "abuse prevention officers" for all cadet programs, and will investigate, and prosecute if necessary, every case. Six months later, in December, three cadets at CFB Borden, near Barrie, Ontario, were charged with assault causing bodily harm when three new cadets told their parents about a hazing ritual that included serious beatings throughout the night.

While it is laudable that they recognize they have a problem, as in hockey no one inside the culture is asking *why* they do and why the problem of sexual abuse appears to be common to all groups of males gathered to exert their masculinity in a physically aggressive manner.

In 1994, American writer Susan Faludi went behind the scenes at The Citadel, the military academy in Charleston, South Carolina, which was made famous by Shannon Faulkner when she didn't reveal her sex in her application to the college and was accepted into the all-male fortress.[4] Faludi describes in her article published in the *New Yorker* in 1994 the stall-less showers and toilets, which cadets say is "at the heart of The Citadel experience." Hockey, too, provides this experience. "When I covered the Swift Current team," says a Saskatchewan reporter, "I was always amazed at how small the shower area was and how they all moved around in it together. I saw a great deal of strutting going on, with these guys in the nude just showing off to one another. There was a very strong group feeling there."

Jim Donlevy, education consultant to the WHL, acknowledges the group showers of hockey can get a little steamy, with players slapping each other and flicking towels. "There's no question about it," he says, "it's masculinity – perhaps a form of war games for control," he muses, "or to test the mettle of one another, I'm not sure. Whether it's driven by society or genes, I'm not in a position . . . to comment. All I can tell you is, when we travel, we would never sleep in the same bed."

The cadets at The Citadel all have their own beds, too, but that doesn't stop the camaraderie that takes place at bathtime. "I know it sounds trivial, but all of us in one shower, it's like we're all one, we're all the same, and, I don't know, you feel exposed, but you feel safe. You know these guys are going to be your friends for life," says a recruit.

"We're all suffering together. It's how we bond," another recruit told Faludi.

The military, just like hockey, sexualizes the initiation. "They called you a 'pussy' all the time," one former knob (first-year student) told Faludi, "or a fucking little girl." When their heads were shaved (a practice Ladds has no problem with in hockey), they were told, "Oh, you're going to get your little girlie locks cut off?"

If knobs appeared afraid, they were told, "You look like you're having an abortion," or "Are you menstruating?" This forcing of the younger boys to "play the part of the girl" is very similar to the sexualized initiations of rookies in hockey.

It is also similar to Don Cherry's Sport Select Lottery commercial, where he tells the team they aren't at a ballet practice when he wants them to work harder, or tells one player after he falls to give his skates back to his sister. Or when he called journalist Lyndon McIntyre "Linda." There is no worse insult, in the world of hockey, than being told you are no better than a girl.

When there are no women around to provide an example of inferiority, Faludi observes a "gender battle, a bitter but definitely fixed contest between the sexes, concealed from view by the fact that men played both parts. . . . If they couldn't re-create a male-dominant society in the real world, they could restage the drama by casting male knobs in all the subservient feminine roles."

Brian Pronger, a sports ethics professor at the University of Toronto, is the author of *The Arena of Masculinity: Sports, Homosexuality, and the Meaning of Sex*.[5] In it, he refers to the paradox of orthodox masculinity. In a highly homophobic climate, a great deal of time is spent trying desperately to be a man's man. If a man feels the need to prove his heterosexuality, he engages in homo-social activities such as male-only sports, or joins other male-only organizations. Within those subcultures, though, is a highly eroticized but completely denied atmosphere that tries to re-create the outside world and uses the new entrants – the rookies or knobs – as the designated females. He is his older teammate's "bitch," to use the expression of the Guelph Gryphons. We socially construct both feminine and masculine roles, so all hockey players and soldiers, no matter how brutal their behaviour, are simply acting in ways they believe real men should act. Consistent in every expert's analysis above is the degradation of women, or of designated women from a subservient male group.

While there are numerous similarities between the military and hockey teams, they both have a great deal in common with gangs. "It doesn't matter if it's the Cryps and the Bloods, or two hockey teams going at it," says sports sociologist Greg Malszecki, "the need to belong to a designated male group that will look after you seems essential to young males who feel insecure about masculinity."

Clinical psychologist Dr. Fred Mathews studied Canadian gangs for the federal Department of Justice from 1992 to 1993.[6] He broke several stereotypes, one by showing that Canadian gangs, unlike their American counterparts, mainly consist of middle-class youth who come from two-parent families, have plenty of material comforts and goods, future careers, part-time jobs, and other supportive structures. They have, in fact, the demographic profile of most boys who enter junior hockey.

Mathews's definition of a gang is "a group of three or more youths whose membership, though often fluid, consists of at least a stable core of members who are recognized by themselves or others as a gang/group, and who band together for social, cultural, or other reasons and impulsively or intentionally plan and commit anti-social, delinquent, or illegal acts." He also observes that "group members sometimes . . . wear common articles or styles of clothing [sweat shirts, baseball caps, football jackets, bandannas, etc.], or have some type of 'look' that signifies membership."

How is one able to prove membership and honour in such a group? Mainly through acts of physical intimidation in front of your peers, says one member. "I mean if you see someone quivering at your feet it makes you, like, 'Yeah, I have power over this person.' It's a head buzz. It's better than actually really getting high. Even though the guy might be six-foot-six and you're only five-foot-ten . . . you've got four of your friends [so] this guy is scared of you. I mean one on one you would never do that. It's a really big high. It makes you feel untouchable. If somebody sees a pair of shoes that they want and they're in a gang, [they] and three of their friends will go up and take this kid's shoes just because one guy wanted it. Even though he might be able to afford it, that's not the point. The point is the thrill of watching this person take off his shoes in front of you to give them to you because he is scared."

This behaviour is reminiscent of hockey initiations. Both acts are about intimidation and humiliation, although hockey initiations have sadistic elements too.

The study points out that male victims of gangs are silenced because of the shame they feel over being victimized and unable to "stand up like a man." Mathews believes that because of this, the sexual and bodily assault of boys and young men is under-reported.

The need to gain favour from one's peer group through violent intimidation and assault occurs not only between same-sex hockey players, but also when players are together engaging in sexual acts with one female. Like hockey teams, gangs also prey on girls and young women. If a girl is a member of a gang, or the girlfriend of a gang member, she is expected to have sex with the other members. She may submit to this unwillingly but be so terrified she won't report it to the police. The likelihood that she will be seen as a slut is enough to silence the girls. Sadly, this is also the case for girls who "service" hockey teams.

Another parallel between hockey teams and members of crime-focused gangs, who are often known as "players," is the role of father-figures. There are not only leaders, or captains, in gangs, sometimes there is also a higher authority. "The owner of the gang [I was in] was forty-five, fifty," says an Ontario gang member. "[He] had the full intention to develop a gang and have younger people running it for him so that he could make money and profit off it. That was the intention of the gang that I was involved with."

Like hockey players, both on and off the ice, gang members objectify their victims. A former gang member talks about life in a gang compared to his new life away from it: "I never thought about other people as having feelings. I just thought of another person as a thing or an object . . . we could go up [to] and beat the crap out of . . . not even thinking about life in general." Once away from the gang, he realized life offered much more: "It's not about gangs and money and power and violence."

The initiation in hockey is supposed to welcome the rookies into the family. Time and again, players and coaches refer to the team as "family." Gangs are also viewed as family by their members. Says one victim: "[The gang] becomes sort of a peer family for the young people in a sense of belonging. I think they need that. It's a replacement for a family that they may not be interested in being involved in, which is typical of teenagers."

Images of degrading hazings, homosexual or homophobic ritual abuse, and gang activity is not what comes to mind for Canadians when the word "hockey" is mentioned. Hockey, as a sport, as a game played in the richness of Canadian winters, can be a beautiful and wonderful thing. But what happens in the name of team loyalty and in the tradition of "masculinity" has nothing to do with a great game of hockey. It is about men who use boys for their own sport.

# CHAPTER FIVE

# When You Know You Just Have to Score

## *A Game Only the Boys Can Win*

Guelph, Ontario, lies approximately one hundred kilometres north-west of Toronto. Populated by 110,000 people, and surrounded by farmland and small industry, it is a vibrant community, with a down-town within walking distance of the University of Guelph. While the university may be the intellectual centre of the city, Memorial Gardens, where the Guelph Storm play, is the centre of passion.

Junior hockey has a lengthy history in Guelph, starting in the 1940s with the Biltmore Mad Hatters. The club started as a farm team for the New York Rangers, and was sponsored by the local Biltmore Hat Company. An immensely popular team, the club won the Memorial Cup in 1952, when future NHL players Andy Bathgate, Harry Howell, Ron Murphy, Lou Fontinato, Dean Prentice, Ron Stewart, Bill McCreary, and Aldo Guidolin all played for the team. Pretty amazing considering there were only six teams in the NHL in those days, which added up to a total of just 120 positions.

Not only did the team deliver players to the elite ranks of the sport, some claim it was the origin of one of hockey's most endearing phrases. Legend has it that every time a junior player scored three goals in one game, he was given a stylish Biltmore fedora. The feat soon became known as a "hat trick."

The Biltmores were owned by a group of local businessmen called The Big Ten and drew an average of 3,600 fans per game from the town. That was more than 10 per cent of the population, and the number grew to more than 4,000 as fans packed the arena during the playoffs.

Over the thirty years between the heyday of the Mad Hatters and the arrival, in 1982, of the Guelph Platers, the city of Guelph saw many changes in junior hockey. In 1963, Guelph lost its major-junior team to Kitchener, and later the Biltmore Hat Company lost a major manufacturing contract and was bought out by the American Stetson Company, which had no interest in junior hockey.

But in 1982, local businessman Joe Holody brought the Guelph Platers to town, naming the new team after his electroplating business. He'd been running a successful Tier II junior club, one division below major-junior hockey, and upgraded it to major-junior level when he was able to secure a CHL expansion franchise. The team thrived, winning the Memorial Cup in 1986, just four years after they landed in the "Royal City." But in the 1987 season Holody started grumbling about the contract he shared with the City of Guelph. Like virtually all major-junior franchises, the team benefited greatly from municipal facilities. For the first five years of the team's life, the two parties had a contract that stipulated the City would pay all arena operating expenses for the team in return for 15 per cent of the net revenue. Joe's son, Rob Holody, said their financial needs couldn't be met with this split. For two years both parties were in disagreement, and then in 1989, the Guelph Platers became the Owen Sound Platers, and Guelph was, once again, without a major-junior team. The city did without for only two years this time, and in 1991, a consortium of twenty-one businessmen, called the Guelph Community Hockey Club Ltd., bought the Hamilton Dukes, a failing franchise to the south of the city, for just under one million dollars.

The consortium was made up of leading men in the Guelph business and industrial sector. Bill Amos, president of Pizza Delight, joined forces with the likes of Steno Carniello, of Steno Electric, Frank Cernuik, of Cernuik Construction, John Woytkiw, president of Royal City Chrysler, and Sam Sorbora, president of First Paridien Realty Corp. But also on the roster were Dave Kendrick, a city alderman, the City of Guelph itself, represented at the time by the mayor, John Counsell, and Jim Rooney, principal of Bishop Macdonell High School, where most of the junior players would end up attending school. By the start of the 1991–92 season, the team, renamed the Guelph Storm, was on the ice, and Rooney was president and governor of the club.

Like a lot of new teams, the Storm didn't start the first season off with a bang. In fact, they finished at the bottom of the Emms Division with only nineteen points after four wins in sixty-six games, a new record low. Only one player, Sylvain Cloutier, made it into the OHL final stats, when he came third overall in rookie scoring. The team tried not to dwell on their poor performance, and instead committed themselves to achieving a better record the following year. Meanwhile, disappointment would be drowned in an end-of-the-season bash.

The March 14 party was a must-attend for the kids at Bishop Macdonell, who saw the players as stars newly arrived in their midst. They might have come last in their division, but the team had still put an end to a two-year hockey drought.

The party was held at the billeting house of a player in Guelph.[1] At the time, the billeting parent was home, and both he and the player stood at the door, checking to see who was coming in. They allowed approximately sixty people through, and perhaps all but two of the Guelph Storm were there.

The billeted player wasn't old enough to drink, but he made sure there was plenty of alcohol for those who chose to indulge. The beer was stacked up in anticipation of the event, and a bathtub was well stocked with ice and booze. There was an informal guestlist, but soon no one was checking and plenty of uninvited kids dropped by. One of those who said she'd been invited by the team was seventeen-year-old Cindy Green. She not only was in Grade Twelve at Macdonell, she worked at the arena as an usher, and thought of the Storm players as her friends and classmates.

The party got off to an early start in the basement rec room, although Green, who had got a ride with a friend, didn't arrive until ten. Green, a minor at the time, says she drank "two small glasses of vodka and grape juice," but one of her friends had got quite drunk, and at one point they went outside so Green could hold her hair back while she vomited. After that, they became separated, and when she looked for her ride home, she found that the driver had left without her. Not only that, the ten dollars she'd put in her cigarette pack for an emergency cab ride had disappeared, along with the cigarettes. She looked around for a ride, but realized that none of the players left in the rec room was in any shape to drive, and that one of them had passed out. The other players who were still left "were all sitting around talking," according to Green, and when she asked if someone could give her a ride home, the billeted player confirmed her suspicion: everyone was too drunk. Green didn't want to stay, because she was the only female amongst six males, but, she says, the billeted player replied, "You can stay upstairs. We'll have you home by morning." By this time, it was one-thirty.

After she realized she couldn't get home, Green stayed in the basement, along with three players. The passed-out player was in another part of the basement that had been partitioned off. Green says two of them picked her up and threw her "jokingly" on a sofa-bed that had been pulled out. They went no further when she told them what they were doing wasn't funny and to stop it. There were two other young men in the room at the time who weren't players, and the players told them it was time to go upstairs. After this, the television was turned on, and Green sat with two of the players at the foot of the sofa-bed to watch. But soon Green tired and, even though the lights were on, she climbed back onto the sofa-bed to lie down and quickly fell asleep.

She woke up when she felt someone undoing her pants, told whoever it was to stop, and pushed an arm away. By this time the lights were off, and she couldn't see who it was, but someone told her to go back to sleep. As she did her pants up, she felt someone trying to undo them again. Her eyes were getting used to the dark, and she could see there was a player on either side of her and a third was at the foot of the bed.

Her clothes were removed, and sexual intercourse occurred between Green and the three players. Sometimes there were two of them trying to put their genitals in her mouth while she was being penetrated vaginally. When it was over, Green says she gathered her clothes, got dressed, and rolled over and lay crying on the sofa-bed.

After this, someone went upstairs and returned with a can of whipped cream. Green's pants were pulled down again, one player penetrated her, and another sprayed his genitals with whipped cream and pushed them in her face. Eventually it ended, and Green went upstairs, where she was sick. She woke up in the morning on the couch in the living room, fully clothed, with blankets and a pillow.

Green maintains none of the sex was consensual, and that she struggled and cried and told them to stop. The players agree with her description of what took place that night, but say she was a willing partner.

The next day, when she had returned home, Green realized she had bruises on her arms, back, inner thighs, and breasts. The next day, March 15, she went to the Emergency ward at Guelph General Hospital, where she was advised to see her own doctor. She did so, and on March 18 she went to the police. Six days later, Guelph police issued arrest warrants for the three players (one of them a minor) and charged them with sexual assault under Section 271 of the Criminal Code.

Sergeant Brian Larkin of the Guelph police conducted the criminal investigation. The police knew the case would be a powder-keg because it involved the Storm. "We knew right off the bat this was going to be a delicate case, but we didn't treat it any differently than any other," says Larkin's colleague, Inspector Rob Davis, who also works in sexual assault. "Every sexual-assault case is treated as genuine until we have evidence that is it not. The benefit of the doubt definitely goes to the victim." The medical reports, he says, were consistent with force being applied in a sexual assault.

Lawyer for the players, David Smith, says his clients agreed with what Green said happened that mid-March night in the basement.

But they say Green consented. The case went to a preliminary hearing presided over by Judge Marita Roberts. She found enough evidence to go to trial, setting the date just over a year after the incident occurred.

Meanwhile, the defence turned up more evidence from the party. The player who passed out had earlier videotaped much of what happened that night. "There was no sexual conduct on the video," Crown prosecutor Alex Smith says, "but I think it's fair to say the behaviour of the boys is not the behaviour parents could feel proud about. Two of them were under nineteen and there was a great amount of alcohol consumed. . . . That's not to criticize the parents. Whoever was or wasn't telling the truth, it was a bad ordeal for all involved."

The evidence was strong enough for Smith to believe he didn't have a case against the defendants beyond a reasonable doubt. It was a difficult, but realistic, decision. The three teammates, accompanied by family and friends, filed into the Guelph Provincial Court House on the designated date, but Smith announced he was dropping the charges given the new evidence submitted by the defence. Two minutes later, the players, friends, families, and billeting families were in the hallway congratulating one another and distributing hugs all around.

"I know my son," said one mother, as she stood in the main lobby of the courthouse. "He's not capable of anything so horrendous. Those girls just want to be stars, and they think if they sleep with the boys they'll get lots of money when they play in the NHL."

So moved by the chain of events was this mother that she wrote to the editor of the *Guelph Mercury*, the daily newspaper that covered the case. In the letter, which was published by the paper, she said she had taken up her pen because:

> I know of no other way to thank a huge mass of supporters – youths and adults alike – for the support given to my son . . . and myself in light of the alleged sexual assault charges made against him and his co-accused a little more than one year ago.
>
> As you are aware, these charges have now been withdrawn by the Crown attorney.

I would like to thank each and everyone [sic] who was there for us from the bottom of my heart. [My son] and I both will be forever grateful.

The city of Guelph brings much heartache to mind, but it also brings much gratitude for good friends and supporters. . . .

Perhaps what is most interesting about this loyal mother's response to the case is the denial that her son could have committed the sexual acts Green said he committed. She referred to "horrendous acts," but her son had admitted to his lawyer that he and his teammates had performed these acts. They only disagreed over the issue of consent. It's perfectly legal to have group sex any way you want, if everyone is in agreement, and her son agreed he had vaginal sex with Green and then oral sex with her at the same time as his partner while their teammate vaginally penetrated her.

But this particular mother was not alone in the way in which she framed the case. The mother of the player who had videotaped a portion of the party and then passed out on the basement floor calls Green "a vindictive little slut." She blames the controversy on the girls who hang out at the rink. "If it was one of my girls, I'd break her neck. But the boys are nice and polite to everybody. They're not going to tell a kid to take a hike. She stayed because she wanted to. She crashed it; she wasn't invited. She just wants to make a quick buck when the boys turn pro."

Only one in 250 junior players actually makes it to the NHL, but both mothers believed their sons would be among those who do. They say any girl who gets herself invited to a junior-hockey social event is just looking for a future NHL husband.

But the second mother does take exception to one claim made by the management of the Storm. "I just read an article by [the general manager]. In one part he said the boys were well monitored. That's a crock of shit. The boys were not monitored after the season. My son was at the party. I don't like the circumstances around that party. It was at one of the billeting houses, and there were plenty of under-agers there.

"But I still think it's a quick buck. When it's evident the boys aren't going to make it, the girls drop them. I hope the team has learned from this."

The brothers of one of the accused also played OHL hockey. They supported their brother during the year-long ordeal, one of them claiming: "The girls just want to be stars and say they slept with one of the Storm players. But as far as I know, I don't know any guy who would go out with a groupie. Anyway, I bet she [Green] has slept with three-quarters of the team by now."

The billeting mother for one of the players supported him all the way. "They definitely weren't guilty. I've been getting to know [him] for some time. He's level-headed."

But what about alcohol? Could it have impaired his judgement?

"I don't know about alcohol, but he boarded with me for the season, I went to the games, and I came to court. If I'd found anything like that, I never would have allowed him in my house. I have a fifteen-year-old son. I wouldn't let that kind of influence occur."

The player who got so drunk he passed out does admit, however, that the party was a little out of control. "When we were at the rink, and not in the playoffs any more, we decided we'd have a party in a few weeks. Everybody found out about it through the grapevine. Sure, there was drinking. Everyone was having a good time. Only a couple of people weren't under age. It was a challenge to hide it all from the police."

He claims he can't remember a thing about the party after he passed out. Once his mother is out of earshot, though, the story starts to change. "I purposely did not go near her, because I didn't like her the first time I met her. I think there was almost no sex. I didn't hear nothing. Nothing went on. The parents were upstairs, and she says there was an attack in the basement.

"Maybe there was sex. . . . They were in one part of the room; I was in another. It was two or three o'clock in the morning. Hey, I don't want to say exactly what they said. They joked around and that was it. I hated her anyway. There was just something about her I didn't like.

"When the charges were laid, and I came back in the fall, I thought, This is just a joke. Something probably happened to her, so she blamed it on someone else."

Not everyone sees the relationship between the players and female fans quite that simply. Crown attorney Alex Smith believed Green's story and never doubted consent was not given. The evidence submitted by the defence, he says, "does not prove rape didn't occur. It just makes it difficult in a court of law to prove that it occurred beyond a reasonable doubt. I stand by the story the victim told at the preliminary hearing, but I didn't want to put her through the kind of ordeal this trial would entail when there would be next to no chance of winning a conviction. . . .

"If a 'puck bunny' [a term Smith had never heard before] is someone who seeks sex from a hockey player, I don't view the complainant as a puck bunny. People in the community may not agree with me, but that's very unfortunate if the community interprets going to a party as consent for sex.

"We take hockey players and we heap praise and privilege on them. It seems to me the message they get from that is they aren't governed by the same rules of society. One only has to look at the conduct of the Montreal Canadiens a few years ago when there were allegations they were having sexual activity with quite young girls. There's a lot of bucks, and an artificial life-style."

Inspector Davis doesn't want to get started on what he thinks about sports heroes. "All I can say is it's unfortunate the charges were withdrawn. That's not a decision the police participate in. Something happened at that party, and it was definitely more than the victim wanted. I'll stand by our investigation."

Davis says the biggest problem Green had after the incident was not that the police and the Crown didn't believe her, but that her own community refused to believe hockey players are capable of such acts. "One father chewed me out for half an hour, saying the police jumped in too soon," he says, while a Storm fan told him he'd "jumped in blindfolded." But, says Davis, "It doesn't matter what kind of a rape it is, you follow the same steps every time."

Mike Kelly, the general manager of the Storm at the time, has a survival-of-the-fittest analysis of teenage relationships. Days after the trial, he is in his office at Memorial Gardens. "In many ways this attitude is one of a wolf pack," Kelly says of how junior hockey players act off the ice. "There's strength in numbers. I don't know if it's primeval. It started there, and it's gone to team sports. That could be the make-up of sport.

"Females, up until now, were not an important part of their lives," he says of life before junior hockey. "But the male gender seems to think it's important to participate in sports. Yet there's a difference between team sports and individual sports. Girls seem to be attracted to the pack. Maybe the bigger the pool, the better the odds. Girls compete against each other for boys. They can get very catty – try to outdo each other – to attract the opposite sex. Again, though, age is a consideration here.

"Like anything else, with guys it's hormones," Kelly adds, "and skates and skirts don't mix. It's a truism, but something else, other than hockey, has entered their lives, and it's puberty."

In terms of the Guelph case, Kelly believes parenting is key. "You have to have the well-being of your kids at heart. Sure, go to a party, but an all-night party where there are girls? The players there were breaking curfew.

"I feel for her parents. The hearsay around town is not nice. It's the same about her reputation. But it was consent. They had enough evidence to show that. People were home upstairs. There was a mixed group to the end. She could have gone home with her friends. One thing led to another. There was heavy drinking, and she had problems. She probably felt she'd get killed if she went home at that hour."

Kelly appears to accept that the dynamics that night weren't as black and white as family and fans at the courthouse had painted them. He's been around hockey a long time. Does he wonder if girls are even sure of what sexual assault is?

"Yes," he replies, he does wonder, "and boys don't know what assault, sexual or otherwise, is. But that was group sex at the party. It's as simple as that. Fourteen- to twenty-year-olds are having regular sex at parties, that gets back to hormones. We have dietitians, nutritionists, the RCMP in to talk to the team about good health. There's always talk about safe sex in the dressing room. Safe sex, girls that hang around the arenas looking for attention and prestige, it all gets discussed. I would guess, looking at dating patterns, that girls tend to be more aggressive than boys."

Kelly continues that players on the team who have sex with female fans are now afraid of becoming the victims of false allegations of sexual assault because of their status in the community. "We need to better educate the kids," he says. "What's a good situation and what's a bad one."

Kelly led the Guelph Storm, after three years at the bottom of the Emms Division, to OHL championship contention in the next three seasons. The team made it into the OHL playoffs in 1997, but were ousted in the semi-final in seven games by the Ottawa 67's, who had finished at the top of the league's regular-season standings. At the end of the 1996–97 season, Kelly was hired by the Calgary Flames of the NHL as assistant general manager.

As of the 1996–97 season, Jim Rooney is still president of the club. Bishop Macdonell High School closed in 1995, and Rooney took over as principal of Our Lady of Lourdes High School in the same year. "I've been involved with junior hockey my whole life, and I think what we try to do in hockey is create a culture which supports values that recognize the dignity of the person. What happened back then is a frustrating situation. It should have never happened," says Rooney.

"But hockey is something you do for your community, as an educator, as a human being, as a person. It is a tremendous avenue for growth," he continues, saying hockey should not be judged on the basis of the odd bad apple. "Four out of the five last national junior teams had one of my kids on it. Hockey is the fabric of Canadian community."

Does Rooney think all those values supported by hockey are positive? "Absolutely. Hockey enhances family values. I don't think what happened a few years ago is appropriate – anywhere, anytime – even if everyone fully consents. I was raised to value abstinence, and it is those kinds of family values I try to instil in the players."

Cindy Green went back to her job at the arena for a while. But the stigma of the assault and the dropped charges followed her. She felt that the entire city of Guelph had turned against her, and found it impossible to live there. She moved away to pursue a post-secondary education. Her mother, who still lives in Guelph, says her daughter wants to put the ordeal behind her. It's something the whole family would like to forget.

Alan Johnson was a star of an Ontario junior hockey team.⋆ So great was his presence on the ice that he remained a celebrity in his home town long after he departed to pursue his hockey career farther afield. Johnson chose to continue to come home for the summers, however. It was a time to stay in touch with old friends like Doug Schultz, with whom he played hockey as a youngster.

One summer evening, Johnson and Schultz attended a local party, where they crossed paths with Theresa Saunders.[2]

Saunders, too, was an accomplished athlete. By age fifteen she had won many high school and county swimming events. Her life revolved around swimming, and she was hoping to win a sports scholarship to an American university some day.

That summer night, her friend Emily Samuels had invited her to come along to her parents' house for dinner and a party afterwards.

Then Samuels suggested they go to a party at the house of Saunders's next-door-neighbour – a boy who attended their high school. Saunders had never been to a party without grown-ups and wanted to see what it would be like.

She was disappointed. People were just sitting around and drinking, and the conversation wasn't about anything she found interesting. She remembers she looked like a real jock, with baggy jeans and no make-up. She never wore make-up; it would just get all sweaty during her workouts in the gym.

One of the young men at the party suggested they leave and have a smaller party at his house. Saunders and Samuels got into a car with Johnson, Schultz, and a number of other people and drove to the young

---

⋆ The names of the people involved in this case and some of the details have been changed.

man's house. Saunders says she hadn't heard of Johnson before. In fact, she didn't pay any attention to hockey games, as she was too busy with her own sport.

While she was in the basement, she was joined by Johnson and they played some pool. Soon Johnson suggested they make the game more interesting and turn it into strip pool. She "passed it off as a joke" and continued to play. Eventually her friend came downstairs with Schultz and the young man who lived in the house, but Samuels and the young man went into a separate room, leaving Saunders alone with Schultz and Johnson. They turned on some sports on TV but she was soon nodding off on the couch. It was somewhere between one and two in the morning.

Later Saunders awoke, she says, to find Johnson kissing her. She says she told him to stop, that she wasn't interested in him and had a boyfriend. But, she says, Johnson ignored her, and said, "You know what I'm going to do to you?" Then he picked her up and took her into an adjoining workshop.

It was a small room, crowded with a workbench and tools, barely large enough to turn around in. He put her on the floor. "He took off his clothes in front of me, his pants and underwear, and I didn't, I just stood there," says Saunders. "And then he started to undo my blouse and . . . he kept on saying, 'Oh, you know you want me.' Like, 'Everybody wants me.' And, 'You don't know who I am?' And then he removed my clothes."

He picked her up again and put her down by the workbench, had already undone her blouse, and took her bra off, throwing it on the hamper. "Spell my name," she says he told her, as he kissed her and took off her underwear. Once he achieved an erection, he pushed her against the freezer and had vaginal intercourse with her.

She says she told him, "No," "Stop it," and "I have a boyfriend," and even named the boyfriend, but it was to no avail. Partway through, says Saunders, Schultz joined them. He asked Johnson, "Why didn't you call me? Why didn't you wait for me?" and then told him to hurry up, Saunders alleges. Schultz had vaginal intercourse with her, too. She says that she protested again, telling him to stop it, that she had a boyfriend and he had a girlfriend, but he continued. Though he did tell her, she says, not to tell his girlfriend.

When Johnson finished, she says, he put his penis in her mouth and then forced her to get on her hands and knees and sodomized her. Schultz was telling him to hurry up, and when Johnson was finished, he sodomized her as well, says Saunders.

Saunders says she was in shock – paralysed with fear. The two friends went upstairs when they were finished with her. She knocked on the basement bedroom door where she thought her friend had gone with the young man who lived there. Her friend asked her if she was okay, and Saunders said she was fine, nothing was wrong. Her friend asked again, and Saunders said nothing was wrong but she needed a blouse because she couldn't find hers. Later Samuels would testify that Saunders was "a little frightened, shaken up and crying."

They found a blouse for her, and Saunders went upstairs to wash. Schultz and Johnson were lying on two beds across the hallway from the bathroom. "Good morning," Johnson said to her. She smiled, washed her face, and ran home as fast as she could. Blood was dripping down her leg by the time she got home. She had been a virgin.

Saunders said nothing to her parents, but in the ensuing months she spent many hours curled up in her closet with the door shut. "There were three walls and a door. It was quiet and closed," she says. "I knew I was safe. Picture walking around every day and wondering, What's going to happen to me? On the street is there somebody behind me? If they're capable of doing that to me, then anyone's capable of doing anything to me."

She felt a black hole swallowing her up. Often she'd wake up screaming with nightmares. "I should not have to live with those dreams. That's not fair. I shouldn't have to live like this," says Saunders, six years later. "On the outside I look really strong, but I'm damaged."

Two months after the incident, she started talking to counsellors at the town's crisis centre. The visits became frequent, and she has been in counselling ever since. Somehow word of the incident got out at school, and before Saunders knew it the high school turned against her. Kids called her "slut" and "liar" in the halls. One girl scratched "slut" into her locker door. One day, while walking home from school with a friend, another girl called her a slut from across the street. Saunders had taken enough abuse. She lunged at the girl and hit her head repeatedly against the concrete. Her mother happened to see what was going on from their house, and she rushed out and pulled her off the girl. As soon as they were home, the story of what happened that summer night unfolded.

Saunders went to her doctor six months later, and eventually broke down and told him what had happened. His medical notes from their meeting confirm that she was badly traumatized.

Saunders says she also told her school guidance counsellor about the alleged assault. She says that was a terrible mistake. Despite the fact he had been a counsellor for twenty-four years, she says he broke confidence and told others, both teachers and students, about her ordeal. What was worse, she says, he wouldn't take her seriously.

She tried to tell the story in other ways as well. One day in a self-defence class she had a flashback that brought it all up again. Her instructor was demonstrating a defence and asked her if she would act as the victim. When he touched her, she retaliated by hitting him as hard as she could. She says being in close proximity to a muscular male body reminded her of how Johnson had straddled her while she was on the floor. To this day she is revolted by muscular legs.

Later, she asked her instructor if he knew how long someone had to report an incident. Then she broke down and told him about the evening as if it had happened to a friend.

Eventually she decided to lay criminal charges after a long session with her English teacher. "I had to keep being excused from class to go to guidance counselling," says Saunders, "and one day she asked me if there were any problems. I told her what happened. I needed to tell her. She was really good about it. It took four hours at the police station."

Johnson and Schultz were each charged under the Criminal Code with sexual assault. When the local newspaper announced the arrests, people phoned in and wrote to the paper declaring they would no longer subscribe if they continued to libel Johnson. Shortly afterwards, the sports section published a story on Johnson, saying ever since the charges were laid "his life has been under a cloud."

After many delays, the trial finally got under way. The defence selected trial by jury. By then, Johnson had graduated to one of the NHL feeder leagues. Saunders had left town and continued her schooling with family in Sudbury after the taunts at school became too much to bear. Before she left, she says, Schultz would come to the restaurant where she worked after school just to sit and stare at her. The first time this happened, Saunders, who had developed stress-related illnesses, started to throw up blood, and called the police. They removed him and charged him with breaching his court order, but Saunders was unable to explain exactly what kind of stares he had employed, and the court decided he hadn't made physical contact or spoken for any length of time with her, and acquitted him. Physical ailments continued to plague her. She was no longer able to swim; she blacked out in one race and suffered severe cramps in others. She experienced recurrent rectal bleeding, especially during each of the lengthy court appearances.

Saunders says the sexual-assault centre provided essential support. "My counsellor, and another counsellor, were so great. They came to the trial. Even one of their husbands came. If a girl doesn't get counselling, I think she'd probably want to die. I wanted one nice week without any nightmares when I lived in Sudbury. Just one week. I think part of me wanted to die. I took a whole bunch of sleeping pills to knock me right out, but I ended up going to the hospital. I'm not that stupid, I really wanted to sleep, only part wanted to die. But I think someone without any help would just want to die."

During the trial, Saunders often broke down under cross-examination. Counsel for Johnson suggested that the sexual intercourse with the two men was consensual, that it was only after word got around and Saunders's reputation was at stake that it became non-consensual in her mind. He also said she didn't like it when Johnson didn't call her afterwards. "I'm suggesting that's when it became a non-consensual sexual intercourse," the lawyer told her.

"No, you're wrong," she replied through tears. She had no desire to see him again, Saunders told him.

Schultz's lawyer told Saunders she had framed herself as a victim so people would feel sorry for her.

"I was always a victim," she replied.

One observer at the trial says Saunders "fell apart" on the stand, that she was much stronger during the preliminary hearing, a common phenomenon in sexual-assault trials. The defence chose not to call Johnson or Schultz or any other witnesses.

In the end, it was Saunders's credibility that was at stake. The Crown attorney told the court Saunders was a typical teenager. She had gone to a party, and stayed out later than she was supposed to, and wanted to please her parents. Why on earth would she fabricate such a horrific story?

He argued that both Johnson and Schultz had tried to get Saunders to drink alcohol, that she had been carried into the workshop from a couch. Why would anyone who was consenting to sex move from a couch to a cramped workshop? The Crown attorney also said the two men had planned the attack on the evidence of Schultz's comments to Johnson when he arrived in the workshop.

After seven days the case ended, and before the jury filed out of the courtroom, the judge instructed them to disregard the Crown attorney's speculations. "I suggest to you there is absolutely no evidence whatsoever to justify such a submission," said the Ontario Court General Division judge. He also instructed them to take into account whether or not Saunders had kicked and screamed when looking at the issue of consent, even though the Crown had pointed out to them that Saunders had repeatedly said "No," that she had said she had a boyfriend, and that many sexual-assault victims don't scream, kick, or fight. The Crown had contested, as well, that leaving Saunders in the workshop after anal, vaginal, and oral sex and going off together was consistent with a brutal attack rather than consensual sex.

The jury was sequestered for twenty-four hours. At nine o'clock the next night, they returned. They needed clarification. Could they find guilt on one charge, but not the other? The judge didn't know what they meant. Did they mean, Could one of the defendants be found guilty and the other innocent? Or did they mean, Could they convict both on one charge, but not the other? He said he was not allowed to instruct them either way. They left the courtroom once more.

The Johnson family looked at each other in astonishment after the jury made its request. It was as if they hadn't imagined there could be any doubt. The next day the jury returned. They found Johnson and Schultz not guilty on both counts. Saunders fainted and slid between her chair and the table, crumpling on the floor. She was taken by ambulance to hospital.

Before the criminal trial had got under way, Saunders had filed her own civil suit against her alleged attackers. This would now be her only possible recourse. In early 1998, the case had not yet gone to trial.

In the 1996−97 hockey season, Johnson played for a farm team of an NHL franchise. It appears unlikely he will graduate to the NHL. Schultz continues to work in his home town, and still sees the woman he spoke of in the workshop in the summer of 1991.

Saunders is optimistic about her future. She has become an accomplished chef, competing in Berlin in the Culinary Olympics, and is planning to participate in an exchange program next year so she can train in Europe. She hopes someday to get back into swimming and make a full recovery.

"I still don't understand how people could believe what happened that night was consensual. I was on the couch when I fell asleep. If we were having consensual sex, why did we move into the workshop?" says Saunders as she sits beside her mother in a restaurant booth. "He closed the door so no one could hear what he was doing.

"Hockey players think everything is theirs, even if it says, 'Private, keep off!' I don't think they even think about it. I don't think they have a conscience that would tell them no. They're inhuman. When I was born, nobody told me people were going to control my life. Like there's no paper I signed where I said, 'Yes, I agree to you controlling my life and doing what you want.'

"I hate driving to [her home town]. I love my parents, but I hate visiting them there. As soon as I'm educated, I'm moving far away."

But the experience has also prompted her to help others who are dealing with their own pain. While still in her home town, she volunteered for the Children's Aid Society to drive to counselling young girls who had been sexually assaulted by family members. She says people from all over Ontario supported her throughout the trial, sending her faxes and notes of encouragement. "I didn't have the courage to write back at that time, but I want to do that now. I want to thank everyone, because I don't want them to think of me as rude and selfish. I do realize there really are some good people out there."

Janet Saunders watches her daughter as she speaks. They look at each other. "I couldn't understand their pain," says Saunders, referring to her parents, "because I was too busy with my own. Now I can."

"There's nothing there to support the parents," says Janet. "At one point we asked if there was any support group for parents who have to go through this, and there's nothing. There should be something for the family.

"Your prime focus as a parent is your child. We did a lot of talking. We talked about every aspect, about everything surrounding the whole thing. But over these last years, we've seen [Theresa] change and develop as a human being. . . . She's a better person after all this, because she rose above it. We're so proud of her."

In 1995, another gang sexual assault by a major-junior hockey team was reported to police. The circumstances, however, made it very difficult to determine whether it was the young woman or the players who were telling the truth. The twenty-four-year-old woman agreed that she had met three members of a team in a bar frequented by hockey players. All four of them drank together in the bar and later went back to her apartment. It is here, she alleged, that the sexual assault occured.

On February 20, the three players were charged with two counts each of sexual assault. They were released from custody on the condition that they not drink alcohol or make contact with the complainant. But other events happened. One of the players' lawyers released the complainant's name to the media, and announced that his client and one other player had a combined twenty-one-million-dollar lawsuit against the complainant. The lawyer and the chief of police went head to head on a townhall meeting broadcast live on CBC Television, debating the unorthodox approach of releasing a complainant's name.

The chief was known for his work with sexual-assault victims, and argued that if women knew their identity would be public knowledge, they would never press charges. The lawyer replied that complainants should be treated the same way as the accused – both should have their names released to the public.

In the end, the Crown believed there was not enough evidence to go to court, and dropped the charges. The complainant's friends, who were at the apartment in another room, said they did not hear anything to suggest that a struggle had occurred, or that she had told them to stop. As well, the complainant did not file a statement in civil court defending herself against the libel charges, which was seen as an admission that she had given consent. When the charges were dropped, the players dropped their civil action. The complainant was a waitress and a single mother; it was obvious she could not pay the amount they had alleged she had damaged them.

The case is interesting in that both sides may be telling the truth. If the complainant went to the bar, and was open to having sex with one or more willing hockey players, she was certainly free to do so. But, as the Crown in the case says, "in the context of vigorous alcohol and sexual activity, [changing one's mind] may not be communiciated in any fashion that would later convict someone. You have all these cases where the tenor of the activity changes. It's so hard to separate what happens in a bedroom."

Indeed, if sexual assault is one of the hardest crimes to prove beyond a reasonable doubt, add alcohol and initial consent, and the case becomes next to impossible. Did the complainant consent to group anal sex, followed by the players laughing at her and walking out, telling her on their way that they were going to find someone else they could do this with now? Or did she just want a night of fun with a hockey player so desirable that later he would be paid millions to sign with an NHL team? It is quite possible she hadn't imagined that being sodomized by hockey players, and then being ridiculed for it, was part of the contract she signed as soon as she started drinking with them that night.

"You know what they say in junior hockey?" says a well-known sports journalist. "The girls don't complain until you roll them over."

Sodomy, especially by a group, simply isn't what most women have in mind when they imagine an evening with a hockey player.

The above cases are examples of Ontario hockey players who were involved in cases where gang sexual assault was alleged to have occurred. None realized any convictions, and two out of the three resulted in civil actions by the accused against the complainants.

It appears that the accused sincerely believed consent was given. Yet the complainants, and virtually all police investigators and Crown attorneys, are equally compelling in their belief that consent was not given. Is it possible that both parties are being honest? What does consent mean? How do junior hockey players hear, or not hear, what girls and young women are telling them, and is their ability to listen any different from that of their friends who are not involved with violent team sports?

A player who engages in group sex, who long ago shut down the voice inside him that questions if the woman has really consented, does so because he needs to meet his own standards of masculinity and gain the approval of his teammates, who will judge him not as a compassionate human being, but as a hockey player. His actions have nothing to do with providing sexual pleasure and respect for a woman and everything to do with being seen as a man in his world. He does this because being a "team player" is good for his game, his bank account, and his future worth in hockey.

Lawrence Ellerbee, a psychologist and the clinical director of the Forensic Behavioural Clinic at the Health Sciences Centre in Winnipeg, is an expert in the field of sex offenders. For the past twelve years he has worked for the Native Clan Organization, a First Nations association that treats and tries to rehabilitate sex offenders. Ellerbee says there are three ways one can deal with a sexual overture. One is to decline verbally, and, if that is not enough, put up some form of physical resistance or try in any way to prevent abuse from occurring. With a negative response such as this, the meaning is obvious to the offender.

Another reaction is to comply, which doesn't necessarily mean consent. The victim in this case obeys the commands of the offender, and is most likely afraid to reject that person openly.

The third response is to give consent. Consent and compliance are the two responses most often confused with each other. Any time the person who has made the sexual overture is more powerful in any way than the person who is receiving it, the grey area between compliance and consent broadens greatly.

Dr. Stanley Yaren, Director of Forensic Psychiatry for the Province of Manitoba, believes men who behave in this way know what they are doing is wrong, but they shut down the voice, the internal inhibitor, that tells them to stop.

"Internal disinhibitors give permission to act inappropriately. That's why we know there's nothing spontaneous about what they are going to do. Sex offences are premeditated and rationalized in the offender's mind. As well, alcohol is an example of an external disinhibitor if these guys think they need help convincing themselves what they're going to do is okay," says Yaren.

While psychologists such as Ellerbee look at what goes on in the mind of individuals, sports sociologist Kevin Young at the University of Calgary looks at how those individuals are shaped by their sport. In particular, he examines the way in which male athletes learn that violence committed against their own bodies, and committed by them against other bodies, is a consensual agreement that confirms their masculinity. Young also asks if true consent is really given by the athlete to have his body subjected to such violence. In English common law, people in a contract assume the risk involved in the job, and all parties should understand equally what that risk entails. In sport, he argues, the players do not. Acts of violence occurring outside the rules of games or after the play has stopped add even further unacknowledged risk. But even before a Canadian boy steps on the ice, he has already been conditioned to disregard pain. Young believes that the televised writhing body in "super slow-mo," coupled with the approving commentary of TV personalities, diminishes the player's pain and renders it an artistic and sensual sports commodity.

He concludes that the athlete can either acknowledge this reality and raise his concerns as health and safety issues – given that no other workers in North America are certain to be seriously injured several times on the job – or he can keep playing in the league. But he really has no choice. Not only is his job on the line, his masculinity is as well, and he certainly can't "go soft," as Malszecki would say. He must be able to take pain like a man.

If hockey players themselves have to ignore the issue of their own consent to expose themselves to the risks of the game, is it surprising they sometimes ignore the right of others to withhold consent?

After the 1991 incident involving the alleged rape of a seventeen-year-old by four members of the Washington Capitals, Ken Dryden was interviewed on the CBC's "As It Happens" radio program about the incident. He said athletes "take their 'groupness' with them." The emotional relationship that has been forged in the physical nature of sport doesn't end when they leave the arena. "In the situations where all of the restraints start to disappear, then groups start to become dangerous. . . ."

This isn't the behaviour of most men. Most men don't sexually assault, and fewer assault in groups. It is the behaviour of certain men who travel in groups and have a great deal of power. The question is, why do these particular men behave in this way? It is as if the cognitive distortion in the individual becomes a collective distortion. It is as if the power of men together – especially men who are usually rewarded for their aggression and are using alcohol – distorts their perception to the point that they consider almost anything they do to be acceptable, because the flip side to thinking like this – that their behaviour is in fact criminal – would call into question everything they take for granted.

No study has been done in Canada that compares the rate at which junior hockey players commit sex offenses with that of their non-hockey-playing peers. But American anthropologist Peggy Reeves Sanday, a professor at the University of Pennsylvania, has done extensive research on the kind of culture that produces what she calls a "rape-prone society." It is defined by "high levels of violence, more emphasis on male toughness and competition, and a low respect for women as citizens."[3]

How does this translate to the locker-room culture of male team sports? American sociologists refer to the locker room as a "rape culture." In 1995, a study was conducted on division-one NCAA basketball and football athletes and rates of sexual assault.[4] Todd Crosset, Jeffrey Benedict, and Mark McDonald, of Northeastern University in Boston, looked at the "police records at 20 institutions from 1991 to 1993, and the records of 10 judicial affairs offices" over the same time period, at the "top twenty" basketball and football schools. The study showed that "male football and basketball players comprise 30% of the student-athlete population, yet are responsible for 67% of the reported sexual assaults." It also showed that male student-athletes made up 3.7% of the total male student population and "represented 9.1% of reported sexual assaults." A further study showed that while there were proportionally far more sexual-assault charges laid against male college and pro athletes than there were against the male population as a whole, they received far fewer convictions.[5] Researchers believe that because of their status the athletes can afford the best legal defence, team management can call into doubt the word of the complainant, and often the only witnesses to the alleged offence are the athlete's own teammates.

"It's the 'groupie defence' that these male athletes are using in court now," says cultural anthropologist Allan Klein, who was one of Benedict's advisors. "When consent is at issue, and it's the word of a powerful male athlete versus a female victim who slept with him, it's a foregone conclusion in most people's eyes that she wanted it. We're finding in the U.S. that women simply can't win in these cases."

Klein says that large amounts of disinhibiting alcohol are part of the aggressive "bachelor subculture" of sport. "This subculture has rape written all over it," he says. "The notion of putting these men together is so dangerous. They may be dangerous on their own, but together they're completely frightening, not just to women, but also to men, because at the highest level, their culture always values aggression and dominance."

Why is it that these kinds of studies have not been conducted in Canada? While the small Canadian cities and towns that are home to most major-junior teams have sexual-assault centres, they are not particularly visible, and girls and young women may not even know of their existence. This is unlike the environment in which the American studies of sport and sexual abuse have been conducted. University sport in the United States is the equivalent of major-junior hockey in Canada. But on the university campus there is greater access to sexual-assault centres and academics are far more aware of the sport being played on their doorstep. The fact that major-junior hockey is so isolated from the academic world may be one reason Canadian academics haven't rigorously studied it in a way similar to their American counterparts.

When this subject *is* aired in the university setting, stories of abuse emerge. The following story is told, not by a female complainant, but by a male varsity hockey player.

"I can't believe what's happening out there. I don't really want to play hockey any more. Hockey's not supposed to be so violent – rough, tough, and bang-bang. There's the social issues, too. You have to be very careful. You're a top prospect and you get vibes from one girl, then you meet another one and you get the wrong vibes. There's so much stardom, glorification of elite athletes, and you get caught up in it.

"My friend told me about [a major-junior] initiation where they had to have sex with this one girl in a hotel room. After the fourth guy, she told them to stop it. They were hurting her. My friend knew she didn't want it. There were eight guys altogether. He didn't want to do it, because he knew he was about to rape a girl, and he knew he wasn't a rapist.

"But he knew what the team would do to him if he didn't rape her, so he did. He feels so terrible about it. . . . But the girls are seen as fresh meat, and these guys are the wolves."

# CHAPTER SIX

# The Empty Net, Part One
## *How the CHL Fails Young Women*

"It's a man's world in hockey," says Bonny Cleary, who, with her lawyer husband, Hank, has billeted many players over the years in their home.★ "It's an attitude of, 'Boys will be boys, just don't get caught.' Sometimes I think I'm the only person who tells them they're hurting people. They're idolized like gods. Hockey puts them on a pedestal, but when I see them, I don't see a hockey player, I see a kid without a home. How do you learn to have a considerate caring relationship unless you've experienced one? They tend to cling together when they come here. Perhaps this creates the perception of being unfriendly and stuck-up. I think they're intimidated."

But in the fall of 1989, Wayne Heath and Ed Dimech – brother of a star in the NHL – were not strangers to the prairie town that is home to the Clearys and to one of the powerhouse teams in the

---

★The names of the people involved in this case and some of the details have been changed.

WHL. Heath had grown up sixty kilometres away, while Dimech was in his third successful season with the junior team and boarded with Pete Fuller, then the president and governor of the club.

The love affair with the team faltered on October 3 that year, though, when Corporal Ben Clegg of the town's RCMP charged both Dimech and Heath with the sexual assault of a seventeen-year-old girl.

Both players were immediately traded, but before they could get him out of town, Dimech told the officer, "I think it's a big joke. I think the cops are wrong. I think you let everything get out of control. I don't think it should have been in the press, and I think we were screwed because of it. I think that girl should be punished and the cops should be punished about the unfair press."

Harold Marshall, acting as counsel for the players, quickly threatened a civil suit against the police department for libelling his clients. Team officials circled the wagons, remaining tight-lipped and making no more comments to the press.

Everyone agreed the girl involved, Sandra Brown, had phoned Dimech on the evening of September 26, 1989, and asked him to come over to watch TV, and that he agreed to come only if Brown invited a friend along and he could bring his teammate Wayne Heath. The two versions of what happened that night didn't differ substantially, but the intent behind what happened, say the supporters of each side, certainly did.[1]

Heath and Dimech pulled up outside the Brown family's apartment building at seven-thirty, "honked a couple of times," according to the players, went around the block, drove past again, parked, and started to honk once more. Brown and her friend Carrie Sinclair, whom she had called while the players were on their way over, came down from the apartment to meet them. When Brown asked Dimech if he wanted to watch TV as planned, he said no, and held up something neither Brown nor her friend had seen before, but "were pretty sure was a condom box."

According to Sinclair, Dimech told Brown, "Either we fuck you or you never call me again and I'll never talk to you again." She said Brown replied, "Are you going then?" Dimech responded, said Sinclair, by saying, "Just wait a minute. [Wayne] might take my car and I'll come in."

Sinclair decided she really didn't want to watch TV, said goodbye, and turned to walk home. Heath drove away in the car, and Brown and Dimech went upstairs to the apartment.

During the trial, Dimech said he had known Brown for two years before that night. He'd gone out with her a couple of times, and had planned on phoning her the night before the incident to tell her not to call again, because he didn't want to speak to her. But when she phoned, he "suspected sex of some sort, so we – whatever. . . . [Wayne] and me had a discussion and we decided to go. We had nothing better to do."

Dimech continued to describe the evening, his version only slightly different from Sinclair's. After the teammates arrived and met the girls on the street, "we were just chitter-chatting, and then all of a sudden we just – I just asked, 'Well, do you want to get laid?' Like I was very direct. And me – [Wayne] looked over to me and he couldn't see Sandra, and then she started winking at me. So I thought that was yes, and it was." He added Brown smiled at them and that her friend left.

During cross-examination of Dimech by Brown's lawyer, Arnold Coulter, Dimech admitted that instead of asking, "Do you want to get laid," he had said, "Do you want to get fucked?"

Once they were inside the apartment, said Dimech, he and Brown just "talked and stuff." Soon they had moved into the bedroom, where, he said, both of them undressed, and after perhaps "a couple of kisses," she performed oral sex. He said she didn't object in any way. Afterwards, he got dressed and left, but a few minutes later came back with Wayne Heath. Brown let them both in, and he told her, "Well, if you want to go out with me, you got to be with [Wayne]."

Dimech said she laughed and told him, "no, because she thought her parents were coming, and then I told her to take off her clothes and she just went into the room." He gave her a couple of minutes before following, and then, finding her only partially undressed, said, "Well, get undressed or we're going to go." At that point Heath entered, and Dimech removed himself to the living room. He could hear no objections from Brown, he said, and when he opened the door, "she was giving him a blow job." Dimech said he started to laugh, and so did his teammate and Brown. After this, he said, Heath had sex with Brown on her bed "in the normal position . . . like her on the bottom and him on the top."

But as Coulter continued his cross-examination of Dimech, more of the story came out. Dimech admitted Heath "was telling her to try. . . . And then after a while she said, 'No, no, no,'" at which point Heath said, "Okay, [Ed]. Let's go. It ain't worth it. Ain't worth it." Dimech said Heath got dressed, and he told her, "Since you don't satisfy [Wayne] . . . I won't go out with you."

Brown didn't want them to leave, though, according to Dimech. She "came out and she said, 'Please give me another chance. Please give me another chance,' and she grabbed his [Heath's] hand."

According to Dimech, Heath continued to resist her, saying, "Naw, it's not worth it." But after she pleaded once more, he relented. He would give her one more chance.

This time, according to Dimech, Brown lay face down on the floor. His teammate was successful in entering her. Dimech stood "pretty close" and watched. When Heath was finished, he got dressed, and on their way out, Dimech said he told Brown, "We won't – I don't want to go out with you."

After describing Heath's encounter with Brown during cross-examination, Dimech said he couldn't remember if he showed her a condom, nor could he remember any blood in her apartment. He did have oral sex with her, and had tried to have vaginal sex afterwards, but the condom broke.

Dimech said Heath dropped him off at the Fullers' house, and shortly afterwards Brown called and told him she was bleeding. "That's when she told me she was a virgin, so I just said I thought it was only natural."

During cross-examination, Dimech admitted to hitting Brown on March 20, 1988, after she became upset when he told her he "was interested in her friend." He said he didn't have a temper, but that Brown had struck him and cursed at him for talking about her friend in a derogatory way. He denied saying, "I'd like to fuck your friend every night." He also said he had repeatedly rejected Brown, but nonetheless expected to have sex when he went to her apartment on September 26. When questioned by Judge Jeremy Harding, the presiding judge at the trial, Dimech also admitted he told Brown not to talk about what had happened that night, "because it would have been embarrassing if she told like the people at school."

Wayne Heath's story started to change as police and lawyers delved further into the case. When Corporal Ben Clegg originally took a statement from him, he denied being in Brown's apartment at all or even having met her. Later, once he had talked to Dimech, he admitted to police that he had been at the apartment and had had sex. He said, though, that Dimech had told Brown that Heath was "going to screw" her, and that if she wouldn't let him, Dimech didn't want to go out with her any more, because she wasn't able to meet the conditions of the agreement. Heath admitted that he heard Brown say she didn't want to have sex and that she didn't want to take her clothes off.

When Heath attempted to penetrate her, he remembered her saying he was hurting her. But she begged him to keep trying nonetheless, and penetration eventually occurred. When Heath was finished, he realized she was bleeding.

Brown's story to the court was somewhat different. She said she longed to be one of the "in group" at school that hung out with the hockey team. On social occasions Dimech was mean to her, as if he was angry at her, she told Judge Harding. Dimech only seemed to be interested in girls if he could get sex from them, and then talked about them later as "sluts." But Brown didn't imagine herself in that category. She wasn't a slut; she just wanted to be a girlfriend. Still, she said Dimech had hit her twice in the past, after she hit him for saying he wanted to "fuck" her girlfriend. (Dimech admitted to having hit her, but said it was only once, and claimed he had said only that he was "interested" in her girlfriend.) After hitting her, Brown said, Dimech told her, "If you ever hit me again I'll break your nose." She hadn't talked to him face to face since that incident, only on the phone.

She testified that when Dimech asked her, "Do you want to fuck?" and showed her a package she thought contained a condom, she answered no and concluded he was joking, because he had said the same thing to other girls.

When they went into the apartment building together, she said Dimech pulled his cap low over his eyes. She said he stayed in the apartment for ten to fifteen minutes without incident and then left abruptly when a neighbour's kid knocked on the door and told him Heath was downstairs waiting for him. But five minutes later, the doorbell rang, and when Brown opened it, Dimech and Heath walked in. She said she distinctly remembers saying she didn't want them to enter, but they came in anyway.

According to Brown's story, Dimech ordered her to take her clothes off. She went into her room, and then came back out to the living room. He ordered her again, "Go into your room and take your clothes off." She wouldn't take them off, and soon Dimech "got really angry – like I never had – I still had my clothes on, and he got really angry with me. He had those evil eyes. . . . I was disappointed . . . and hurt about how he was treating me. . . . And then [Ed], he came back into the room and he looked behind the door and I still had my clothes on, and he got really mean with me, and his eyes stuck out very shiny. And he told me to take my clothes off, and I told him I didn't want to. And he told me, 'I want you to fuck my partner.' And I said, 'No.' And he wanted me to, and he got really mean with me . . . so [Ed] got out of the room and I had taken my sweater off, my bra, my jeans, and I left my underwear on. And I . . . grabbed my pink nightgown and I stood there against the wall. . . . He came in and he looked behind the door, and he told me to lay on the bed. So I got really scared and I had laid on the bed with my nightgown on top of me. And I had closed my eyes because I was scared of what they would do to me. And then I opened them up and [Ed] and [Wayne] were standing in the doorway. . . .

"[Ed], I guess, like switched the lights on, and [Wayne] told me, 'Give me head.' . . . And then [Ed] goes, 'Yeah, give me head.' And [Ed] was standing right beside [Wayne]. . . . And he forced his penis in my mouth. And I got it out of my mouth and I quickly turned my head. And then [Ed] was still standing in the room watching. And [Wayne], he got on top of me, and I told him to get off me. And he pulled my underwear off and ripped the elastic off my underwear. And then he pushed my body up against the wall. Like I hit my head against the wall. . . . And I remember [Ed] walking in front of the desk. He said, 'Oh fuck . . . get lost.' He said that more than once. And he also said, 'If you don't do it, I won't go out with you any more.' And at that time it didn't make sense to me 'cause we've never gone out before. And I remember [Wayne] on top of me and he couldn't do it to me. I wouldn't let him do it to me, and I didn't – like I didn't want to do it . . . and he told me, 'Relax.' He said that more than once."

During this time, Brown said, Dimech winked at her, then started to tap the toe of his boot on the floor to show her where he wanted her head while his teammate tried to penetrate her. Brown testified that Dimech ordered her to lie on her stomach on the floor. She was terrified, and did as she was told. Heath straddled her, and lifted open her legs while Dimech looked inside her. Heath then forcibly entered her, said Brown. "And I remember it was very painful. . . . It was a very sharp pain. . . . And . . . [Wayne] had said, 'There's blood.'

Later, Arnold Coulter, Brown's lawyer, confirmed that his client alleged that anal sex also occurred.

As the players left, said Brown, Dimech told her, "I never want to see or speak to you again." Brown continued to bleed heavily that night, and intermittently for the next few days.

The above testimony was given not at the sexual-assault trial of Dimech and Heath, but at the public-mischief trial of Sandra Brown. Before the case went to trial, police stayed the charges against the players and instead charged Brown, saying she purposely misled them when she told them the sex was not consensual. Brown had been asked to come to the Crown prosecutor's office on November 1, 1989. Meeting her there was Hugo Matheson, who at the time was the regional Crown prosecutor for the local branch of the public department for the province's justice department. He also happened to be a former law partner of Hank Cleary, part-owner of the team on which Dimech and Heath played. He told the court during the public-mischief trial, a "reliable witness" had alleged "some previous misconduct by [Brown]."

Another team member, Joseph Frick, told Matheson the defendant had had oral sex with Frick and Dimech on a previous occasion. No reason was given during the trial as to why oral sex is considered "misconduct" for females but not for male hockey players. Matheson believed, since Brown had had sexual contact with Dimech in the past, that her story was suspicious. He never asked whether the contact was consensual. He felt she hadn't put up a good enough fight against the players to convince him rape had occurred. He also doubted her word because she hadn't told police that she'd found a condom on her dresser and thrown it away. He called her "street-wise." Matheson made no mention of the fact that Heath initially lied to police by telling them he didn't know Brown and had never been in her apartment. His second story was accepted without question.

The police interrogated Brown several times about what happened that night. RCMP Constable Michael Murray had originally been assigned the case. He says the charges against the hockey players were justified. "Everything I said in court, I'll stand behind," he said later. "I was one of the people who charged those boys right from the start. But I don't have a good feeling about this case. I wish it had never happened, from the time the offence occurred to the trial. It was horrid. It's important to make sure this stuff gets written about, but it wouldn't be professional of me to comment any more than that. I have to live in this town."

Murray, who was trained in investigating sexual-assault cases, was taken off the case and replaced by Corporal Ben Clegg. In the five years Clegg had been on the force, he had investigated three sexual assaults. In court he said he told Brown he "didn't believe her. . . . I felt it would be impossible for a male person to hold a woman down, take off her clothes, and put on a condom." During his interrogation of Brown, Clegg told her he "didn't believe her story and that things didn't really happen the way she was telling" him. Finally, after two more hours of interrogation by Clegg, Brown agreed it was possible she hadn't said no. At that point Clegg read her a caution and charged her with public mischief. Brown had become the accused.

By this time Brown was in counselling and had contemplated suicide. Clegg, however, said he found Brown to be "remarkably controlled and remarkably at ease," when he was interrogating her. He did admit under cross-examination that he knew Brown had talked about suicide, but said he did not believe she needed to be accompanied by a crisis worker, parent, or lawyer during the two-hour interrogation.

The last witness called by Coulter during Brown's trial refuted virtually every reason Matheson gave for pressing mischief charges. Dr. Madeleine Petrov was brought in as an expert witness. As a clinical psychologist and university professor, she had researched and written extensively on post-traumatic-stress syndrome and how it is manifested in rape victims. She told the court that victims often react to rape with disbelief, dislocation, rationalization, denial, anything to help them survive the experience. Women who measure their self-worth by other people's reactions to them often blame themselves. When they are told they should have known better, or weren't really being honest, they often believe it. If anyone in authority questions their motives, they are especially likely to blame themselves. In other words, she said, the defendant was acting like a typical rape victim.

The hockey players, on the other hand, still said they believed that Brown *had* given consent.

As the trial wore on, accumulating one thousand pages of transcripts, opinion in the town started to change. Coulter says 90 per cent of the conversations in the coffee shops at the beginning of the week had it that Brown had charged Dimech after he dropped her. Dimech had a cheering section of young girls noisily supporting him each day until Judge Harding ordered them to leave the courtroom. But with each day the number of Dimech and Heath supporters dropped dramatically, until it was more like 90 per cent were supporting Brown.

When Judge Harding found her not guilty, the courtroom burst into applause. In his judgment, Harding said that as a result of the "degrading and disgusting" incident, Brown "suffered considerable physical and emotional pain. . . . That's not sympathy. That's fact. . . . It became clear to her that [Dimech and Heath] had no feelings at all for her, and had merely used her for their sexual gratification. . . . [S]he honestly believed that what happened to her . . . was not by consent."

With the trial over, the players went back to their new teams, two time zones away. Three weeks later, their old team won the province's team-of-the-year award. Brown received counselling for the next four years.

Bill Pritchett, who heads the governing body for all sports in the province, said if there's a problem with an award they plan on giving, they don't give the award out. He didn't see a problem giving the award to a team that had Dimech and Heath on it.

Sportswriter Linda Berman says she confronted Pritchett about what happened in the town shortly after the team was given the award. "I was working as the sport historian at the sports hall of fame," says Berman. "I had to talk to Mr. Pritchett about something else, and I asked him how on earth the team could win the award after what those two boys had done. He complained about me to my boss, and I left the job a month later."

The legacy of the case has not been forgotten by those who know Sandra Brown. Both pastors from her church believed her and formed a support and prayer group of up to twenty-five people, which met regularly over the entire period. Even Arnold Coulter attended the sessions before court opened. "I'm quite proud of the congregation," he says, years later. "I'd never worked with a support group before. There was a lot of self-education for me, and I could focus on the legal matters, because I knew there were people looking after the emotional ones."

One of the pastors remembers it all as if it were yesterday. "The hockey people in this town were going to teach her a lesson, and the hockey buffs include a lot of lawyers. They can't let anything happen to their little darlings. This shows how attitudes toward athletes have to change. But it backfired on them. She was acquitted. They interrogated her alone. It's not difficult to catch someone up in those circumstances. There were a lot of people covering for those boys."

After the trial, Dimech's and Heath's old coach, Grant Hayes, was staying late in the arena after a game. He said the combination of girls, sex, and hockey comes with the territory. "We've had a situation here recently where a woman has gone out and said, 'I fucked six players.' I think it might have been one or two, but alcohol, group morality, peer pressure . . . it adds up.

"The girls are young – sixteen, sometimes younger," said Hayes as he rested his foot on the bench in the home box. "The girls who are a little older, who have moved away to school, are less attracted. But the people in both cases are naive, experimenting, don't have a good self-image. I hope it's been a learning experience for us. I can't say it's something we bring up. These two guys got in trouble; now we're trying to put it behind us."

Hayes said the players could go to their guidance counsellor with their problems, and he said there were plenty of them. "They're young, away from home, in the spotlight, horny. Girls are very attractive, and they desire to be with a hockey player. It keeps going. In the towns with professional players, they're always going out and getting fucked. I'm sure the women think it's an accident that the guy just happens to be there, but the guys are caught up in themselves, and in the spotlight.

"I know of guys who have hundreds of names of women they could phone up in every major-league city," Hayes continued. "I went out with a friend in a bar, and at least thirty girls would have done anything to him. I think it's wrong to blame just the girls or just the boys. Some women are actively involved, they seek it out. I get phone calls at one in the morning, four a.m., on weekends: 'Is your billet home?' It's infuriating when they phone late at night. But at twenty-six and twenty-seven, they're still phoning in the NHL.

"I doubt there's a whole lot of passion involved. In the change-room they don't have respect for girls. They spend hours talking to girlfriends, but they don't like the girls at the rink."

On October 16, 1989, while the charges were still standing against the players, Judge Maurice Liddell of the Queen's Bench set aside a publication ban previously issued by Judge Morley Hedges. The request for the ban had come from Hank Cleary, who argued through the players' lawyer, Harold Marshall, that it would protect the players from embarrassment and potential financial loss. When asked, Cleary said that in fact he was only trying to protect Brown's reputation.

The ensuing media coverage cast serious doubt on the legal procedures that had taken place. Arnold Coulter, Sandra Brown's lawyer, publicly requested an inquiry, saying his client's case had been seriously mishandled. In May 1990, an article appeared in the press stating that the province's Minister of Justice had declined to launch any inquiry. The minister told the press he had conducted an internal review and was "confident that all the relevant issues were properly and thoroughly examined. My officials, as well, are satisfied that the police investigations were handled properly in a manner which was believed to be fairest to all parties involved."

But this doesn't satisfy Arnold Coulter, who still maintains the justice department tampered with the case and points to the fact that the minister is a friend of Hank Cleary. After the minister refused to launch an inquiry, Coulter told the press he viewed the internal review of the justice department "as no investigation at all. [The minister has] gone back to the same actors and said, 'Did you do a good job?'"

Despite everyone's protestations that justice was served, the reversal of charges happened like clockwork. Brown's family first came in to see Coulter on November 18 because they felt the police were turning against their daughter. Coulter assured them that couldn't possibly happen. But on November 20, 1989, Coulter was notified by Ben Clegg that they would be laying mischief charges. On November 21, he was contacted by the provincial director of prosecutors, Mary Innes, about the case. Innes now sits as a judge on the province's Queen's Bench. But the information Clegg gathered and passed on to Innes during the interrogation was later seen as inadmissible during the trial. Judge Jeremy Harding ruled in a *voire dire* that Clegg's taped conversation with Brown during his interrogation of her was inadmissible because he did not warn her to bring counsel with her during the interview, even though he was reasonably sure he would be laying charges against her that night.

Coulter says the decision back in 1989 to stay and then drop the charges was an example of how the law of the land simply doesn't apply to the world of hockey. "After [Brown] was acquitted, they could have proceeded with a preliminary hearing for the players. They didn't attempt to establish whether or not there was enough evidence for a trial. I think we heard during the first trial that there's plenty of evidence.

"It's not unusual in small towns for the Crown attorney to be the former partner in a [local] law firm," continues Coulter, "but it does mean there needs to be rigorous ethics at all times. I believe there was some contact between [Matheson and Cleary]. He [Matheson] took a young and very upset girl into his office with the assistant prosecutor. There was a discussion in their office, later she's picked up at night, taken to the police, and charged. There was a terrible amount of pressure on her.

"It's my view that they had people who had known each other for a long time. It was time to call in the IOUs. Once [Brown] was acquitted, they had a year to act on those charges against the players and resurrect the case. From the very beginning they tried to stop this case. My client was brought into the guidance office at school, and the counsellor tried to convince her to drop the charges. 'They're nice boys,' she told her. 'They wouldn't do that.'"

The guidance counsellor denies she instructed Brown in any such way: "That's nonsense, absolute nonsense. I have never in my life advised someone to drop charges. It's not my decision. Somehow [she] interpreted it that I was trying to influence her, but my God, if someone has committed a crime, they should be tried for it."

On a day in early March 1996, the wind chill hovers at -30°C as a group of teenagers finds refuge at the food court in the shopping mall beside the Marion Graham High School in Saskatoon. The kids wrap their hands around Styrofoam cups and unzip their jackets. They are middle class, the trendsetters for other schools. But what really sets them apart from the other kids is the fact that the city's junior hockey team, the Saskatoon Blades, also attends Marion Graham High.

The teams packs thousands of spectators into Saskatchewan Place – the state-of-the-art arena the Blades moved into in 1988 – all hoping to spot a junior player on his way to the NHL. The "young turks," as they are affectionately called by the media, are front-page news at the Saskatoon *StarPhoenix*. Local radio and television cover them live. They're always willing to sign autographs and make special appearances at McDonald's.

The club began life in 1964, when Jim Piggott, who was originally from Saskatoon and owned the Los Angeles Blades in the then soon-to-be-scrapped World Hockey League, turned the Saskatoon Quakers – a farm team for his pro franchise – into the Saskatoon Blades. The Blades competed in the Saskatchewan Junior Hockey League until 1966, when the WHL was born. In the early years, the team saw players such as Bobby Schmautz, Keith Magnuson, and Herb Pinder, and played in the old Saskatoon Arena.

In 1976, developer Nate Brodsky bought the club from Piggott, and for ten years the team got by with mediocre to poor performances. Then Brodsky hired Daryl Lubiniecki, a former Quaker coach, as coach and general manager, and neither man has looked back since.

Over the years the team has sported several brother acts: Bernie and Ken Federko, Gerry and Herb Pinder, Ross and Lane Lambert, Dan and Darryl Erickson. But the family everyone remembers is the Clarks: Wendel, Donn, and Kerry.

Today, the kids in the mall don't seem to care one way or another about the team or its history. In fact, they don't judge them by what they do on the ice, but rather what happens when they're off. "Those guys don't even do drugs," claims one of the boys at the mall, and the rest of the kids laugh. But the lone girl in the group corrects him. "Mainly, they drink, but some do drugs. Remember that party?"

The party. But it was only marijuana, and that doesn't count, the kids say.

What about that girl, Linda Sterling, who alleged a sexual assault after a team party?

"Yeah, sure. That's what she says," one of the boys replies. "She just doesn't want to admit being a slut." They all laugh.

"She met them at the door in a negligee," the girl adds.

How does she know? Was she there?

"Of course I wasn't there. I wouldn't hang with her," she says with disdain. "Everyone knows she's a slut. No one likes her. I just heard. That's all."

But the incident didn't occur at her house.

"Whatever."

This is not a terribly friendly group, but perhaps they know where Linda is now?

"She isn't here any more," says one of the kids, "not at our school. Not even in Saskatoon."

"She's gone west," says another. "She's playing with a different team by now." They burst into laughter at that one. They toss Sterling's name and reputation around like a punching bag, all taking a jab. Getting what she deserves, they say.

"Hey, I know who might know," one of the boys finally says. "This guy John Smith, on Meadowlark. He used to date her sister. He's in the phone book."

There is a pay phone just outside the food court, and Smith is at home.

"I can't remember, it was so long ago," he says of an event that happened just the year before. "I didn't know her. I just went out with her sister for a while, and she's not around any more. I don't know where she went. She's not in Saskatchewan any more."

As Smith speaks, one of the kids from the mall walks toward the pay phone with an official-looking woman.

"Excuse me, but what are you doing here?" asks the woman, who is the mall manager.

Perhaps she knows where the girl who alleged a sexual assault by the Blades in January 1995 can be found. She went to Marion Graham High, next door to the mall.

The mall manager becomes very polite. "Well, I'd like to help you, but normally, if you want to talk to people in the mall, you have to work through the manager's office. These kids told me you were bothering them, so I had an obligation to make sure everything was all right. Just contact me if you want to talk to anyone."

While there appears to be a collective amnesia at the mall, members of the media are more helpful. Vance Oliver, who covered the Blades for the *Saskatoon StarPhoenix*, talked to the team's general manager, Daryl Lubiniecki, after the incident was alleged to have happened.

"Lubiniecki didn't deny it happened," Oliver says, "but he said it was consensual. I understand there was a party, lots of booze, and under-age kids. The girl went back to school – to boast, I guess, to her friends – and a couple of them told her they didn't think it was a very good thing. A few days later she went to victim services."

In a separate interview another reporter on staff has more. "They did it all right. It was after a team function, and the players went off to one of the houses for a party. She was passed out on the floor when they had their way with her. Lubiniecki knew about it, because he told me personally there was no doubt in his mind that they had fucked her. Those were his exact words. He said he saw the condoms in the bathroom garbage later on.

"The cops said she didn't want to co-operate, but two of the assistant coaches on the team are city police. She identified five guys at the party. It started as a team party. Hockey players are gods out here, so these things don't go any further."

Lubiniecki has a different take. "It made us aware that people can make up stories, get you in trouble. We've been thinking of charging the girl with mischief," he says over the phone.

But why make up such a story? Who would want to disclose such intimacies?

"Obviously you guys [the media] will have to ask her that question. Your TV stuff is ridiculous. . . . There was a bunch of bullshit in the press. But you made us aware that we have to watch ourselves . . . be on guard all the time."

So can hockey players live normal teenage lives?

"Our kids are front and centre. And let's face it, boys and girls are going to be in trouble. The boys are athletes, and women are going to follow them around. But this thing is history. There's been a lot of mischief."

Ed Chynoweth, who was commissioner of the WHL at the time, confirms his statement in the February 11, 1995, *Saskatoon StarPhoenix*: "Certainly if the reports I'm getting [are true], this wasn't her first time in the kip," meaning she had slept with players in the past. Still, it's hard to imagine Lubiniecki and Chynoweth are talking about the same incident as Mary Lissel, who worked with Sterling at the Saskatoon Sexual Assault Centre.

"She seemed to be friends with a lot of the girls who wanted to be with the Blades, girls who have low self-esteem," Lissel says. She confirms the newspaper reporter's stories. "It's hard to give consent when you're unconscious. She was very drunk. Sometimes she'd wake up during the ordeal and see faces and hear voices. She positively identified five players.

"I accompanied her to the police station when they requested further interviews. I've been doing this for five years, and I've never seen anything like it. They had her father in another room. She and her father were not getting along. They wouldn't let me be there with her, but we could hear what the staff sergeant was saying. He kept telling her, 'You're lying, you're lying. Tell the truth. Your story doesn't match the hockey players' stories.' He was abusive to her. How would anyone feel after being a victim of a gang rape, and having their relatives present during questioning? She wasn't living at home at the time because of her father. It was done in a very unprofessional manner."

Jim Cox of Youth Services of the Saskatoon police says a thorough investigation was conducted, with no conflict of interest on the part of the assistant coaches, who had nothing to do with the case. But since no charges were laid, the case was over.

For Sterling, it had just begun.

"After the police dropped the case, [Linda] tried to save her reputation," Lissel says. "She had very low self-esteem, just shattered and crushed, crying all the time and very upset. She transferred schools, attended Holy Cross, and changed her name. You could see the difference in her body language. She walked tall until the kids there found out who she really was. Then she had to leave. She left Saskatoon altogether. It was terrible. Now I don't know where she is."

Holy Cross is across town from Marion Graham, with a different set of kids. They mill around the front entrance at the end of the school day. It's still very cold, but the kids stay outside, defiant in open jackets and without tuques or mitts. There is a group of girls around the same age as Sterling. Do they remember a girl named Linda – tall, long dark hair, really pretty? Attended their school in the middle of 1995?

The girls look at each other, slightly puzzled, and then a knowing look takes over.

"Yeah, she was here until we ran her out," says one matter-of-factly.

"She had a bad rep, and we found out about it, so she got run out of this school."

Another girl looks uncomfortable. "We're pretty brutal on people. I don't know why," she says. "It wasn't very nice."

Inside the school, the secretary at the office calls on Assistant Principal Guy Cyrene. A concerned look crosses his face when he hears Linda Sterling's name. "Yes, that poor girl. She was only here half a semester and had to leave. I don't know where she is now, but I wouldn't be able to help you. We're very strict about student confidentiality, especially in a case like that."

He sighs and closes his eyes briefly. "I wish I could help you with this," he continues, "because I will tell you one thing: this story needs to be told. It's a terrible thing that happened to her. I hope and pray you find her."

"I have no comment. I can't comment," Dennis Ens, the principal at Marion Graham, says over the phone. "She's not a student here, nor was she at the time."

He does confirm, however, that at least half the Blades attend Marion Graham. "That's all I have to say," says Ens, and abruptly hangs up.

But he is contradicted by his own students, who clearly remember Sterling attending their school. They are at the Blades game, at Saskatchewan Place, a short cab ride from Marion Graham and the mall. Between periods, young women congregate in the foyer in groups of twos and threes. Despite their attempts at looking sophisticated, with coiffed hair, tight jeans, and short jackets, adolescent faces peer from under heavy make-up. Some claim never to have heard of Sterling, but two of the girls will talk about her.

"She ran away from home and stayed at Clara's house before it happened. I have her number, call her up," says one. The other has a number of another girl who, she says, was at the party. Both deny being her friend or being at the party.

"Linda got beat up in the washroom at the mall," one of them adds. "A girl called her a slut, and she tried to fight back, but she got beat up pretty bad."

"I didn't hang with her, and I don't know where she is now," says one of the girls when phoned. She also denies being at the party.

There is a click on the line, and a man's voice comes on. "I don't want you talking to my daughter. We have nothing to say, so don't call back." The phone goes dead.

"Linda stayed with us before the incident," says the second girl, "but I don't know where she is now. Girls get a bad rep if they're with the Blades. We call it the McBlade Club, because the players act like child heroes, but they're just assholes. The girls are called puck bunnies, because they get passed around from player to player like a puck.

"I can give you another girl's number who hung with Linda. Maybe she can help."

The third girl is named Nancy. "I've heard a lot about the Blades," she says, "and it's all bad. They only want one thing. If someone is seen too often with them, she has to move out of town because you get such a bad reputation."

Sterling did leave. It turns out she stayed with an aunt and uncle who lived a few hours outside of Saskatoon. It takes several months to locate them, and a few more before they see their niece, who had eventually moved even further away to escape the past. Perhaps the distance has done her some good; Linda Sterling finally feels ready to tell her story.

"The party was at Rhett Warrener's house, he's a player," says Sterling from her new city and province. "The parents were upstairs, but no one wanted to go upstairs and get the Coke for the rye. . . . See, we had this big thing of rye. So we drank it straight.

"I was with [one of the players] that night. Supposedly we were dating." She says the player had taken her out a couple of times before the night of the party. "He treated me well, but not for long. We went up to a bedroom to make out, and then I don't remember anything after that. I blacked out, I drank so much. Then later, I started to remember. I wasn't aware of it that night. They passed me around like a puck. I thought I was going to be popular, that I was going to be liked by the Blades. My parents were away, so I thought I'd go to this party and I'd be popular."

Sterling speaks in a matter-of-fact voice. She's started a new life in a new city as a part-time fitness instructor, waitress, student, and volunteer. She says she likes helping people, and feels she must constantly clean. Cleaning at the hospital where she volunteers is one of the few things that makes her feel good. "I feel like I've accomplished something," she says, which she hasn't been able to do in the rest of her life.

"I didn't have any support from my parents; I'm not close to them. My mom's not really my mom. I can't talk to her. I can't go to them and say, 'How was your day?' My parents are into money a lot," continues Sterling, "and it's always my brother who gets all the attention. He plays hockey – they go to his games all the time.

"I didn't want to tell my mother about the rape. When I phoned her from the police station, she told me it was my fault. 'You dress like a slut,' she said. My parents still go to the Blades games. Can you imagine the type of parents who would support the team that raped their daughter?"

Sterling's voice becomes emotional. "I'd never been through anything like this before. I was going crazy. Even before it happened, I'd run away from my parents before. Twice I went to Vancouver and OD'd on cocaine. After this, they weren't supportive at all. I didn't want to tell the truth, because I couldn't count on my parents."

It wasn't just Sterling's parents who failed to support her, she says. She had switched schools at the beginning of Grade Ten, and entered Marion Graham because she thought of it as "a high-class school, and I'm a high-class girl. I'm a snob. I like all that clique stuff, I like brand names, and high-class cocaine. I'm not a very good student; I get distracted. But I was the new girl at school. I just wanted to fit in, but I was only in Grade Ten, pretty young and naive."

Sterling had imagined people would like her if she was a friend of the hockey players. At first she thought she was popular because the Blades knew her name. But in the second semester, after the Blades incident, everything changed. They ganged up with the rest of the school, she says, and used her. "I've learned it's good to have a couple of good friends instead of a bunch of bad ones. They didn't beat me up in the washroom at the mall, I got away from them, but a whole bunch came to Holy Cross when they found out I was there and tried to beat me up. I kept running – I was always running. I was afraid to get on a city bus, because someone might be following me. I had to leave the city."

Sterling's life was becoming a nightmare. If it hadn't been for a few key people, she says, she wouldn't have made it. "My auntie and uncle were great. They just let me stay with them, and talked to me. They were friendly. So was Mary at the sexual-assault centre. She used to pick me up at school and take me for a coffee, and we'd just talk. But when she went to another placement I didn't go back.

"My principal at Holy Cross was so nice. I really like him. He really understood me. I had to tell him what happened to me, because it was kind of late to register in the middle of the year. He was so nice."

She's surprised Dennis Ens denied that she went to Marion Graham, but she adds her English teacher there said she was "wild."

"He said that about me. That's the type of school it is. They thought I gave consent just because I was drunk. I was vulnerable, but that doesn't mean I wanted six guys to have sex with me.

"First of all, we went to one house," she says, coming back to the night in question. "There was music, and the hockey game was on. The parents were upstairs. Then the party was transferred to another house. I went to the bedroom with [the player with whom she had come to the party], and I don't remember anything after that. When I came to I was all by myself. I was still drunk and not thinking clearly, but I remember thinking, Where is everybody? I saw that they had pulled my tampon out, and there were condoms all over the room, and all my clothes were off. I put them back on and took a cab home. It woke my mom up, but I went straight to bed.

"The next afternoon I had cramps, I wasn't feeling very well, and there were bruises in my groin area.

"The Blades are so phony. They don't care about anyone else – it's their hockey, and that's it. The girls don't say anything about what they do to them, because they know they'll get in trouble."

Her former boyfriend, Neil Sawyer, had gone to Marion Graham for four years. He was well aware of the Blades and how girls could get into trouble. "They always had a reputation at school," says Sawyer, who kept in touch with Sterling and remained her friend. "First of all, we used to say they were in the six-year program, because they weren't always passing in class because they missed so much school. But a lot of guys knew they had a certain attitude towards girls, and I advised Linda not to go to this party. She was just asking for trouble. I knew about their history and ego problems. They think they can get away with anything.

"But Linda kept saying they were really nice guys and I was mis-judging them. There will always be some girls willing to go along with them and take whatever they dish out. They have low self-esteem, and what the players do is all about boosting their ego. They use this locker-room talk, it's very disrespectful of girls, and then they tell everyone what they've done."

When Sterling realized what had happened to her, Sawyer drove her to the police station to report them. But going to the police was interpreted by the rest of the kids at school as an act of hostility towards the Blades. "Some of those girls thought the Blades were still okay guys. They were friends with the players who screwed her, and they couldn't handle what Linda was saying.

"Alcohol makes people do strange things," continues Sawyer. "I asked her, 'Are you going to do anything about this? I think you should do something.' She's not one of those girls who would agree to do that. I had to go down to the police station and make a state-ment, tell them what she told me. She said she passed out, and when she woke up there were condoms in the garbage, her clothes were off, her bra was missing. Then a player who was there phoned her. He wasn't necessarily doing it, but it was a way for him to admit what his teammates had done. He put the rest of the pieces of the puzzle together for her. There's no doubt in my mind they raped her. Sometimes Linda embellishes stories, but not this one. I saw the bruises on her hips, but the police didn't take pictures right away. They waited a few days."

Sterling says a member of the Blades didn't just phone her, he took her out for coffee and explained what had happened. Sterling takes out her address book. "I'll give you the names he told me, and billeting parents' phone numbers," she says, and writes down six names. When she went to the police, though, she says they weren't the least bit helpful.

"The police wouldn't tell me anything. They came to my house and asked for pubic hair samples. They told me, 'If you don't give them to us, we'll take you away in handcuffs, and force them.' I was really down by then. I just said, Forget it. No one wants to help me. I'm on my own now. The police were really mean."

Sergeant Whitsone of the Saskatoon police is friendly enough, but he's not interested in talking about the thick file on the case. "If you want any information, you'll have to get the permission of all involved, and then go through Freedom of Information," he says.

One by one the players on Sterling's list acknowledge they were at Rhett Warrener's party, but maintain they were not among those who later went to the second house. Their bonus money had been adding up, says one of them, every time they won a game, and "it went towards beer that night. . . . There was hard liquor, too. I think some players abuse it. . . . The coach didn't know how much they drank. It was always a game, trying to do it without getting caught."

No one was there at the second party, no one knew Sterling, and no one can remember much anyway. One of the players goes so far as to claim he was no longer even on the team by that time. But that's not how one of his teammates remembers it: "Oh, he was there, all right. You could say he 'introduced' her to the team." The little that the players say they do remember from that night is inconsistent; none of their stories match. And then during one of the conversations, a player decides to talk. "I'll tell you what happened if you don't use my name," he says. We agree the story will be anonymous.

"We were a really close team back then," he says. "I don't think we tried to have a contest together, but we were so close, we had the same girls. I think it was a game [for the girls] to see what guys they could get.

"She'd been with three or four of the guys on the team – different guys on different nights. I don't know exactly who she was with that night, but from this occasion, when this girl went to school the next day, people were giving her a hard time.

"She ended up dropping out of that school and going to a different one," he continues. "It wasn't fair, those people that were saying that don't know exactly what happened, because they weren't there.

"She seemed proud of it. But it made it embarrassing, and she ended up going to the cops."

Can the player remember anything else?

"I'll tell you my story on it," he says. "I was actually with her the weekend before. She was drinking quite a bit that night [at the party], but she seemed to be all right. Then she was kind of, like, all over me. I didn't like that in front of the guys, so I said, Why don't we go somewhere? . . . So we went [to the second house]. I'm not going to tell you exactly what we did, but it took a few hours, then I wanted to go home. She wanted to stay there. I walked back. She was conscious when I left. . . . I don't know if she was unconscious or not. There were three or four guys still left at the party, and I heard they went to [the second house] after that. There may have been those three, another girl, or some guys."

Why did they think she wanted more sex?

"The things she was doing to me at the party in front of everyone were pretty . . . They thought she wanted it."

Do five or six players often have sex with this one girl?

"Generally she's not the only girl. There were other girls as well," says the player. "It's not a group of guys, but two guys. It happened quite a bit. We'd have different girls together. I think it happens . . . I'll be honest with you, I've done it with another guy, the guys I did do it with were really close to me. I didn't feel uncomfortable."

Did he have sex with other players without the girl present?

"There's always a girl. I couldn't imagine it without the girl. I don't know if I feel intimate towards him [the teammate], but I think closer is the best word."

He names the other player he paired up with to have sex with a girl. "We did it quite a few times. We had respect for her, and we treated her right. We made sure that was what she wanted, and if she didn't want it, she was to let us know."

Did they ever ask the girl what she would like to initiate?

"Oh, I never thought about that," the player replies.

By the winter of 1997, Linda Sterling had changed her identity. The long brown hair that, together with her dark skin and deep brown eyes, identified her as a young native woman, is gone. Her hair is cut above her shoulders, and bleached blonde. She says she doesn't know, or care, what First Nation her mother comes from. She sits in the bar where she will soon be working the evening shift. Celery sticks are arranged beside her on a plate. This is lunch, though, without being asked, she vows she loves food and does not have an eating disorder.

There are plenty of men in the bar, but they look nothing like the inhabitants of the high-class world Linda imagines for herself. Three TVs are tuned into sports. The other waitresses appear to be the same age as Linda. All have blonde hair, tight T-shirts revealing plenty of midriff, and short shorts.

"I used to want to play ringette when I was little," says Sterling as she lights up a cigarette. "But now I wouldn't go near an arena. Don't ever have a relationship with a hockey player. They'll just pass you around like a puck. They can do whatever they want. I wish I'd known they'd save their own butt before they'd save mine. Everyone lied. When I think about it, I start to cry."

"People think I'm happy, but it's a lie, too. I hate my life. I hate all the things that have happened to me, and I'll never forgive my parents for this and all the other stuff. My step-uncle sexually abused me when I was young, and he abused my cousin, too. A retard like that gets two months for doing that to us. What's the point in trying?"

Sterling's friend sits beside her. They both live in the same trailer park. Her friend's been great, says Sterling. Thank God for her, and people like her aunt and uncle and Mary from the assault centre.

"Mary was like a lawyer for me, and like a mom. A total sweetheart. She took me for pregnancy tests, and STD tests. She was so nice. She did everything for me.

"I'm just going to make enough money to get out of here," continues Sterling, as she butts out her cigarette. "I'm moving to the West Coast. I can be a fitness instructor and a waitress out there."

It's time to get changed into her T-shirt and shorts and start working.

In parting, Sterling says she wishes she knew the full extent of what happened to her that night, and reaches out for a hug before she leaves.

Peggy Reeves Sanday is a professor of anthropology at the University of Pennsylvania in Philadelphia. She studied campus fraternities for two years in the early 1980s before writing *Fraternity Gang Rapes*.[2] In 1996 she wrote *A Woman Scorned: Acquaintance Rape on Trial*, which includes a historical look at how attitudes and laws concerning rape were formed.[3] She says the incidents of fraternity gang rapes are very high, but American research has shown that sports-team gang rapes have surpassed them.

There are many similarities between the two. While girls are called groupies, pucks, puck bunnies, or dirties by hockey players, the fraternities refer to a woman who they believe will have sex with any or all of them as a party girl. Both groups, as well as other male sports teams across North America, have developed a vocabulary to describe sex with these women. The "show" occurs when one of them has sex with a female and the rest watch. The "rodeo" occurs when she tries to get out of the room (if she's conscious), and the "train" is the line-up of men waiting to have sex with her. "Pulling train" refers to the process of one man after another having sex with a groupie or party girl.

"Gang rape goes beyond the passive photograph and the singular act of masturbation that porn provides," says Reeves Sanday, but "the men still have this belief that the woman has no sexual agency, that she is purely a commodity, and that her passivity should be there to accommodate their sexual needs."

The sex should not be mistaken for heterosexual sex, says Reeves Sanday. Instead, the group masturbation for sports teams that is accommodated through the presence of a female body is really a homosexual act. The reason for this, she says, is that the emotional relationship exists between the men, not between the men and the woman, and her body services their need to perform for each other. Her presence allows them to come as close as they can to an intimate relationship with each other while at the same time presenting visible "proof" of their masculinity. The real meaning of the words *homo* as in "same," and *sexual* as in "an act of sex" gets blurred simply because a woman's body is being penetrated, but without female sexual agency, without an appreciation and respect for what her body desires, a woman may as well be a blow-up doll with three orifices. The only emotional relationship the athletes have with the female in this situation is one of contempt. This hardly fosters appreciation of female sexuality.

Reeves Sanday hadn't heard about the sex scandals that rocked hockey in 1997, but her analysis sounds as if she'd been reading Canadian newspapers for the entire hockey season.

"I was obtaining very secret information when I wrote the fraternity book," she says. "It's still difficult to get information. These are highly secretive organizations. But the rituals of the actual rapes of young women are the acting-out by athletes of their expectations, and their experiences.

"The boys learn they are items to be exchanged by older men in sports. It's the sports trade, which of course is the analogue to the girls in the sex trade, but the girls don't get paid much, while the boys do, if they make it. The point is, both are reduced to being an item for purchase.

"There is a relationship between the cultural image of a hockey player and the commoditized body of the player that is being put into circulation for money. We can measure the financial cost of producing a young man like this, but we never measure the human cost. He is a highly sexualized, and highly homoeroticized commodity, but the homophobia and the secrecy of this culture don't allow us to take a good look at how men 'rape' these boys, and then how they [the hockey players] translate that into raping young women."

Reeves Sanday says that most rapes of young men occur by men who identify themselves as heterosexual, because of homophobia. In fraternities and teams, much of the sexual abuse occurs in initiations. The initiates are caught, not only in a homophobic culture that, paradoxically, has just abused them, but they can't face what has happened to them, because to do so would call into question the whole world of male sports, the father-figures who run it, and what passes as family values. Instead, says Reeves Sanday, they express their "feelings of debasement" through "sacrificing the bodies of young women, who are thrown away, just like they'd like to throw away their own feelings, but they can't. As any psychiatrist will tell you, you don't get rid of feelings by acting them out. Yet they have to constantly act them out, over and over again, because they can't face them.

"The naming of sexual acts is important if we're going to be honest about providing real family values and respect for women," says Reeves Sanday. "What's happening now is young men are starting to say that they've been raped by men; they're beginning to name what really happened to them."

She believes if we're going to address the problem of gang rape, women also have to name what really has happened to them. When a renowned study on the frequency of rape was conducted in San Francisco in 1978, researchers asked if women had experienced "unwanted" sex while "asleep, unconscious, drugged, or otherwise helpless."[4] Many said yes when the question was expressed that way. Comparatively few women felt that they had been raped. Researchers have come to agree that when the word "rape" is avoided and phrases such as "forced to have sex," "sex against your will," "physical force used to obtain sex," "sex with someone you hadn't intended to have sex with" are used in surveys, far more women respond in the affirmative.

In Steven Ortiz's four-year study at the University of Berkeley conducted with the wives of professional male athletes, only one wife out of forty-seven said there was any physical abuse in the marriage, and none said they had been raped by their husbands.[5] But several described sex with their husbands as forced and devoid of any emotional attachment on his part. Sex in these marriages was also infrequent, because the players used groupies and girlfriends for sex.

Brian Pronger, a sports ethics professor at the University of Toronto, echoes Reeves Sanday's analysis. In *The Arena of Masculinity: Sports, Homosexuality, and the Meaning of Sex*, he argues that pro sport is a homoerotic culture in a homophobic climate. "This is a male-only club," says Pronger of pro sport. "Whether it's in the locker room, the playing field, or a team party, there is no interest in really including women.

"Gang rape is really an excuse to have sex with each other. The woman is the intermediary; she disappears as the vessel while the real sexual exchange is between men," he says. "Homophobia and misogyny are a double-edged sword. These men fear the loss of masculinity if they actually have sex with each other. Instead of loving each other, they abuse a woman and use violent sport as the way in which they try to bond with each other. Why can't they accept what they are doing? What's all the nakedness in the shower room about, what's all the play and towel-snapping if not a form of affection?

"The tragic part of all of this is not that the men in charge of hockey have worked it out and let it happen, it's that they haven't figured it out at all. The coaches set the culture, they're teachers and mentors. Sport isn't really about getting a puck in the goal, it's about socializing and educating boys that this behaviour towards women is okay, and that homophobia and denial reign. Those who run sport are guilty of negligence, of not really thinking about where it can lead."

The behaviour of many young hockey players is much like that of the egocentric child: selfish in gratification, and boastful afterwards. They need to show off to their peer group to gain status. The culture of junior hockey feeds their childish egos and tells them they are all that matters. The trouble is compounded by the lesson of the initiation and the aggression of the game: they cannot afford to be distracted by their pain, and, consequently, are oblivious to the pain of others. They are damaged children in the bodies of men.

Conversely, girls and young women are still not allowed to be their own sexual agents. It's perfectly normal for teenage girls to want to experiment and enjoy sex, but they should be free to do so in conditions that honour and respect them. This is certainly not the case in junior hockey. While our culture must stop worshipping young men just because they're good at sports, it must also allow girls to love their bodies and realize that the best kind of relationship, either sexual or nonsexual, is the one that dignifies and pleasures the complete female self.

"The girls become surrogate victims," says Peggy Reeves Sanday, of sex practised on girls by survivors of initiations, "a person upon whom all the undesired feelings in a man can be visited. She's debased and degraded, because they have what they consider debased and degraded feelings within themselves, because they are engaging in homosexual acts in a highly homophobic sport."

Reeves Sanday argues, like Pronger, that gang sex has nothing to do with female sexuality, but is rather the legitimization of a sexual relationship between men by the addition of a female body.

Certainly, in the Blades case, if Sterling wasn't conscious, all the interaction had to be between the hockey players. In the Ed Dimech and Wayne Heath case (both names are pseudonyms), it is obvious that the two players were the real couple in much of their own testimony. Dimech would often start his sentences with "we" and then change to "I" halfway through. He not only watched closely while his teammate had sex, he choreographed it, pointing his toe to where he wanted the girl's head to be. Since she "couldn't satisfy" his friend, Dimech wouldn't "go out with her any more." In another case discussed in this book, the complainant could only have the star of the team if he brought two of his teammates along, and in another, one of the defendants asked another, "Why didn't you wait for me," when he walked in on his friend having sex. Two Guelph Storm players tried to put their penises in a woman's mouth at the same time. Who would receive the most physical pleasure from this? They also wanted to know "who was best," as if the sexual act were a continuation of a team practice.

"Girls may see themselves as being brought into the rarefied world of male athleticism when they get invited to these parties or go home with three hockey players," says Reeves Sanday, "but they don't understand they're extremely bit players in the religion of hockey. Women need to be far more selective about their sexual partners. If a woman knew she was really just going to facilitate sex between a bunch of hockey players – that they're much more intent on each other – I doubt she'd want them as sexual partners."

# CHAPTER SEVEN

# The Empty Net, Part Two

## *How the CHL Fails Young Men*

Brian Bell of the Calgary police is working the night shift in the general investigation unit in the city's Sixth District. The police station is tucked into an industrial park. Later on this mid-March night, Bell and his two colleagues, who "do everything from assaults and frauds to B&Es," are going to stake out a location only blocks away, where they suspect thieves will be hitting a warehouse. They are dressed casually for the occasion. The walls have "wanted" posters, and a map of the district, but no adornments that would speak of the personalities of the office inhabitants. This is determinedly a place of work. A coffee urn looks as if there's something stale and warm in it, but it's still early, not quite midnight, and it's as good a time as any to take off somewhere for a coffee break.

The undercover cops pile into a booth at a nearby cafe, and Bell looks down at his fresh cup of coffee before speaking. "On August 23, 1996, Sheldon Kennedy gave us a statement of fact. He came to the police station with a friend, and it gave us the opportunity to talk to him many times in the future," he says. "Slowly, he started to open up. It took two or three interviews, working with specialists in the field of abuse. He kept giving us pieces of information."

As police started to piece together the story that would change hockey's image forever, so did the media. A tip to the *Calgary Sun* that the police were investigating a possible sexual-abuse case involving a hockey coach moved the investigation beyond the control of the police. The story broke on September 7 when the *Sun*'s Eric Francis and Suzanne Wilton published a story under the headline "CITY POLICE INVESTIGATING FORMER COACH." They were saying something players and fans couldn't believe: long-time junior coach, hockey mainstay, and *Inside Hockey*'s Man of the Year for 1989, Graham James, had resigned from his job as head coach and general manager of the Calgary Hitmen while police investigated allegations of abuse against him. "I don't think he really wanted to leave the team. He was a good coach and we all liked him," Hitmen winger Tomas Migdal told the *Sun*. Lorne Johnston, president of the Hitmen, added, "Graham was a friend and was looked up to as one of the best coaches in hockey."

Calgary police had been quietly looking for other victims with the aid of the Swift Current, Regina, and Winnipeg RCMP, but once the case hit the media, says one officer, the leads dried up. "The victims were compromised, the investigation compromised. The accused had to do some damage control. We could just imagine him on the phone calling up all the victims and telling them not to talk.

"We had complete lists of all the teams, right back to the 1982 season when Graham was in Winnipeg, and had to get a hold of all of them. There were brainstorming sessions with the Crown, and inspectors, in all areas he had coached in. It was Corporal Rick Newstead of the Swift Current RCMP who found the second victim. He did an excellent job."

By mid-September, police believed James had assaulted twenty to twenty-five players in Swift Current, "with a ceiling of a hundred in total, from the time he spent in Manitoba and Swift Current, and four or five at the barest minimum," said a police source.

Still, players defended him. "This is one of those situations that, by being accused of it, you're pretty much considered guilty," said Tim Tisdale, who played for James from 1986 to 1989 and was typical in his response. He told the *Calgary Sun*, "I've never seen anything that would make me believe he did anything wrong. Until there's proof somewhere that convinces me otherwise – which I don't think will be the case – I'll support him. The way I look at it, there weren't that many kids at that level that were that vulnerable. I feel he honestly cared about his players and that's not a crime."

Tisdale is now head coach of the Kimberley Dynamiters in the British Columbia Tier II league.

The police didn't expect all the players to come forward at once, given how difficult that can be for the victim, but they were hoping for co-operation, because they believed James was a dangerous offender. "It took Sheldon five years before he could look at this problem, but a coach like Graham James can see a kid who doesn't have the support children need a mile away," says an officer who believes that lack of support and affection from parents makes children vulnerable to sexual assaulters. "I coined the phrase 'serial sexual predator' with James. I told him, 'You hunted these kids out.'"

James, like many sex offenders who prey on young people, used the power he held over his charges to extract what he wanted. "He plugged himself in," says the investigator, "took them to Jamaica, Europe, showered them with all this stuff." This officer describes the coercion in terms similar to earlier descriptions of rookie initiations. "You're locked in, because you're a part of the dirty secret now. Unless a victim is willing to throw away all the resources, all the chances of going on in their sport, they'll stay quiet."

By September 1996, it was James who was keeping quiet, giving just one interview to Francis and otherwise making few comments to the media or not saying anything at all.

Graham James had led an outwardly quiet life in Swift Current while not coaching, and had had an unremarkable upbringing. He was born on February 7, 1952, in Summerside, Prince Edward Island. His father was a member of the Armed Forces, and moved frequently to various military bases across Canada. When he was thirteen, his family moved to Winnipeg, where, in 1972, James played hockey at the Sturgeon Creek Community Club. Twelve years later, his coach from those days, John (Jack) Charles Nelson, was convicted on two counts of sexual abuse and one of indecent assault after three teenage players came forward to police immediately after an incident. Nelson died in 1995, and James has never said whether or not he, too, had been a victim.

He continued to play hockey at the St. James Community Centre, near his father's air base, and stayed on in Winnipeg as a university student, studying English Literature at the University of Manitoba while the rest of his family returned to the Maritimes. He was forced to give up amateur hockey at eighteen because of asthma. For seven years he worked as a substitute teacher and began coaching the St. James AAA bantam and midget hockey teams, various community teams, and with the Armed Forces.

But in 1977 he was fired as the coach of the bantam team. The reason given was that while at a tournament in Minneapolis he was found playing video games with his players at their hotel well past curfew.

This setback, however, did not seem to hurt James's coaching career. In 1979, he coached the Fort Gary Blues, a junior A hockey team, and by 1983 he had coached both the Blues and the Winnipeg South Blues to provincial titles and was working as a full-time hockey scout as well. It was while coaching at the Andy Murray Hockey School in 1982 that James first came across a talented thirteen-year-old named Sheldon Kennedy.

Kennedy started playing hockey at age four in St. James, a suburb of Winnipeg. At six, after his family moved to Elkhorn, Manitoba, he began playing in organized leagues. By the time he enrolled at the Andy Murray School, he was playing for the bantam team in his home town, but the junior rights for him, and for his older brother, Troy, were already owned by the Brandon Wheat Kings. In 1984, James, now coaching for the Winnipeg Warriors, made arrangements to trade away one of his players, Randy Cameron. In return he was given the rights to Kennedy and his brother, and asked the impressionable younger Kennedy if he would like to play for the Winnipeg Warriors.

He called the boys' parents, who were flattered that a coach from the city would be so interested in their sons. "That seemed like a chance of a lifetime," said Kennedy later. "My family couldn't get me on the bus fast enough."

It was April in that year that James made his first move. He invited Kennedy to play in the Lions Tournament in Winnipeg and offered to put the fourteen-year-old up for the week in his one-bedroom apartment. Kennedy would later recall that the windows in the bedroom had been covered up with cardboard, making the room very dark. A cot had been set up for him beside James's bed.

On the first night of his stay, Kennedy was almost asleep when he heard James crawl over to his feet. He kicked out from under the covers, and heard James retreat. Then he heard noises. The coach was rummaging around the closet. The light was on by this time and Kennedy could see James was holding a shotgun. He had a strange look on his face, and wanted to talk about his duck-hunting excursions. Kennedy was terrified as his coach started jumping about the room with the gun.

Eventually James put the gun away and turned the lights off again. Approximately one hour later, Kennedy heard him crawl across the floor again. He started to rub the player's feet but Kennedy pretended to sleep. James then began to masturbate above the player's feet, and eventually ejaculated on them. Then he moved up and placed his mouth around Kennedy's penis. Kennedy had been wearing underwear, but James had pulled them off. The player rolled away. After the first attempt at oral sex, the coach didn't try again, but he did continue to touch Kennedy. This went on for more than an hour, and during that time neither coach nor athlete said a word. For the next four days, James made Kennedy take showers and steambaths with him, while wearing swimming trunks, and twice more ejaculated on his feet. They were the first of more than three hundred assaults that lasted until 1990, when Kennedy left the Broncos.

He was a vulnerable target. "My dad and I weren't very close," Kennedy said. "I don't know how Graham could tell, but he knew." James could see that Kennedy was ready to leave a troubled home, and was dreaming about making it into the NHL. "You do not have a clue what to do," Kennedy said later. "You tell your mom and she makes you come home. You tell your friends and they will just portray you as a gay guy, and your hockey career is finished. It's just a very scary thing."

James later visited Kennedy at his home on three or four occasions. The player was sleeping in the family's unfinished basement, where there were a number of beds. His coach joined him, and after approximately an hour James would get out of his bed and masturbate on Kennedy's feet while he massaged them.

While Kennedy became locked into the relationship, James's career was on a roll. As an up-and-coming coach, he wasn't going to pass up any opportunities just so he could stay in Winnipeg and be with one fourteen-year-old.

In 1984, when the Winnipeg Warriors were bought by the town of Moose Jaw, James simply moved Kennedy with him, arranging for him to play on a AAA midget team, and approximately fifteen to seventeen junior games. It was at this point that the relationship transformed into "a religious thing," according to Kennedy. He was billeted with Joe and Arlene Dessert, but was told by James he would be spending a good deal of his time at the coach's apartment. Every Tuesday and Thursday evening between six-thirty and seven, as long as they didn't have a game, Kennedy was summoned. The evening would start out with some television or videos, and James would make flattering comments about his player. Then, between ten and ten-thirty, he would take Kennedy into the bedroom, get him to lie down, and mount him, putting his penis between Kennedy's legs. James would get him to ejaculate on his testicles and into his mouth.

There were approximately fifty such episodes that season, one of which occurred at a motel near the Max Bell Centre in Calgary in March 1985.

Kennedy remembers one instance where James told him if he would suck his penis, he would buy him some new clothes. The player declined. As well, there was a request for anal sex, when James told Kennedy that other players allowed him to "go up [their] bum." Kennedy declined.

Graham James lasted only two years in the new location. In the 1985–86 season, he was back coaching in Winnipeg for the Winnipeg South Blues. It wasn't until after the Kennedy story broke that Barry Trapp, who was general manager of the Warriors when James was head coach, finally spoke out, in 1997, about why James's tenure was cut short. Trapp had phoned James in August 1985 to set up a meeting to discuss team business. James told him he was unavailable because he was going with some friends to Minneapolis to attend a ball game. Later it was revealed to Trapp that those "friends" were really players from the team. He told James he thought his behaviour was inappropriate. "I had no proof, only suspicions," Trapp would later say. "My antennae went up that day. Something just didn't sit right with me. Graham didn't say, 'I'm going to Minnesota with a couple of our players.' As far as I'm concerned, he lied to me. Everybody had concerns, but until you have proof, it's hard to accuse a guy."

Trapp gave the board of directors an ultimatum: they could keep James or him, but not both. The board chose Trapp. "I took a lot of heat for that," Trapp said. "And I never told anyone else why I really did what I did. I just kept telling everyone, 'It's in the best interests of the Moose Jaw hockey club.' I didn't want to be around the man. I wanted nothing to do with him."

James told people in Winnipeg he had been "Trapped." The animosity between the two remained throughout their careers, but James had taken his prize player with him, so the assaults on Kennedy continued. Kennedy's parents were concerned, but for a different reason. They told James the move back to Winnipeg represented a demotion for their son; he was going from the WHL to the Manitoba Junior Hockey League. James responded by employing all his powers of persuasion to convince them it was in their son's best interests. After he returned with Kennedy to Winnipeg, there were at least seventy assaults.

James wasn't out of the WHL for long. In 1986 he became head coach of the new Swift Current Broncos franchise. Trapp wasn't surprised. "Graham was very popular. Everyone liked him and he was a real rising star." The rising star brought his own young star with him to Saskatchewan.

In James's first season, in December 1986, the team suffered a hor-rific accident on the way home from a game when their bus hit ice on a bridge and careened off the road. Four players died. After the accident, James told Kennedy that if the young player had died, he wouldn't have been able to go on. The coach was credited with helping the players through the ordeal and, in the following years, putting them back in the running for the WHL championship, and eventually the Memorial Cup. In 1989 the team had the most suc-cessful record of any junior hockey team in the history of the CHL, with fifty-five wins, sixteen losses, and one tie.

James's young protégé showed plenty of progress, too. In the 1987–88 season, he earned 63 goals and 54 assists, following it with 58 goals and 48 assists in 1988–89. In 1988, Kennedy was selected to the national junior team that won gold at the World Championship in Moscow, setting the standard for many more junior world victo-ries in the future.

But off the ice, Kennedy, now eighteen years old, remained under the control of James. James re-instituted the Tuesday and Thursday night get-togethers, and added punishment, such as grounding Kennedy, if he acted up. It was a perfect system. Kennedy would exhibit the self-destructive behaviour typical of abuse victims by drinking and driving, and using illegal drugs. And the more James abused Kennedy, the more he could be assured of behaviour calling for punishment, and the more isolated his player became. James rep-resented the player as a troubled young man whom only he could tame. "He would always put you down, so you would have to look to him for help," said Kennedy, who admitted alcohol had affected his career, but did not consider himself to be an alcoholic.

When he was grounded, Kennedy was only allowed to venture out to his coach's house for tutoring. The system was inadvertently strengthened by Kennedy's billeting parents, Colleen and Frank "Digger" McBean, who was part-owner of the team. If Kennedy ever resisted James, the coach would become very upset, but Colleen, who was also a high-school guidance counsellor, would "encourage him to go over to James's place to work it out," according to the statement of fact filed by Crown attorney Bruce Fraser of Calgary. Kennedy was often in tears in the McBean home when he got off the phone with James after being told he must go over to "do his school work."

"I never opened a book over there, not once," Kennedy said later. "He kept me with him all the time, on all the trips. It was like we were married. It was unbelievable. There is no doubt that Graham loved me, that he was infatuated with me. But it is not right. I told him that time after time, that it was not right. He was just a very smart, manipulative man."

So sure of himself was James, he could display his preference for Kennedy in public with no questions asked by management. Not only did he include Kennedy in everything he did, and arrange for him to come along on vacations, he also threw tantrums when Kennedy didn't do as he wanted. At one point, he chased Kennedy around the dressing room until the player escaped and ran to the McBeans' home in full equipment and skates. During this three-year period in Swift Current, Kennedy estimates there were more than fifty incidents of abuse each season.

As Kennedy descended into despair, James climbed. In the 1988–89 season he won the Man of the Year award from *Inside Hockey* magazine. He took the team to victory at the Memorial Cup in 1989, the ultimate measure of success in junior hockey and an incredible achievement for the young team, still recovering from the tragedy in 1986. They had an amazing 55–16–2 record, and won every one of their twelve playoff games.

The club thrived off the ice, too. Though the largest share in the team was owned by a tight group of Swift Current businessmen, 175 townspeople had shares in it, with another 150 volunteers working as "The Hockey Hounds." Hot games drew as many as three thousand fans, providing approximately eight hundred thousand dollars' surplus for a franchise that drew from the league's smallest market.

Murray Costello, president of the Canadian Amateur Hockey Association (now the CHA), wrote to James after the Memorial Cup win, telling him what a good role model he was, and that "hockey is skill and leadership and not violence and intimidation." Costello finished off the letter saying, "Your leadership, which goes right back to the drafting process, where you emphasize skills and not intimidation, in any way, shape or form, has been exemplary."

Meanwhile, as Kennedy finished his last year in junior hockey, he knew – as all players do – that in large part the door to the NHL could be opened or shut on the say-so of his club coach. He was drafted by the Detroit Red Wings in 1989, but felt he didn't perform anywhere close to his potential. Worse, life off the ice continued to be painful. While playing for Detroit in 1993, he was convicted for reckless driving and ended up spending fifteen days in jail when he violated the parole conditions of the charge. When he returned to his home province of Manitoba in January 1995, he was charged with possession of marijuana. (The charge was later dropped.) Before long he gained a reputation in the league for his drug, cigarette, and alcohol abuse dating back to his days in junior hockey, and he bounced up and down from the NHL to the AHL, trying to find a niche in one league or the other.

In the summer he lived out of his car, staying with various friends across the continent and trying to distance himself from James. "But he would always find me," Kennedy would later tell the *Calgary Sun*. There were a couple more assaults, but as he put more distance between them, Kennedy did manage to stay clear of James, if only physically. Psychologically he suffered from extreme loneliness. "I have always felt like I was not normal," Kennedy told Eric Francis of the *Sun*, adding that alcohol numbed him into a state he learned to think of as normal.

Branded a troubled player, Kennedy didn't just shift up and down from the NHL to the AHL, he also moved laterally, as different clubs tried and later traded him. Detroit sent him to Calgary, but after he became a free agent in 1996, he moved again, to the Boston Bruins. His life and career were in turmoil, yet his old coach seemed never even to falter.

While the Broncos didn't win the Memorial Cup again, James took the team to the WHL playoffs each season, and won them in 1992–93, going 49–21–2 the same year. He had created one of the most successful franchises in the CHL.

As well as producing a winning team, James had a reputation for colourful and questionable antics. He drew continent-wide attention to Swift Current in October 1990 when he disagreed with a ref's call during a game against Medicine Hat. He threw the team's sticks and waterbottles out on the ice and did a strip tease from the home bench. The players dragged him into the dressing room before he could remove his briefs. Footage of the rant aired on the David Letterman and Johnny Carson shows, and on sports channels across the country. In 1992 he was charged with assault after an altercation with a heckling fan in Moose Jaw. But he was also known as a highly intelligent coach who didn't drink or participate greatly in the raunchy hockey social scene outside of the arena. He was an outspoken opponent of hockey violence and arranged sponsorship of the team by the Dairy Council, making sure there was no endorsement of beer companies or initiations.

Typical of Graham James's fans in those days were Marg and Ken Cobbe, members of the Hockey Hounds, the Broncos' booster club. In 1993 they retired from the government co-op ranch they ran for years outside of Swift Current. Now they devote as much time as possible to the Hockey Hounds. They're the friendly, salt-of-the-earth kind of people for whom the prairies are famous. "Graham James tries to make real gentlemen out of those boys. They're polite and well-behaved," said Ken in the summer of 1993 as he took a break from the Broncos lottery booth in the mall. Yet just the previous season, James had been charged with the assault in Moose Jaw. But the Cobbes only go to the home games. They make the rink their "second home for the winter," to promote raffles, sales, and special events that help keep the Broncos solvent. They say they'll never go south as long as the Broncos are playing. "Winter without the Broncos would be empty, terrible," said Marg, also taking a break from the booth. "The Broncos are our winter entertainment."

Despite the team's successes, and the respect James had earned in the community, he suddenly departed Swift Current after the 1993–94 season when his contract was not renewed. At the time, the *Regina Leader-Post* ran an article quoting Broncos president John Rittinger, who had resigned from his position in Swift Current to become one of the owners and business manager of James's new team, the Calgary

Hitmen. "The groundwork Graham laid here will last for a long time," he told the paper.

Rittinger is also quoted as saying, "What astounds me is the number of calls Graham gets from alumni. Every day, he hears from somebody like Geoff Sanderson, Joe Sakic, Sheldon Kennedy. The only disappointing thing is that most of them call collect."

Bronco right winger Ashley Buckberger added further praise, saying, "Graham believed in freedom and letting players do as they may on the ice with creativity. He was a very open coach and a player's coach . . . probably the most colourful coach in the league."

The article, did not, however, say why he would leave such a successful franchise. By the next season James was part-owner, general manager, and head coach of the Calgary Hitmen. Aside from Rittinger, his business partners included NHL star Theoren Fleury of the Calgary Flames, and also two of James's regular NHL collect-callers from the Swift Current days, Joe Sakic of the Colorado Avalanche and Geoff Sanderson of the Hartford Whalers. Bret "Hitman" Hart of the World Wrestling Federation and Maple Leafs scout Anders Hedberg were also part-owners, as was Sheldon Kennedy.

The team didn't play in the 1994–95 season, and as a novice team it wasn't expected to shake up any of the top Western teams the following season. By the end of the 1996–97 season, they had yet to make it into the playoffs. Six months earlier, on September 5, 1996, James tendered his resignation as head coach and general manager. The *Calgary Sun* story about sexual-assault allegations appeared two days later. On September 9, Francis wrote another piece entitled "COACH: 'I'LL GO ON LIVING.'" "I don't want to say it [hearing of the allegations] was worse than the day of the bus crash, because no matter what, there's no recovery for those four kids," James told Francis. "I'll go on living. That's more of a chance than they got.

"The bus accident put hockey and life in better perspective, but I'm not sure anything could have steeled me for this," James continued. "It's been a very difficult time in my life. I don't know how to compare them – they're two different things. This affects me personally and in an ongoing fashion, but you can't be lower than seeing four people you know and like die.

"Right now I'm expending so much energy worrying and thinking about things that I'm mentally drained. Sleep hasn't been a problem.

"I've received quite a number of phone calls – that's keeping me half sane," said James of friends who had called to give him support. "At the right time I'd certainly like to [address the issue], but that's not now."

James went on to talk about the Hitmen, who were on the road playing an exhibition game, but said, "It wouldn't be appropriate for me to be there, and I think that would be too difficult." He had called each player at home on the night of his resignation, saying he "just wanted to say goodbye to everybody. I obviously cared a lot about the team and the individuals that are a part of it."

Both of James's brothers – Rusty, who had been the Hitmen's assistant general manager, and Dennis – flew in from the Maritimes to be with their older sibling. "I go through times when I would rather be alone," continued James. "They kind of look like me, so I'm not so sure how glad I am to see their faces."

The *Sun* continued their investigation. Francis, who was a golfing buddy of James's and as stunned as anyone by the allegations, began a five-month series of articles on the case. In a September 11 article, entitled "COACH'S FRIENDS SHAKEN BY ALLEGATIONS," he interviewed Colleen McBean, who had not only billeted dozens of Broncos players, but was educational advisor to the team.

"I'm one of the people," she said, "that says to the parents who are giving us their seventeen-year-old child, 'Don't worry, we'll look after them for you.' There's nobody on the planet that feels more devastated by these allegations than me.

"Everyone liked him," she continued. "I could only say I think everybody here is shocked and feeling very horrible."

On September 12, another of Francis's articles, "PUCK HOTBED STUNNED," ran in the *Sun*. In it, he quoted Scoof Kruger, who had had three sons on the Broncos team, one of whom died in the 1986 bus crash. "He was a helluva good coach who knew his stuff. Graham threw the odd tantrum. I don't know how many of the boys' ghetto blasters he smashed, but there aren't too many better in junior hockey that I know of."

Francis and McBean weren't the only ones who had completely misread Graham James. Pete Montana, who is a sports broadcaster in Red Deer, couldn't believe the news either. "I've known Graham for a long time, and we had no idea why he resigned from the Hitmen," said Montana in September 1996. "It's hard to believe anyone of Graham's stature and ability would be mixed up in something like this. He always did what's right for the players and the organization. . . ."

"I've seen some things that go too far," says Montana of male-on-male behaviour in the sport.

The story made its way into newspapers' sports sections across the country, but as the World Cup of Hockey commenced, the regular junior and NHL seasons took off, and a police investigation that wasn't about to suffer any more leaks continued, it receded in people's minds. That was until October 29, 1996, when the *Calgary Sun* broke the customary practice of not releasing a sexual-assault victim's name and ran a story entitled "EX-FLAME INVOLVED: SHELDON KENNEDY AN ALLEGED VICTIM IN JAMES CASE."

Kennedy refused to comment, but his agent, Tom Laidlaw, was reported to have said that Kennedy was not playing for the Boston Bruins at the time, because of "personal reasons." He hadn't yet played in the 1996–97 season, but was expected to do so shortly and was "absent from the team with permission." No other media source revealed Kennedy's identity, but on November 2, the *Toronto Star* ran a short interview with James. In it he said, "Right now, in effect, I am already in jail because I can't do anything. I need some end to that. I need the next step of whatever is going to happen."

It had been almost two months since the allegations were first made public. "I think something will probably happen within the next week to ten days but I have thought that for a while now," James continued. "I would like to see some end in sight. . . . I am not looking for anything right now but for this to come to an end."

In fact, James and his lawyer had already admitted to Crown attorney Bruce Fraser that the abuse of Kennedy had occurred. On November 23, the waiting game ended. Calgary police charged James with sexually assaulting Sheldon Kennedy and another player between 1984 and 1994.

To no one's surprise, when James walked into the Provincial Court of Alberta on January 2, 1997, with his lawyer, Lorne Scott, he pleaded guilty to Judge Frank Maloney on three hundred counts of abuse against Kennedy, and another fifty against the other complainant.

On behalf of his client, Scott entered a statement to be considered in sentencing. It portrayed James as a highly intelligent, articulate, and motivated man, with a dedication to hockey and hockey players that few could surpass. Letters of reference from former players and colleagues gave shining reviews of James as a coach and human being. At least two of the letters were written before James was formally charged.

One of the letters came from former player Brad Blizner, now a lawyer, who had remained friends with James after his hockey career. In part, Blizner's letter read: "I can say without reservation, without exception, the individual outside of my own family who has had the greatest impact in allowing me to achieve whatever degree of success I have experienced in my life is Graham James. Graham took whatever trust I placed in him and responded by fostering that trust and helped it to be molded into friendship, which has been as important to me as any I have known. Graham has always been the first one to lend to me his support when it was most required, and I hope that, through this letter, I am equally able to support Graham at an uncertain time of his life."

Another letter came from Kimbi Daniels, who played for the Broncos from 1989 to 1993, and lived with James even after his father moved to Swift Current. Daniels wrote, "Mr. James was an excellent teacher of the game. . . . He treated each player fairly and was able to relate to them on a level most coaches can't. He never used threats or bribes to get a player to fulfill their potential. . . .

"I don't ever recall anyone saying anything bad about Graham. I considered Graham to be a great friend because of his honesty, humour, intelligence, and willingness to help, if need be. . . .

"I wish I knew more people like him."

Even after interviews with detectives, Daniel Lambert, who played from 1986 to 1990 with Sheldon Kennedy for the Broncos, also wrote, "I am not ashamed and I know in my heart that Graham James is a great coach and a great person."

John Rittinger wrote his letter of recommendation on November 22, 1996, the day James surrendered voluntarily to the police. In it he praised him for eliminating hazing on the team. He talked about the numerous times he had the coach over for dinner and commended his "attitude towards employees, players, all the persons that he would have come in contact with . . . over the years that he was with the Swift Current Broncos."

Lorne Scott also revealed that Kennedy was a minority owner of the Hitmen, along with his former Bronco teammates Sakic and Fleury. He acknowledged that James was a homosexual, who "made a very significant and serious error in judgement in becoming emotionally attached to these men, and in particular, to Mr. Kennedy. And you have heard my friend relate the depth of the feeling that Mr. James had for, and continues to have, for Mr. Kennedy. This is not an uncaring, unfeeling individual simply going and preying upon two people for whom he has no feelings whatsoever other than that of sexual gratification."

James was truly remorseful, Scott declared, and wanted to save the two complainants the stress of going to trial by pleading guilty. He did, however, have a different recollection of certain events than the two players did. James admitted to mutual acts of masturbation, and confirmed the players' assertion that no anal penetration had occurred. But James did not remember "having any sexual activities with Mr. Kennedy in his parents' home," Scott told the court. "Now we have reviewed this very carefully. Mr. Kennedy is adamant that it did happen. . . . Mr. James has his recall as well, but that does not undermine the fact of the sexual assaults to which he has admitted, and numerous sexual assaults as well."

Scott continued to rationalize his client's actions. "Mr. Kennedy was a person who, you know, without a doubt, Mr. James loved. And as I pointed out earlier, it is not a case of simply taking advantage of a young man for the purposes of straight sexual gratification. He considered Sheldon Kennedy to be his friend, his 'great friend.' He does not point a finger at Mr. Kennedy stating that Mr. Kennedy, who he thought felt the same for him, has now complained about the activities; he acknowledges what he did was wrong.

"With respect to the gun incident, he acknowledges that there was an incident, he recalls it taking place in Swift Current, not Winnipeg, and that it was more of a joke. He never intended to threaten Mr. Kennedy. Mr. Kennedy may have viewed it as a threat, he was 14 or 15 years old at the time, so he was a young person; Mr. James was in his thirties. . . ."

In answering the victims' charges that James bribed them, and became angry if they didn't do as he wanted, Scott said, "He never did anything or offered anything that [he] felt in his mind was a bribe. . . ." He also said, quoting his client, that James would on occasion "pout and whine," and that perhaps Kennedy and the other victim had interpreted that as anger.

"He never made any physical threats to either of these men . . . ," Scott continued. "We must bear in mind that, by the time these various incidents did end, these young men were big . . . nineteen-year-old hockey players; they're not little children. I'm not trying to undermine the seriousness of the offences . . . but one cannot ignore the ultimate age of these people."

Scott also tried to make the case that James believed Kennedy did indeed return his love. He presented a Christmas card sent by Kennedy after he began playing for the Detroit Red Wings and was out of James's clutches, or "arms," as Scott said. Kennedy wrote a postscript that said, "If your job is on the line, Woody [James's nickname], tell me, and I'll pay cash for the team." This was an act of friendship, said Scott, who interpreted the lines to mean, "If they're giving you a hard time, then I'll buy the team and you can run it for me."

Scott finished by arguing why James should receive three and a half years, saying that apart from the revealed assaults and the emotional harm that they presumably caused the victims, the extent of which was not known, there were no other aggravating factors in James's crime. He had no prior record, and he stopped the acts voluntarily. He had "absolute, total, complete remorse," said Scott, and "has attended a psychologist. He was found not to be a pedophile. He is a homosexual. . . . I submit there is little . . . risk of re-offending. Mr. James has recognized his wrong. He is not in a position at this point to be in contact with young hockey players."

Scott confuses homosexuality and pedophilia. The mere fact that James is a homosexual does not explain why he chose to prey on a fourteen-year-old boy. And in fact, according to Sandi Kirby, a sports sociologist at the University of Winnipeg, most researchers believe the choice of child victim has nothing to do with his or her sex and everything to do with the victim's apparent vulnerability.

Scott also argued that James is "not a danger to children. He . . . sought counselling before detection." With these remarks, Scott finished his submission.

Bruce Fraser, the Crown attorney, defended Kennedy's recollection of certain facts. "The fact that Mr. James doesn't recall any activity in his parents' home, I can tell you that I have canvassed that with Mr. Kennedy vigorously, and he has a clear memory of this. . . . In relation to the gun incident that took place, whether it took place in Saskatchewan or Winnipeg, as I understand it, he is accepting the fact that it took place. . . . As to whether he intended to scare Mr. Kennedy, I can only advise you that he certainly did scare Mr. Kennedy, and through his eyes, at that age, he was a very scared individual."

Justice Maloney ruled that these facts would not be disputed and that three and a half years would be an appropriate sentence. With that decision, James admitted he had "preached selflessness but I was selfish." He was led away in handcuffs and leg-irons, and would soon enter the maximum-security Edmonton Institution.

The Swift Current Broncos and the Western Hockey League had spent the months between James's resignation and the sentencing doing as much damage control as possible. Other players had been given the opportunity to come forward if they had suffered any abuse, but none did so. Police believe they had been advised by agents, managers, and coaches that it would be better for their hockey careers if they kept quiet.

Even so, uncomfortable questions were being asked about the complicit role the WHL and the Broncos may have played in turning a blind eye to rumours, innuendoes, and signs in Swift Current that something was wrong. And what role did other members of the Broncos team play? Were Canadians to believe that no one – administration, owners, members of the board, and players, especially those close to Kennedy – detected any sign of abuse during all those years?

If police were upset with the media leak, they were appalled at the role the WHL and the Broncos played in the case. "The amount of people I was dealing with, the number of people bailing out, telling barefaced lies to me, covering up, was unbelievable, astounding," says one investigator.

They believe a deal was struck: James would plead guilty to the charges before the court, and no one else would come forward with information that would incriminate him further. He'd serve his time, get out, and everyone could put the case behind them. But by the time the sentencing date rolled around, the net of suspicion was being cast widely by the media and experts in sexual abuse. The Broncos announced they would conduct "an internal investigation," while the WHL issued a gag order to all its members.

Despite attempts to control information, certain people did not stay quiet. The first to speak out was the father of the second complainant. On January 4, he told the media that his son had alerted Broncos management to James's behaviour three years earlier and they chose to ignore the criminal ramifications of the matter. "They knew about it," said the father. "He went to people involved in the Swift Current organization. . . . They let him [James] resign to protect themselves.

"They let his contract run out because they knew something could happen. It bothered my son that they let him go to Calgary, where he could continue," he said, adding his son had lodged the complaint with the Broncos' chief scout, Doug Mosher. When asked if his son had explicitly told Mosher about sexual abuse, the father replied, "I don't know that. I do not know that he specifically said he was being sexually abused. But there are all kinds of abuse and he told them."

On January 16, newspapers across Canada ran the second complainant's father's open letter to "All Hockey Parents." It read as follows:

From the time of birth, if your child needs you, they let you know. If they are uncomfortable and hungry, they cry. As they get older and they get hurt, they come running to you to show you their cuts and scrapes so you can make it better.

As parents we believe that our children will always confide in us in their time of hurt or need. Maybe we are being naive. But one thing we have learned is that when your child is being sexually assaulted, don't count on them confiding in you or asking your advice. Maybe it is a feeling of guilt or shame but we think more than that, it is mental manipulation.

They will be brainwashed into believing that they have no friends and not even their own parents care about them. And that they have no future and their best hope of success is totally dependent on this person. We always thought that sex offenders or pedophiles were sick and stupid individuals and we have learned otherwise. They are sick and disgusting but they are not stupid.

Graham James proved that. He plotted and planned each move he was about to make. He had answers for every question he was asked. James made us believe that he had our son's best interests in mind. We knew that it was within his power as a coach and GM of a major junior hockey team to either give or take away a dream our son had of becoming an NHL hockey player.

Looking back on our experience now, hindsight has been a good teacher but not one I would wish on any other parent. Beware of situations where one person is both coach and general manager. In our minds, they have too much power and control over the players. There are no checks and balances on them over that power.

We as parents demand respect from our children and we also demand that they respect their elders, their teachers and yes even their coaches. If your son or daughter leaves home at a young age, remember they are now depending on these people to take your place in their lives to help and guide them.

Remember mind manipulation can start very quickly. Watch for signs of a problem such as wild mood swings or sudden disinterest in things that were important. In our son's case, it was junior hockey. Watch for a loss of interest in close friends, extreme anger at you or someone else around you over something that seemed to you at worst a minor annoyance.

A coach has a job to do in developing your child's talent. They should not want to spend large amounts of time with that child in off-ice situations or out-of-season activities. Watch for more than normal phone contact, especially in off-season or during holidays. Be concerned if they are spending money on your child.

Like us, our sons and daughters have dreams and aspirations. As parents we have always tried to keep those goals realistic. I have often told my son making the NHL is like winning the 6/49 Lottery. It won't happen to a lot of people. However, in a lot of cases, our children would do almost anything to achieve their goals.

But, remember, there are people out there like James that, given the opportunity, will take advantage of your child's desires to achieve and be successful. They will put their own selfish desires on a list ahead of your own son's dreams and in order to satisfy them they will destroy your child's life.

It is not an easy thing for my wife and I to talk about but we feel some good must come of this. If by speaking out one child or parent will be spared the ordeal we have gone through, then in some small way we have helped.

 – *Victim's Father*

The next day, Grant Fleming of CBC Radio Sports interviewed the unnamed victim, whose voice was changed to protect his identity. He confirmed he filed his complaint about James with Doug Mosher in the winter of 1994. After the meeting, James left him alone, but continued to coach. The victim felt the administration had not taken the complaint seriously. Mosher, who had transferred to the Medicine Hat Tigers, where he was the general manager, denied any knowledge of the incident, as did John Rittinger. The latter simply repeated what he had said in his letter of recommendation – that the players "adored" James – and told the *Calgary Herald*, "No player ever came to me when I was in Swift Current and said he'd been sexually or criminally abused. I would have referred it to the police immediately."

The day after the father of the second victim first spoke to the press, Sheldon Kennedy revealed his identity to media beyond Calgary. On January 5, 1997 he met with a selected group, including the American sports network ESPN, and *USA Today*. He told them of his ordeal, and allowed them to identify him as the first victim.

He spoke about his life during and after the abuse, and how messed-up and alienated he had felt during what were supposed to be his formative years. The change in his life that prompted him to do something was his relationship with his wife, Jana. In the spring of 1995, while Kennedy still played for the Calgary Flames, the couple were married. In the same year, Jana became pregnant with their daughter Ryan. Kennedy knew he had to do something if the past wasn't going to wreak havoc on his future. His bottled-up pain came tumbling out during that summer as he described to his wife the nightmare that was still playing out in his mind.

"When my daughter was born, and I thought if anything ever happened to her in the future like what happened to me and I never did anything about [James], I'd feel pretty bad about it," Kennedy told the *Globe and Mail*. "I'd feel like I should have done something."

Two days before that interview, Jana Kennedy had told the *Calgary Herald* of the day in the spring of 1996 when she confronted Graham James about the abuse. "He called to find out why Sheldon hadn't played and what was going on," she said. "I had known for almost a year at that point, and I had never said anything to him because I was trying to respect Sheldon's space. I just basically said, 'Do you want to get into this with me right now, Graham?' and right there he knew. And he just started to backpedal, and tried to justify his actions. He tried to keep me on the phone for a really long time, just justifying.

"I finally said, 'Graham, there is no justification. He was a child and you're an adult and you abused your power and your trust and I have nothing else to say to you.'"

From the start, Jana was her husband's strongest supporter. "Obviously when I married him I thought he was a really great person and had a lot of great qualities. But to be honest with you, I didn't know about all of this when I married him and I found out shortly after," Jana told the *Herald*. "And as the year went on I was completely amazed and I am to this day completely proud of him."

In the spring of 1996, when Jana Kennedy confronted James, Sheldon Kennedy and the Flames were trying to stay in the running for the Stanley Cup. On April 17, after their game, Kennedy shared his story with his teammates.

"We were in Chicago during the playoffs," says Flames teammate Dean Evason from his Calgary home. "There were around five of us sitting around the hotel room, talking and having a few beers. In the middle of this, Sheldon blurted out that he'd been sexually assaulted by Graham James.

"I've known Sheldon since we were kids in Manitoba. We're both from small towns and we'd visit his family for two or three weeks every summer while we were growing up. We've continued that friendship through hockey. But the other guys didn't go so far back with Sheldon," continues Evason, who, at thirty-two, has spent twelve years in the NHL, playing for Washington, Hartford, San Jose, Dallas, and Calgary. "They started to filter out of the room, but one of them said to me, 'Maybe we shouldn't let him go to sleep by himself.' So he and I ended up going to a coffee shop for three or four hours. What he really wanted was to get it off his chest.

"The behaviour Graham used was exactly what would work on a fifteen-year-old whose goal it is to make the NHL. 'I won't or will get you drafted if you'll do this.' If you can get on the inside track, you can get into the NHL.

"Sheldon went into particulars, and I asked him if he had slept with the guy. He replied that they hadn't actually had sexual intercourse or oral sex. Then I asked him how many others he thought Graham had abused. He said he thought it might be from two to ten, but he was sure he'd started again with the Hitmen. That's the thing that really bugged me. I don't have a problem with Graham James being a homosexual. Big deal. But I have a big problem with him doing it to a fifteen-year-old. He had a team here that was very young.

So my young kid is on a team with a guy like this? There were so many people of influence who didn't do anything. If you don't want to believe it, you won't see it.

"Looking back, my mom said it was very scary. She took me, when I was fifteen years old, two thousand miles away to a junior-hockey town. You're giving your kid away to this man. They're very fortunate that he treated me like a son. If you think there's something going on, and you say your son's not going to play, it won't work. He'll do anything to play, to get back in the line-up."

Evason is well aware of the pressure and rewards of junior hockey. In 1982–83, he won the player-of-the-year award in the WHL when he played for Kamloops. He was drafted shortly afterwards into the NHL, and during those years in the two leagues, he saw a lot of things he couldn't fathom. He sees the Graham James case from this perspective.

"This is very complicated. First of all, homosexuality is not accepted in the real world, forget about a place where men beat each other up. There's no way it should matter, but it does. Hockey is small-town Canadian. Yet it's sick the kind of stuff that used to go on. I saw different things a man would do to another man in hockey. It never made sense to me why you'd want to do that. I've seen some really sick things that happen, and I still don't know why people do them.

"But Sheldon's a good person. He experimented with a lot of things, but in this case, he told me his initial thought was that he wanted to prevent it from happening to others. We're all very proud of him."

Kennedy's teammates thought they were the first to know of the abuse, but it turned out that one week before he broke down he had asked the Flames' coach at the time, Pierre Pagé, for help.

"We knew something was wrong," said Pagé. "We phoned his room and he said he wasn't in very good shape. I said, 'Do you want to talk?' and he said, 'Yeah.'"

Kennedy says Pagé "came down to the room and I told him the whole deal and he said, 'All right. I will phone a doctor.' So they phoned the doctor and it was a stress therapist-hypnotist and I went to see him twice. They wanted to relax me and calm me down. They never talked about the Graham thing. They talked about scoring goals. That was the least of my worries."

Pagé tells the story differently. In a December 1996 radio interview in Calgary, where local media had already disclosed Kennedy's name, Pagé reacted to criticism Kennedy directed at the Flames while he was in Calgary playing an away game for the Bruins.

"I don't mind being criticized for some of the record that we have right now, despite the fact that we're hanging in there," said Pagé about the Flames' season, "but to be criticized by Sheldon Kennedy, who has no credibility at all in the world of hockey – I mean, the best news we have is that Sheldon finally accepted help last year. Here we are with a few games left to go in the regular season, trying to make the playoffs. Kennedy is drunk all night, he finally admits the next morning that he can't play. He needs help, we fly him back to Calgary, we get him all the help we can get. And then, you know, my feeling is that this guy should not be playing hockey.

"He's got bigger problems than [Bob] Probert [who has cocaine and alcohol-abuse convictions]. He went AWOL in Boston a week ago, disappeared, and the same thing he's done with Winnipeg, and Detroit, and Calgary. I mean, this guy's big-time problems. He blames [me], blames the coach in Winnipeg, blames the coach in Detroit, blames the last five years. You know, I think he's got to take hold of himself. I can't believe that this guy's got the guts to go and criticize people that tried to save his life. This guy's not fighting for a contract, he's fighting for his life.

"I've got enough experience in this business to know that. It's ridiculous to have a guy like him, who has more problems than Bob Probert, criticize other people. He's got to take the bull by the horns and solve his own problems, get in a rehab centre. The league, you know, has to take action pretty soon on this case, and I don't know if Boston will take action, but they should. I thought we wanted to take action, told [Flames' GM, Al] Coates we should spend as much money as we can to rehab this guy who has serious problems. If the players said what they could say, they would tell you the same thing. This guy needs help."

Pagé later told the media Kennedy had not told him James was his abuser. When Kennedy spoke to Pagé, James was coach, general manager, and part-owner of the Hitmen, and occupied an office in the Saddledome, where Pagé also worked. Kennedy says he did tell Pagé it was James. In the end, he said, he had to live through the terrible memories without the club's help or support.

"It affected me big time," said Kennedy in January 1997. "You feel very awkward in public. You feel people are looking at you. I put up a shield. I didn't let anybody in. It's a very lonely way to feel. You never feel normal. You know something is wrong, but you don't know why it is like that."

"I feel like I am ten months old inside a twenty-seven-year-old body," Kennedy continued. "You are learning to live again. You are learning to have friends, and you have to learn to love and relax. . . . I can't remember the last day I relaxed totally.

"I went looking for a father-figure, and once it starts, once it starts happening, it is brutal. You are always trying to run and hide from him and he is always tracking you down. It is something that you just cannot tell anybody.

"I could not tell anybody because I was so scared to come out and admit it happened to me. I was scared to say I was with another man. I have nothing against homosexuality, but there has to be an understanding if somebody is not willing. That's what I told him many times. Then it is wrong.

"Graham knew I needed a father-figure coming from home because it was brutal at home and he preys on that. He knows. He knows exactly what he is doing. He put me in a position right off the top that screwed my whole life for me."

In the February 1, 1997, edition of the *Globe and Mail*, Kennedy described the isolation he felt as a victim of abuse: "You have to get as low as you can go before you realize you have to do something about it. You can run and run and run and run . . . my running shoes were getting worn out at the end of my days in Calgary. I hated hockey. I didn't like life. I didn't like me. I knew I had more to offer my friends, to people I care about, rather than being in trouble always."

"Calgary knew I had a problem, but they were uneducated about what they were dealing with. They sent me to a doctor. It was a hypnotist who tried to get me to relax and he talked to me about hockey and scoring goals. Graham James's name came up maybe once."

While Kennedy spoke with the media about the lack of support for him within hockey, others had trouble coming to terms with what it all meant. James's former business partner, Bret "Hitman" Hart, a shareholder in the Calgary Hitmen, expressed surprise and a feeling of betrayal once the trial wrapped up. Hart had asked James in the late summer if the allegations were true. "He told me it wouldn't be as bad as made out to be. I had reservations because he wouldn't come clean and say he was innocent," Hart told the *Winnipeg Free Press*. "I feel betrayed. I feel very sympathetic for the victims and the hockey community. Hockey has unfairly taken a black eye. The hockey community is straightforward and honest . . . and then you have something like Graham. . . ."

Hart felt hockey was being picked on by the media. "It happens in churches, schools, and the work place," he said. "You can never understand why."

People in the sports world like Hart were surprised by Sheldon Kennedy's allegation of abuse, but as the story unfolded more allegations were made. Kennedy went public with advice to old teammates. He believed many others in hockey during James's career had been victims. "If I could give them any advice, I'd say deal with it somehow. You can only run from it so long. I know that one.

"I know one person: he's running pretty good right now. I think he has to deal with it before his life gets more screwed up than it is.

"There's a difference between dealing with it and coming forward. If they don't figure they can handle coming forward, then they don't have to. But at least deal with it in your own life.

Kennedy also questioned why no one put a stop to James's abuse. "What bothers me is that people turned a blind eye to it. If there's a problem, what are you going to do, run from it?" he told the *Globe*.

It wasn't the first time Kennedy had asked why it had to continue for so long. During the interview he gave on January 5, when he first disclosed his identity, he told the press, "I know tons of people [who knew]. I was talked to on the ice and guys would say things on the ice. . . .

"I want people to know they can tell somebody. . . ."

And indeed, later that year, new complainants did come forward, and in early 1998 James pleaded guilty to new charges stemming from 1971 in Winnipeg. However, he suffered no further penalty; the new sentence for these offences is to be served concurrently with his earlier sentence. Given this result, it is hard to imagine that many more complainants will consider it worthwhile coming forward.

It wasn't just hockey players who now felt they could "tell somebody" after Kennedy's story of abuse became generally known. One of those who came forward was Martin Kruze, who said that starting when he was thirteen years old, he had been lured into having sex with employees at Toronto's Maple Leaf Gardens. Gordon Stuckless, a former assistant equipment manager at the Gardens, and his boss, George Hannah, who is deceased, had used tickets to games and other incentives to tempt Kruze and many others.

Martin Kruze had alerted Gardens administration to the assaults in the late 1980s, and reached an out-of-court settlement with them at the time, but at no time did the administration go to the police about the case and no charges were laid until Kruze went public in 1997. In March 1997, Gordon Stuckless was charged with multiple counts of sexual assault against boys who visited the arena. John Paul Roby, an usher at the Gardens, was charged with seventy more counts after fifty-one victims came forward.

In November 1997, Ontario Court General Division Judge David Watt sentenced Stuckless to two years less a day, saying Stuckless had recognized the gravity of his actions and had agreed to a program of chemical castration. Victims reacted negatively to the light sentence and verbally attacked Watt in the courtroom. The next week, Kruze, who also believed the sentence was far too light, committed suicide. Justice Watt was president of the Ontario Hockey Federation from 1992 to 1997 and sat on the CHA's Sexual Harassment Committee until September 1997.

# CHAPTER EIGHT

# Covering Up in Swift Current

## *"Everybody in the League Knew About It.*
## *Nobody Did Anything."*

While the CHL and WHL were calling the sexual abuse revealed by Sheldon Kennedy "an anomaly" in the league, media across the country carried stories about Brian Shaw, former owner and general manager of the Portland Winter Hawks and past chairman of the board of governors for the WHL. Shaw, who had held the most powerful position in the league for twelve years during the 1980s and early 1990s, and had died of AIDS-related cancer in 1993, was revealed as a long-term sex abuser.

Jim Harrison, who played for the Edmonton Oilers in 1974 when it was a World Hockey Association team, told the SouthamStar Network that Shaw, who was head coach at the time, would "come in the training room and start rubbing your leg. I lasted until the beginning of training camp . . . and, one day, I just lost it. It was giving me aggravation – I just fired my stick at him and said, 'I can't play for this man. I can't play in this surrounding 'cause it's wrong.'

"I had a no-trade contract, but I just phoned [Alan] Eagleson, who was my agent at the time, and said, 'Get me the hell out of here.' I just couldn't play for the man."

Harrison added that "nobody wanted anything to do with the guy, but what are you going to do? He's the coach and you're making the biggest money you've ever made in your life."

What's most interesting about Harrison's disclosures is that he was the assistant coach of the Moose Jaw Warriors the year after James abruptly left, and knew then that James's behaviour resembled that of a coach he could not tolerate. "I look back now, and we should have done something about him. We're all in the same boat; we're all to blame."

The media pursued the story on front pages everywhere. The *Globe and Mail* reported that not only had Shaw abused players since the 1960s, but that it was widely known by those in power in both the WHL and WHA. The paper quoted "a former club executive," who said he had complained about Shaw to the WHL's president, Ed Chynoweth, asking him, "Why don't we discuss this issue?" To which Chynoweth replied, "Why do you keep raising this?" The club executive retorted, "Because it's an issue."

Chynoweth told the *Globe* that this exchange never occurred. "I can unequivocally say I have no recollection of [a complaint]. There were rumours and innuendo, but it wasn't exactly like you could prove something.

"If I had proof he molested a player, I certainly like to think I would have stepped in and gotten more information."

The former official of the club also made a connection between the league's failure to recognize Shaw was an abuser and the free licence with which Graham James could later operate. "The point is, if you're Graham James and you were looking at this league and saw that this [Shaw's abuse of players] is not a problem, no wonder he felt he could prey on them."

The *Globe* also quoted former players on the subject of their coach, general manager, and owner. "In Portland, I would definitely say there were players being abused," said one. "Do I think Sheldon Kennedy is the tip of the iceberg? You bet I do."

Jamie Huscroft of the Calgary Flames, who played for the Winter Hawks in 1983 when he was sixteen, said, "He called me into his office, reached for me, and said, 'Can I?' I didn't know what to do."

Huscroft made a quick exit, and two weeks later found himself traded with no explanation. Another former player, Cam Neely, said that when the team competed, "You would get barbs. They would call you [pejorative names for homosexuals] just because you happened to play for that organization." He added he also knew that Shaw was taking certain players with him on off-season trips, "but I never heard of anything happening that should not have been happening."

Jim Harrison added to the picture by describing Shaw's behaviour in the locker room. "Any player will tell you that . . . he used to shower with the guys and everything. That's not a common thing for a coach. . . . The stories were rampant."

Shaw's inappropriate behaviour was first apparent when he coached a junior team in 1968. By the 1969–70 season, players realized Shaw's favourites were receiving gifts and trips, and many more athletes were being sexually harassed. They complained to the owner, Fred Muller (now deceased), who fired Shaw at the end of the season. Sources believe that Muller considered reporting him to the police, while one player weighed the benefits of a lawsuit. In the end, no one did anything to stop Shaw, though the Ontario Hockey Association apparently had an unwritten rule that barred him from coaching in Ontario.

The *Globe* also quoted an unnamed former WHL executive who said, "I'm as guilty as the next guy. Everybody in the league knew about it. Nobody did anything; nobody said anything. I watched an interview with Sheldon Kennedy . . . and I cried. I sat there and just cried, watching the pain the guy was going through."

After the Graham James case became public, it didn't take long before Dev Dley, president of the WHL, announced that counselling services would soon be made available to all players in the league. They would be doing police checks on all coaches, managers, and officials, and "talking to the RCMP to ensure if there are further steps we can take, other than those in place, to ensure it doesn't happen again. This is not a knee-jerk reaction."

Dley also pointed out that the league already had a program, instituted in the early 1990s by Ed Chynoweth, and run in conjunction with the RCMP, that matched police and players together. "It has allowed many of the players to try their hand at the shooting range, go on a ride-out in a police cruiser, and get better educated on issues like drug, alcohol, and sexual abuse," reported the *Calgary Sun*.

Sheldon Kennedy had set the ball rolling. Players and former players were going to police with stories of sexual abuse suffered at the hands of coaches at the minor level. One after another, hockey coaches were being arrested, though in the end not all victims were prepared to press charges. Most sought help outside of hockey, from sexual-assault clinics and the Children's HelpLine, although in Manitoba alone, player advocate Don Smith dealt with six cases.

Before Sheldon Kennedy went public, "we used to receive approximately twenty calls a month from men," says Calgary Sexual Assault Centre co-ordinator Danielle Aubry in March 1997. "Now it's twenty a week. Twenty-five per cent have been about coaches, another 10 to 15 per cent about the environment of hockey. One caller had a terrible sexual assault during an initiation. It was really violent, and happened fifteen years ago. He's in a serious crisis about it now.

"This is the time, when a male victim starts to realize he's been a victim of sexual assault – and it can take years before he's ready to face this – that he's most at risk of committing suicide."

Aubry believes that people involved in sports need to think seriously about what happens to boys when they are put into a situation that stresses violence and the suppression of feelings, and meets the needs not of children, but of the adults for whom the children perform.

"People think that male juvenile prostitution only occurs on the 'boys' stroll' in Calgary," she says. "But the real prostitution of boys is happening in other forms. People don't connect these sexual assaults in hockey with the way in which the boys are treated in terms of prostituting themselves to a game, as commodities. People think hockey is 'safer' than being on the street, because from a societal perspective it's more rewarding."

Like Aubry, many others noticed a sharp rise in the number of men calling sexual-assault centres. In Sarnia, Ontario, the CHL's Sarnia Sting set up their own twenty-four-hour sexual-abuse hotline for players.

But by January 14, 1997, Swift Current itself, where all the publicity had started, was back in the headlines. CBC Radio Sports' Grant Fleming interviewed Darren McLean, a member of the Broncos from 1993 to 1994, who said he had met with Broncos management to disclose James's sexual behaviour and was given his walking papers as a result. The left winger told them that not only was James hitting on some players and ignoring everyone else, he was also paying them to have sex with girls while he watched and videotaped the proceedings.

McLean grew up outside of Redvers, Saskatchewan, on his family's farm. He started playing hockey at age five, and at fourteen moved 120 kilometres from home to play for the Estevan Bruins, a bantam AA team in the Southern Saskatchewan Hockey League. At eighteen, in January 1993, he started playing for the Broncos, and remembers thinking the world was at his doorstep. "I felt really good," says McLean. "They were in first place in the standings when I started playing, and they'd won the Memorial Cup a few years before."

But just one month into playing in Swift Current, "one player mentioned something to his best friend," says McLean. "He said he thought another player was having a relationship with Graham. It felt very uncomfortable.

"It was a little obvious," continues McLean. "He spent so much time with this one player, both at and away from the rink. We became suspicious, but we were so intent on winning we overlooked more instances that concerned us for the rest of the season. But that summer there was a bit of a blow-up with one of the players. Graham got into a fight. I think he knew someone was going to blow the whistle eventually, but it was all internal at the time, and we weren't clear on exactly what had happened between them."

The players returned in the fall, and hoped it would be like any other year in hockey. "We had normal good spirits," says McLean. But the season started to fall apart for him, even before it started. "I hurt my shoulder in training camp. It was the seventh time it had become separated, and I was out of most play for a good four months. I was going back and forth from home to Swift Current, and talking to players.

"Staying away from Swift Current for a while gave me a different perspective. It was more and more obvious that something was going on. Certain players were receiving gifts, and holidays. We were hearing about sexual conduct that was unacceptable.

"When I came to Swift Current, I was a new player, but by this time I was a veteran. Some of us were in a position to say something – it was our role to be leaders."

At first, the players thought it might be consensual, but they eventually decided what James was doing was just plain wrong. "Graham wouldn't spend any time with the rest of the players, for the most part he lost interest in us," says McLean. "It had such a negative effect on everybody. We just wanted to play hockey. Our performance began to decrease. There was no team unity, and the players became divided on whether or not they supported Graham. Those of us who opposed what he was doing weren't sure how to deal with it."

Despite efforts of the players to compete in the WHL, the situation grew worse every day. "He didn't care about us at all. We were giving 110 per cent; he was giving us nothing," says McLean. "Then we stopped caring, too. It got to the point that one player would phone Graham and tell him, 'We're out trying to pick up girls.' He still talks to Graham and is friendly with him. At one time he was living with Graham. His way of dealing with it was just to avoid it."

Since many veterans were supporting James, even as his behaviour became obvious, McLean and other veterans decided to approach the rookie players. "We could see Graham had picked out a few of the sixteen-year-old kids. We told them to keep an eye out. Don't do anything you're not comfortable with."

In February 1994, it came to a head. Before a game, the players could hear a yelling match between James and the second complainant who came forward to the police. "There ended up being a fistfight in the dressing room," says McLean. "His special player had bloodied and broken Graham's nose, but we still had to play that night. One of Graham's friends got in a fight in the game, and got kicked out. He stayed in the training room with Graham," preferring to show his loyalty to his coach rather than play. "Graham kept his tracksuit on and stayed away from the bench. Then he lied to every-one, and said the assistant coach slammed the door in his face.

"A couple of days after the incident I talked to the assistant general manager, Doug Mosher. I called him to my house and told him every-thing I knew," says McLean. "I told him about James's propositions to players, and about players having sex with girls in Graham's basement while he secretly watched. I'm sure the girls didn't know it was going on, but the players were being paid money for it."

"He was kind of shocked," says McLean of Mosher. "He said he suspected something was going on but had never imagined it went that far. We were playing Regina in Swift Current that night; it was early to mid-February in 1994. I told him I was finished, I didn't want to play. But he convinced me to keep playing. I played that night, and then after the game we had a meeting. The veteran players expressed their feelings about Graham, and a number of us felt he should be released.

"Doug came over to that meeting. He came to Kevin Powell's billets' house, where it was held. Kevin supported what I said, and his billeting parents were great."

It was an exhausting twenty-four hours for McLean. The team meeting finally ended at two a.m., when Mosher suggested they meet with the team president, John Rittinger, as soon as possible. At eight the same morning McLean met with Rittinger in Mosher's base-ment. "Doug sort of summed up everything that was said at the team meeting, what the players' concerns were, and that Graham was affecting the team negatively. But Rittinger told us he thought it would be difficult to get rid of him. He said you just can't up and fire him. In the end, though, he agreed to tell Graham he'd be relieved of his duties."

Rittinger arranged for the team to gather at the rink at noon that day. When they arrived, he told the team James was going to speak to them. "He pinpointed the players who complained and said, 'How could you do this to me? I gave you money when you needed it. You needed me,'" McLean says. "He went all around the room, and then four or five players said, 'You're right, we respect you.' But I just stood up, and I told him, 'I respect you for what you've done in hockey, but I don't respect you as a human being or as coach for what you have done.' Kevin Powell said the same, but the rest caved in and went along with Graham."

McLean couldn't believe his teammates' lack of resolve. They were willing to compromise and accept a deal proposed by Rittinger and Mosher. "Graham made a promise that he'd put the team first and we'd all make the best of it," says McLean. "They told us, 'It's going to be hard enough to make the playoffs without this. Whatever is said in the dressing room doesn't go any further. Either put up or shut up.' "

McLean walked away in shock at the cover-up. He approached Eldon Molberg, who covered the Broncos' games on the local radio station, and told him what was happening. That afternoon during practice, McLean was called up to the front office. "They'd heard word of me speaking to Eldon," says McLean. "Doug told me I no longer had a position on the team. 'I can't believe you're saying that,' I replied. . . . They told me to leave town. They said they would pay me the equivalent of what I would have made if I'd worked part-time during the season, and handed me a cheque for two thousand dollars."

Today, Eldon Molberg is the public-relations director for the Broncos. Darren McLean hasn't played a game of hockey since. "I didn't want anything to do with it, if that's the way it was going to be run," he says. "I was really confused at the time. 'What the heck did I do wrong?' I kept asking myself. My self-esteem was pretty low, and I lost a lot of confidence. All of a sudden I was off the team and finished with hockey.

"But you should have seen the difference in the players that were involved with Graham. They started carefree, but their dreams were shattered. Some of them hated hockey. One player quit a couple of times, but Graham convinced him to stay. During the whole time, there was a little part of me that said, 'Did I do the wrong thing?' but I know now, especially since Sheldon came out, that the answer is no."

The traumatic days in Swift Current are still not far from McLean's mind. "I know [the second complainant] had confided in Carol Byers. She was the Broncos' secretary, and she voiced her concerns to the organization. I think it's really affected her more than other people. She had to take direct orders from Graham, so if he got her to run errands, or phone players, he'd be able to get [the complainant] to himself. She was really shaken up. But she'd been working for the Broncos for several years, and I think she was caught. It was a very tough position."

McLean believes there are still people not disclosing information to the police. "A lot of players who are loyal to the Broncos believe they never would have made it without Graham," says McLean. "I feel they're afraid to look back for a short period of time, sort all of this out, and then carry on with their lives. They've decided to just carry on and pretend nothing happened.

"But I don't know how they could possibly do that," he continues. "The whole league called us the 'Swift Current Homos,' especially players who had played in Swift Current and had been traded because they were unhappy with the situation. Even the season after [the second complainant] was traded, he still got called 'Graham's Bumboy,' 'Graham's Fag,' those were just a couple of catcalls you could hear on the ice. It's hard to imagine the WHL wouldn't have had any strong suspicions with that stuff going on."

Around the time Darren McLean spoke out, the Broncos were to release a report of their "internal investigation." It was delayed, however, as the club tried to tackle McLean's allegations. "The Board of Directors have undertaken an internal review regarding the various meetings held between players and management," said a statement. "We wish to address the allegation that $2,000 was paid as 'hush' money from the Bronco organization. The Board of Directors wish to advise that in accordance with an internal review of our accounting records and bank records, no Swift Current Bronco cheque or other payment was issued to Darren McLean, other than his regular February 15, 1994, payroll cheque. . . . We find it appalling that anyone would suggest that this Board of Directors would condone and/or cover up such reprehensible conduct. . . . There is conflicting information as to exactly what was said and what can be substantiated. This is full disclosure of the information made available to the Bronco board and any further comment will not be forthcoming."

Kevin Powell, the former player who had supported McLean in his attempt to have James fired, also spoke to the media, confirming that Mosher and Rittinger had been aware of the sexual relationship James was having with a teammate. In reply, the Broncos issued another statement, saying they were "extremely concerned with recent allegations in the media and an internal investigation is continuing."

"My son has gone on the record saying he supported Darren," says Grant Powell, Kevin's father. "Telling the truth has not helped him in his career; if anything, it's hindered him. . . . He knew something was going on with James. They didn't have solid proof, but they could tell things were not right."

One point Grant is sure about, though, is that no one from the Broncos called his son to clarify what went on at the team meeting with Mosher and Rittinger. "Did the Broncos talk to him?" asks Powell. "The answer is no."

It is suggested to him that there seems to be a case of collective amnesia in Swift Current. "More like 'protective amnesia,'" he replies.

The week before the McLean and Powell stories broke, however, Gary Bollinger, vice-president of the Broncos in 1986, admitted to the *Calgary Sun* he had been told James was having sex with Kennedy. "I was told by the father of the player we traded to get Kennedy that [Kennedy] and James were doing it. But I didn't know for sure that [James] was a homosexual." He had no proof, and at the time didn't pursue the matter any further, saying, "I figured if they were doing it, they were doing it with consent."

Not long after James was hired, Bollinger lost his position on the board when he questioned why the coach needed to take a player with him on a scouting trip to Czechoslovakia. "I confronted Graham James and he didn't respond," he said. "The team was in a tough position – I guess they figured, 'Do we get rid of a successful coach or do we get another vice-president?' It's a lot easier to get a new vice-president."

Bollinger stressed in his interview with the *Sun* that he had never told anyone on the board about his suspicions.

Soon he gave a similar interview to CBC Radio and once again said he had been aware that James had appeared to be having a relationship with Kennedy.

The WHL issued a gag order on the entire league, and the Broncos were only too happy to comply. They preferred the treatment they received from the local papers, who buried the story and continued to trumpet the team on every occasion. It was time to get on with the game of hockey. Bollinger now claims he was misquoted in the media. "They seemed to have been good friends," he says from his farm near Assiniboia, outside of Swift Current. "Kennedy really seemed to like him. Who knows what goes on? I didn't think anything was going on. That quote was wrong."

Meanwhile, Ben Wiebe, chairman of the Broncos' board of directors, explained how the internal investigation had been conducted. "Basically the directors of the club took the information we had, and included what we had learned through the media. As a group we had to talk to those involved."

They interviewed former staff and players, including Darren McLean. "We had numerous meetings with Darren after his disclosures to the press," says Wiebe, who is also an accountant, and a veteran of the club since 1986. "We looked at information on press releases, information from numerous players, including Darren, and former staff. There was conflicting information as to what was said at those team meetings. Darren's allegations couldn't be substantiated."

For reasons unknown, the Broncos decided not to interview James. They also decided not to mention that Darren McLean's allegations had been backed by Kevin Powell, nor did they interview Powell. Instead, a press release concluded, "no other player accepted what Darren had said." The internal investigation was over. By the time the summer of 1997 rolled around, Wiebe openly admitted they hadn't interviewed Powell. "Basically, we knew he would have just backed Darren up," he says from his Swift Current accounting office. As well, they hadn't bothered with a written report. "It wasn't really a written thing," he says. "We conducted the investigation verbally."

Wiebe prefers to stress the strong points of the club and the WHL. "There are several WHL initiatives," he says. "There will be procedures and policies in place in the future. We're trying to create an environment so the appropriate person will know. It didn't happen this time. No matter what the screening, someone like Graham could still have slipped through. . . .

"People have put their heads together – we're part of the solution. The individual we have as a guidance counsellor, she is the epitome of approachability. She is trained at recognizing situations where an individual is being abused. . . .

"We haven't lost any support. In fact, it's gone up. There's a strong community and a strong organization. People got caught up in the media circus there before, but we're moving on. There was one bad guy here, but it's all family people who are running this organization. You're just not going to find a group of people who are going to condone that kind of behaviour."

Swift Current's mayor, Paul Elder, was a billeting parent, and hosted social events for the club at his home. In mid-January, he shared his thoughts on James with the *Globe and Mail*. "We thought he made men out of boys. We all are searching. How could this have gone on?" he said, adding that the townspeople had no idea abuse was occurring. "Being a small Bible-belt town, maybe we're naive, especially for a guy you put on a pedestal."

Wiebe's and Elder's conception of Swift Current is somewhat different from that of an investigating officer in the case, who does not want to be named. "You have to look at the social make-up of this town," he says. "I can only comment from a personal perspective, but one should look at the number of churches versus the number of people in town. They're almost cultish. These people go to church on Sunday, but the rest of the week, I'm not sure. We're investigating stuff out of those churches that's thirty years old.

"There's a cowboy mentality here. It's a different community, and I've been in other small communities. A lot of people seemed to put this together after the fact, but other people knew. It's just like the abuse in the churches."

The family of the second complainant in the Graham James case has filed a civil suit against the Broncos organization, arguing that they didn't perform their duty of *in loco parentis*; in other words, that they had assumed parental responsibility for the player while he was in their care and had failed in that responsibility. They say there were signs that something was seriously wrong with the team that normally functioning adults would have been blind not to see.

Apart from widely circulating rumours and James's obvious partiality for certain players, the danger of the situation also showed in the players' behaviour. The team drank vast amounts during James's era. Anger and alcohol became a constant theme for certain players. Some time after the second complainant had his very public fight with the coach in the locker room, he injured himself when he destroyed a plate-glass door at school and needed forty stitches to close the wound. Frank "Digger" McBean's firm represented the player in the legal action that followed. Sheldon Kennedy had a drinking-and-driving charge against him that Digger handled as well. Todd Holt, who was billeted with James, became so drunk by three o'clock one morning, James had to rush him to hospital. There were never any convictions.

Even after someone stepped in and told James to stop abusing and harassing the second complainant, James contacted him continually on a phone he had installed in his billeting house for the purpose of summoning him at whim.

Carol Byers, secretary of the team, is alleged to have unplugged the victim's phone at his billeting parents' home to prevent the abuse from occurring. Observers believe Byers wanted to go to the police, but she was told she would lose her job.

No one is sure just how many players were unwittingly or otherwise influenced by James, but it is known that he sent Brian Sakic and Theoren Fleury to the complainant's home to convince him to play on the team.

Conditions continued to deteriorate. Every time he went out on the ice, the players called him 'Graham's fag.' As McLean says, it appears several in the WHL knew what was going on.

Even so, everyone thought it was business as usual – except for Carol Byers. "As far as I know the gag order is still in effect," she says from the Broncos office in the summer of 1997, explaining why she can't disclose new information. "It's been hell, as you can imagine, but I would prefer to work with the police, and not the media, if I'm needed. It's not over yet. You heard about the cases coming up in Manitoba? Well, there's more here, too."

Byers's observations are hardly surprising. The police believe there were between twenty and twenty-five victims.

The family of the second complainant doesn't just want legal redress, they want to make sure it never happens again. There was a nice-looking boy whom James recruited to the Calgary team in the 1995–96 season. They warned him and his parents to watch the coach very carefully. James had already opened a bank account in the new player's name. The new recruit sat on the bench for more than a month, but for the family it was a sign that he wasn't giving in to James's wishes.

The complainant's family has hired Fran Huck to see the case through. Huck is a long-time lawyer who practises in Regina and is more than a little familiar with the hockey world. He played in the NHL for the Montreal Canadiens and the St. Louis Blues, the WHA for the Winnipeg Jets, and captained the Canadian national team at the 1968 Olympics.

In the summer of 1997 he still looks fit and athletic, still plays hockey and basketball, and trains five to six days a week. Like many former players, he's not huge like the modern Eric Lindros style of player, but believes in a combination of technique and finesse.

"Most of the hockey I played was river hockey," says Huck of his childhood. "The kids themselves did it. There were only outdoor rinks, and none of what we see now with kids being regimented and spending so much time in dressing rooms."

Huck sees a relationship between the old-style hockey Canadians once played – where the game was in the hands of the children who played it – and the safety of those young people. They skated and played outdoors within full view of the community. The game wasn't separated from anyone by walls, boards, Plexiglas, or the price of a ticket. There were no dark hallways and hidden locker rooms and offices where children could be sequestered by adults. Hockey, and the guardianship of those playing it, was for everyone, whether they played or not, and whether they knew it or not.

"There was more fun, and a higher skill level then," adds Huck. "At a young age, we didn't have a team concept like they do today, we just played. Now the kids watch all this nonsense from the NHL and imitate. They don't need to learn certain skills used in professional hockey until they're fourteen or fifteen. Those sorts of mechanics can be taught in a few seasons."

Huck believes the case launched by his clients will help protect the right of young people to a safe environment in which to play hockey. "No one's really looked at sport this way before," he says, "but we've found James's behaviour to be part of systematic abuse in the WHL that goes back to the 1960s. Hopefully, once we show this, more victims will come forward."

While concerned parents have begun to search for signs of abuse, and professionals like Fran Huck have undertaken to seek legal, administrative, and structural changes in the game, there was another group in Swift Current that everyone, including the media that inundated the town, has overlooked.

"They never really did anything *to* me," says Heather Smith, who used to hang around the arena after Broncos games, but has since moved from Swift Current. "They verbally sexually harassed me – at school, in the mall, and at the hockey rink. They'd tell me I wanted to sleep with them. All I ever wanted was to sit and watch a hockey game. I think I've met two hockey players who were decent. Very few are real. Honestly, I don't think they have any feelings," she says.

Smith went to her school guidance counsellor when the behaviour of the Broncos became too much for her to handle. "I went to Colleen McBean. I know her pretty well. I watched her on TV [during the James case]. She helped me out with a lot of my problems. A lot of them were because of the Broncos. She stuck up for me."

The problem was, though, no matter how many times Smith complained about the Broncos, the harassment didn't stop. "I guess I just assumed she would tell them to stop it," she says. "She was [also] . . . the team's counsellor, so I thought she would tell them to stop it."

Smith admits she thought there were plenty of good-looking Broncos, and she would have loved to have been the girlfriend of one of them. But she couldn't believe their definition of what a "girlfriend" was.

It appears there is a real division between the girlfriends, who are often back in the player's home town, and the girls they go after while the season is on. "There was a list when I was in Grade Seven," says Smith. "That was seven years ago. They had a bet going to see who could sleep with the most girls. [One of the players, who became a part-owner of a major-junior franchise] phoned me and told me he wanted to have sex with me," says Smith, whose name was on the list. "I had a big crush on him when I was in Grade Seven." But sleeping with players wasn't what she thought girlfriends did when she was twelve years old, and she says she didn't co-operate.

After one incident she phoned the coach, and told him she would press charges. "I guess he talked to the player, because he called me and told me never to call him again. He freaked out. He thought he could do anything he wanted."

Another girl found out in Grade Eight that she had made the 1991–92 list. "They used to watch me in the mall. I guess my body changed a lot from Grade Eight to Grade Nine. I'd heard about the list, so when they started phoning, I was scared. They start eyeing you early, so by the time you get to high school, they've got you staked out. Everyone started telling me I was going to be a Bronco girl."

A third young woman whose name was on the list said it wasn't smart to be seen with the Broncos. "You get a really bad rep if you hang out with them. Some of them beat their girlfriends and some don't. . . . They can be really rude and sick, but I think they're a good team."

Smith started to realize there was something terribly wrong with the way in which the Broncos were behaving. "There were fights that I saw between the players. They could be pretty mean – flat-out rude."

Of the eight girls interviewed for this book, two denied that they were abused, despite the fact their friends said they had been treated terribly.

"I didn't associate with any of them," says one, who the others say was at plenty of team parties and had sexual intercourse with a number of players. "It's too bad about [James]. I heard they set up cameras so the players could bring girls down to his place. You're just a puck if you get caught up in that. It's always been that way."

What does she think of the Broncos?

"Nine-tenths are scum. The players just want to screw girls. That's why I wouldn't associate with them."

Another young woman explains what happened to the second girl, who says her relationship with a team member was problem-free. "He treated her like shit. This guy, I don't know why he was such a jerk," she says. "I remember she went out with him and then we'd always go down there [to Swift Current], and he'd be rude, and tell her, 'Let's do it,' in front of other people.

"He had a temper all the time. Sometimes, I remember, she'd come out of the room crying. She'd never tell me why. He was very evil. He didn't treat me bad, but I could see the way, at parties, the way he treated other girls and my friend."

Elaine Martin speaks about the players and girls who hung out together. "I don't hang out with those girls now. I don't know. I don't think it ever happened to me," she says of the girls who may have unknowingly been part of the team's pornographic videos. "The players I hung out with were nice guys. There were a lot of other people, other guys who weren't hockey players, who were jealous of them because all the girls liked the players. They put us under a spell."

She says she first met the Broncos when she was in Grade Ten, but corrects herself. "No maybe I met them when I was twelve and a half. When Graham was the coach, we always went to his house. He had three Broncos living with him."

At the time she felt the players didn't like James, who, she says, never seemed to be home when the players brought girls to his place. "None of the girls ever saw him. We thought he was some kind of weirdo. I was never in his basement, but I was with someone in his place – he told me Graham was gone. The guy I was with, he was a slut. I think he was engaged to another girl. There was a big deal. Her mom called my parents, but he's taken a lot of other girls there. He was physically abusive, not to me, but to her. He beat her all the time, and everybody knows he beat her. . . . She'd come to school with black eyes."

Martin says she can't talk about it any more and excuses herself from the phone.

The next evening she calls back and the conversation continues. "Graham always had them [the players] up there [at his house]. Always. When I was thirteen years old, I started hanging out with them. I had a big crush on one of them. I was thirteen and he was eighteen. It was so weird. We [certain girls] were categorized by others like we were sluts," she says. "But we weren't really sleeping with the players, and we weren't disrespected by them, either. It was more like a friendship. I had a relationship with only one, not five, but I think some other girls did."

Martin corrects herself later, saying that what she called a friend-ship wouldn't have occurred if she hadn't had sexual intercourse, and that maybe she *had* slept with more than one. The boys, of course, had sex with as many girls as they liked, but the girls who had sex with them were quickly judged by others in Swift Current.

"We were treated fine by the guys, but we were seen as the sluts of the town. A lot of us weren't like that. I had sexual relations with a couple. Sometimes I still think about [one of them]. For my teen years, I gave myself to [him]. But it bothered me that he would sleep with other girls. I'd say, 'I know you like me, but I hear you were with other girls.' He'd tell me they didn't matter. It was like a trance. He put me under a spell.

"A lot of the guys, I think, thought I was just going to do it for one night. But I'd ask, 'Will we have a relationship now?' I'd hear those words, 'I like you, I want to be with you,' and I'd think they'd want a relationship, but they never did. I'd say to myself, Why are they going to like me? In a way, I really felt like certain ones did like me. For me to give myself to them . . . to give my body, it meant a lot to me to do that. Most of them were so gorgeous. . . . I'd sleep with a guy, and then he wouldn't talk to me after that."

It was the physical abuse of the other girl that distressed her most, however. Yet although she and others knew of the abuse, no one reported it to Colleen McBean.

"I didn't know her too well," she says of McBean. "But it's kind of hard, coming to school with different bruises every day and nobody notices."

There wasn't just physical abuse, says Martin. "One night some of us girls were sitting in a room with them. There were four girls and ten guys, I'd say. . . . That night there wasn't a lot of alcohol. I thought they respected us, but they were pigs. It wasn't really sex harassment, we weren't called whores by them, but they said to us, 'You three − dyke out for us!' Like in front of them. We thought, No, I don't think so, and we left. I was fifteen then."

While Martin wasn't familiar with the Broncos' list referred to by Smith, she said one of the male friends of the team kept one, and that a girl who made it on to that list was treated terribly by the team. "I think they probably had certain girls most of them had slept with. They picked on big, fat, ugly ones. There was one girl, she wasn't a very pretty girl. She was probably with five of the Broncos. She was really disrespected. They'd talk about her really rudely. It was a lay. That's all. That's one person I felt really sorry for.

"Just to hear the words, 'I like you, you're a beautiful girl.' Hockey players like pretty, skinny girls. Fat girls were the joke. . . .

"I'm just glad I'm out. I didn't want to be known as a slut. It was killing me. Everyone knew who I was. I'm glad I'm starting over. It's been a lot better."

Like Elaine Martin and Heather Smith, Jennifer Stewart saw and heard things while she spent time with the Broncos that were deeply disturbing. While she feels she wasn't a direct recipient of abuse, she says she was there when the team decided to test her friend out.

"This is just one example," she says of what might happen on any given evening. "My one friend and I went to a billet's house. This one guy said to my friend, 'Come here, I've got to show you something downstairs.' They all screwed her. One at a time. Each guy would take her back down to the basement. She just let them do it to her. It was so disgusting. Before that, they were all sitting around, and then they started undoing their pants and were beating off. They got my friend to strip for them. So there were eight guys in a billeting house getting her to strip, then they screwed her one at a time in the basement.

"The other guys would be hanging out upstairs. They'd get mad at me because I wouldn't do that. They told me to go home if I wasn't going to put out. They're all pigs."

Stewart says the girls rarely went to games. They waited for a phone call from a member of the team, and then went to a designated billeting parents' home when the parents were away, or to Graham James's house. The age of the girls didn't seem to matter.

"They don't care how old these girls are. I was not even fifteen when I slept with [the player who had also slept with Elaine Martin while abusing his girlfriend]. I was really stupid to keep doing it. He was a Bronco, and he liked me. That's all I needed to hear then. They have so many relationships, too. You never knew how many girls they'd been with.

"After a few of my friends slept with [another player on the Broncos], they found out he had herpes, and there he was sleeping with all these girls at the billet's house when they were away."

Like other girls interviewed, Stewart kept the secrets about the Broncos to herself. She desperately wanted to believe they really were nice boys, and she was convinced no one else – especially her school guidance counsellor – would listen. "I'm pretty sure [Colleen McBean] must have known. I think she did a lot of good stuff, but . . . she saw past all the bad things. They were her little angels. I don't know if girls would talk to her. . . .

"You hear the old people, they talk so good about them. If they only knew."

Marsha Harding is the girl Stewart says had sex one night with eight players. She echoes a phrase most of the young women use to describe the team. "They're all pigs. Honestly, they only want one thing, and we both know what that is. They have no respect for girls. They'd screw anything that moved. Relationships have nothing to do with them."

She says they are not all terrible human beings, but finding one who will stand up to the rest of the team is very difficult. "We were at [a certain player's house]. I was there with Paul Vincent. One of them was drunk, and trying to get my friend to sleep with three other guys.

They were going to videotape it. Paul Vincent said to them, 'How can you treat them that way?'"

Vincent was the only one in this particular group of Broncos who didn't demand sex. "Paul Vincent was actually a nice guy.

"We went over to one of their houses, and there were a whole bunch of Broncos there.

"'If you don't screw us, we'll spread rumours about you being a slut,' they told me. I said, 'Who cares?' Then they said, 'Okay, we'll say you were with five Broncos and there was a big orgy. There'll be lots of rumours.'

"This year, two players started spreading stories around about me. At first I thought they were really nice guys, and then . . .

"They always come on with another, like three or four other guys. They all wanted it at the same time."

Harding also says there were rumours about the team making porn videos when she went to high school. "I heard about it way before Darren McLean said anything about it. It was going around the school."

Eventually, Harding realized she had to extricate herself from the team. "I got sick of the harassment," she says. "My older brother answered the phone once and one of them told him all about what they said I did. I started to be afraid of them. I started thinking, These guys are really scaring me, and that's my mistake, that I let them do those things all that time.

"But I don't think anyone would have listened to me if I said anything. They favoured the Broncos so much. It got so I was afraid to go to the mall, or wherever they hung out, like in the hall at school. I'm glad I moved away."

Colleen McBean says the physically abused girl referred to in some of the above interviews did come to her guidance office to confide in her about her boyfriend's anger. "Yes, I remember her talking about his temper," says McBean from her home in Swift Current during the summer holidays. The counsellor didn't intervene and talk to the player about the abuse. "I guess I've come to the conclusion that you can't help people unless they're ready to be helped," she sighs.

The girl in question received counselling elsewhere when she finally left the player.

The frustration over the Graham James case still haunts members of the Calgary police, despite the fact that the case is now closed. "I know of one other player in the NHL, and one in the IHL, who were assaulted," says one investigator. "They won't face it, but what will happen is they'll turn to alcoholism, or they'll become violent, and continue the abusive behaviour. Perhaps they'll be able to stave it off while they're still playing hockey, and they can push it out of their minds, but after they retire, then what will they do? How will they treat their children?

"Over the years, I expect we'll revisit this case. One player after another is either going to say to himself that he needs help, he can't handle the pain any more, or they'll be criminals themselves. It would be a lot better for us all if people would be honest. They don't have to disclose who they are. The second victim maintained anonymity. Right now, they're not only putting themselves and children at risk, they're helping Graham James get out of prison with a pretty light sentence. I don't consider this investigation over. We'll see the ramifications of this abuse for years."

# CHAPTER NINE

# Changing the Line-Up

## *How Can Canadians Reclaim Their National Sport?*

It is a serious group of men who file into a conference room at the Royal York Hotel in Toronto on January 20, 1997. They are met by an equally solemn gathering of reporters. The occasion is to announce that the CHL has commissioned a "policy development report," to be called "Players First," in response to the issues in hockey brought to light in the Graham James case. "The persons involved in the administration of the League and its member teams," says the press release, quoting league president, David Branch, "have an obvious interest in ensuring that the CHL provides a developmental hockey environment which is as safe as we can possibly make it for the players both physically and emotionally."

Cameras turn to Gordon Kirke, the Toronto lawyer and sports agent hired to write the report. The release quotes him as saying he "was honoured to have been asked by the CHA League to undertake this task. . . . As a parent, I understand the seriousness of the responsibility which I am undertaking, in a sense, for all caring parents."

Kirke had been asked to develop policies for the screening of personnel, using both police searches and psychological testing; the education of players in respect to "this kind of conduct"; the provision of people for players to confide in about personal matters; and the counselling for those who had been affected by "this kind of conduct." Kirke would also be responsible for specific recommendations and suggestions for the above areas, and was required to deliver the report in time for it to be implemented in the 1997–98 season.

Nowhere in the four-page press release did the CHL say what "this kind of conduct" actually was. The CHL did not utter the words "sexual abuse" anywhere in its material. Journalists certainly did, though, and asked, among other things, whether CHL officials had had any warning that players may have been the victims of abuse in Swift Current. Absolutely not, replied the men seated at the press-conference table. We're fathers, and we love hockey; we never would have allowed this to happen.

After the crowds cleared, "the fifth estate" reporter Lyndon McIntyre spoke with David Branch for an update to the "Thin Ice" documentary on sexual abuse in hockey. Branch had refused to speak to the CBC when they were making the first documentary, which aired in the fall of 1996. This time he agreed to comment.

McIntyre asked if the policy would be broad enough to cover not only coaches abusing players, but players abusing each other, and player behaviour towards others. Branch replied, "If we find through the James situation that there's an even bigger need on our part to do it, then by all means we will respond."

McIntyre pursued the point and asked if they would look specifically at sexual abuse of women. "Well, Lyndon," Branch replied, "I think that you've got to carry it right across the board. Like, there's no use sitting down and developing a program if it does not address as many of the concerns that we all have."

Branch also said it was time to lift the veil of secrecy that hid what went on in the locker room. The same went for initiations. Branch reiterated that initiations were not allowed in the OHL [as part of the CHL], and that "if we were to find out about a hazing, we would deal with it in a most serious fashion, take the appropriate sanctions with the people that were involved. But clearly there isn't a team, there isn't a person, there isn't a coach, manager, owner in the league that wants hazing. There's nothing more degrading, and it is not tolerated . . . and is not to be condoned."

On August 7, 1997, Gordon Kirke and the media once again filed into the Royal York Hotel. The sixty-three-page "Players First Report" was complete. On the first page, Kirke repeated what leaders in hockey have been saying since the fall of 1996, when the *Calgary Sun* broke the Graham James story: "Few of us would have believed that such an insidious and destructive crime could have infiltrated the CHL, an institution imbued with Canadian tradition and pride." Further on, he adds, "In the context of this report, nothing is more important than protecting players, whose trust the CHL enjoys, from harassment, abuse, and discrimination, problems which threaten and affect youth in all sectors of our society. These recommendations are a sincere attempt to lay a foundation for that safe environment. It is hoped that they are viewed as a positive step towards a brighter future for our most valuable commodity: our children."

The report recommended the following:

- the institution of a screening process for all CHL employees and volunteers, and anyone else who comes close to the players;
- the utilization of local registries of convicted child abusers;
- ongoing employee evaluations by players and their parents;
- that there be no change to the present draft system;
- the institution of a twofold system within the CHL, where players would attend workshops particular to harassment, as well as "life-style" workshops;
- that a committee be appointed – whose members would include the commissioners of the three leagues, administrative staff from each league, and experts in the field of abuse as ad hoc members – with responsibilities for the appointment of complaints investigators and an appeal body if either players or coaches disagreed with the findings of the investigators into a case, and which would appoint an advisory council for each

team consisting of two to four members who would also be "experts" or very familiar with the issues of abuse;

- that the teams' advisory councils be responsible for implementing workshops, with the "life-style" workshop addressing issues such as "equal opportunities and discouraging discriminatory practices," as well as "but not limited to racism, homophobia, drug and alcohol abuse, mental health, and self-esteem";
- that a nationwide toll-free telephone service be provided to extend support and guidance to players or employees who wish to disclose an experience of harassment; and
- that the confidentiality of all parties be guarded throughout all counselling and investigations.

Two days later, the *Globe and Mail* led Saturday's editorial with a review of the policy, entitled "STOP DRAFTING KIDS INTO JUNIOR HOCKEY." "What if," the editorial read, "you were trying to stamp out a certain type of destructive, antisocial behaviour in your organization, and what if you knew that your organization's corporate structure had been so poorly designed that it actually fostered and encouraged the very behaviour you were trying to eliminate? How would you go about fixing things? Would you leave the organization exactly as is, but try to fight against its noxious incentives by bringing in all sort of 'counselors' and 'monitors' to watch out for abusive conduct? Or would you, more simply and more productively, change the structure of the organization, so that those incentives no longer existed?"

The *Globe* was asking an obvious question, a question no other newspaper or commentator thought to ask. The CHL had investigated itself and had decided to give itself more power by creating new moral watchdog positions to be filled either by the all-important committee recommended by Kirke, or by those appointed by that committee. All of a sudden, men who for twenty years had failed to detect even one of the several predators amongst their ranks – men who had made a career of exploiting the physical abilities of young hockey players – were now supposedly capable of putting everything right.

The editorial continued, "The Canadian Hockey League structure demanded that you keep your mouth shut and do as you were told. Anyone who did otherwise, and to this day, anyone who does otherwise in [major-junior] hockey in Canada, risks never playing again. Period.

"The problem is the draft, under which the top 14-year-olds in Western Canada and 15- and 16-year-olds in Eastern Canada are selected by a Tier I junior team. . . . You report to the Tier I team that drafted you. Even if that team is hundreds or thousands of kilometres away. Even if the coach is a jerk. Even if the coach is a sexual predator on the side. You belong to that team unless that team wants to trade you – in which case, you belong to somebody else."

The *Globe* questioned the fact that the structure of the CHL remained intact and all-powerful. "You will not find any of this in Gordon Kirke's 63-page report on the problems besetting junior hockey, ironically entitled 'Players First,'" it continues. "Give us a break. The league has never, ever, been about players. The league is a business, which is fine enough, but as businesses go, this one is run like some kind of illegal immigrant sweatshop. . . . In Canadian hockey, teams choose, own, buy and sell players, players who are just kids."

The *Globe* questioned Kirke's integrity. "The Canadian Hockey League is not about to empower someone to harm its profitable little operation, so it asked for an investigation that delved deeply into the consequences but never got at the primary cause. And on that request, Mr. Kirke delivered. Just like Canada's junior hockey players whose abuse at the hands of coaches he was investigating, he shut up and did his job."

The editorial concludes, "As we have said before, the CHL should not be investigating this matter. The CHL, and the draft, should itself be under investigation."

While the *Globe*'s scepticism poked a hole in the image the CHL wanted to create, it didn't say who should investigate the CHL or that there are other serious problems with the policy.

Why didn't Canadians demand an outside investigation of the organization? The CHL is not above the values that govern the rest of Canada. Surely Children's Aid and the community and social services ministry in Saskatchewan could have led investigations into the way the players were treated, not only by James but by an administration that sat passively by. When James left the Broncos, it was with the blessing of the Broncos and the CHL to start yet another club. After Darren McLean alleged that players were being paid to bring girls to James's house so he could videotape them having sex, social-service agencies should have stepped in and stated that the Broncos and the CHL should not be allowed to investigate such serious matters.

They are not the only organizations that should have been looking out for the well-being of young people. The provincial ministry of labour might have looked at the work schedule and payment of junior hockey players and compared them to those of young people in other lines of work. In his 1995 scholarly paper "Child Labour, Sport Labour: Applying Child Labour Laws to Sport," sports sociology professor Peter Donnelly of McMaster University quotes the United Nations Convention on the Rights of the Child, saying there is a "current international understanding that, 'Children, because of their vulnerability, need special care and protection.'"[1] He also emphasizes that the Canadian Charter of Rights and Freedoms recognizes "the need of legal and other protection of the child."

Donnelly argues that, "Under adult guidance and supervision, large numbers of children are training and competing under highly worklike condition for long hours, and in many cases for immediate or potential remuneration. . . . Children are also, in some cases, suffering from deteriorating coach and parent behaviour, and there is a growing body of evidence concerning the behaviour of many of these young athletes and their abusive parents and coaches."

"Assaultive ice hockey players" are one group Donnelly identifies in this area. But, he says, amateur sports organizations and government have been slow to acknowledge the risks faced by children in sport. If they were considered employees of the team, there would be several kinds of protection, and, if necessary, the government could step in, fine owners, and even shut them down.

Donnelly recommends a "child centred system in which parents, coaches, administrators, physicians, and educators work together in the best interests of the child athlete under the auspices of the sport governing body." He adds this will not happen, because "too many vested interests and ingrained ways of thinking are embodied in sport institutions, and because the funding and sponsorship of sport governing bodies will likely continue to be based on the achievement of international success."

Kirke's report is devoid of any mention of government organizations whose mandate it is to protect children, and makes no connection, as Donnelly does, between violence on the ice and violence off it.

Given the framework Kirke recommends, with all control held in the hands of the CHL commissioners, we are unlikely to see any real openness. Secondly, why does the policy only protect players and employees, and not young women who allege sexual assaults by players? Why did Branch bother to assure a reporter that "you've got to carry it right across the board," and that developing a program is of "no use" otherwise?

Sadly, even if counselling were offered to female victims of abuse, as part of the "Players First" policy, it is unlikely that any girl would feel comfortable confiding in someone appointed by the CHL in a program set up mainly to serve players; it is difficult enough for a young woman to approach the local sexual-assault centre, which is generally staffed by women. But if the issues affecting girls had even been *mentioned* in the "Players First" policy, at least a positive message would have sent to young women that they matter.

"My mandate was players first," says Kirke. "If the respect afforded women changes in the dressing room, it will evolve to the community. Counselling for girls? It's not what we've been discussing."

But what about those players who have already been abused and have become abusers of women? And is it possible, given the exclusive male-only culture of hockey, for players to have respect for girls at all? David Branch is surprised at the question. "Of course our players respect girls. Family values are instilled on these young men at home," he says emphatically. "I do not subscribe to the belief that our players do not respect young women."

Branch also takes offence at the suggestion that predators have not, as the report states, "infiltrated" hockey, but rather that they have always been on the inside. It was, after all, a highly respected coach and the head of the WHL (not to mention the many coaches and presidents of smaller leagues) we heard about in the winter of 1996–97. These were esteemed long-time members of the hockey community. "I didn't play major-junior, but I did play minor-junior and university hockey, and I was never exposed to sexual exploitation," says Branch. "I'm not going to suggest that it has not happened, but it's not inside hockey."

All three leagues adopted the policy.

With all the decision-making and information in the hands of the new committee, the CHL can put virtually any spin it wants on a story (should it even make its way to the media), when the truth comes down to the word of a lone young woman against that of one or more young men backed by the best legal counsel available and the powerful friends of hockey within the community. The tactic is tried and true in United States, where NCAA and pro athletes hire top criminal lawyers and have influential people backing them to win a case, not just in the courtroom, but in the public arena as well. Mike Tyson's lawyer, Alan Dershowitz, joined forces with the boxer's high-profile supporters to wage a media war against Desiree Washington before, during, and after Tyson's trial for rape.

The fact that the "Players First" policy doesn't acknowledge the girls who are harassed or assaulted by players implies that those in power do not perceive the issue as serious. It sends a strong signal to the community: boys are in need of protection, and girls aren't.

What if Sheldon Kennedy had been Shelly Kennedy? What if, instead of falling victim to Graham James, she had attracted the attention of five members of the team who wanted to watch one another have sex with a "dirty"? Would the hockey establishment have acted on her behalf with the same vigour they, finally, did on Kennedy's, or would they have conveniently shoved it under the rug? If the Sheldon Kennedy story taught us to take better care of our children, the fallout afterwards should teach us not to put our trust in hockey organizations. They have far too much power in the small towns in which junior teams reside.

It was up to Sheldon Kennedy himself to take the brave step of coming forward. Had he accepted the tradition of silenced pain that hockey reinforces in players, who knows who long it might have been before we could get even this glimpse of the crisis in our national sport?

Soon after the Graham James story broke, CHL officials started talking about screening programs that would keep "those kinds of people" out. Branch was vehement that predators were not part of the hockey culture. But those kinds of people aren't on the outside – they are as entrenched in hockey as Zambonis and penalty boxes. Those kinds of people are head coaches, presidents of associations, members of boards of directors, and owners of teams.

Those who have power in the hockey establishment are not going to give it up. They will frame the issue of assault as something that invaded an innocent sport, despite the fact that there is nothing innocent about the business of trading in young men. As William Houston wrote in his May 1997 *Globe and Mail* series, it is a "system that lives exclusively by the cashbox." Thirteen new teams were added to the CHL in the last sixteen years, and three more appeared in the 1997–98 season. The CHL franchises are individually worth upwards of one million dollars, and new ones sell for well over that. Each team has an annual budget of approximately one million dollars.

With the possible exception of Olympic years, all the girls and women in Canada who play hockey would be lucky to have this spent on them collectively in one year.

There are approximately 1,750 regular-season games, plus the playoffs and the Memorial Cup. The CHL employs 1,300 players, and 400 full-time and 1,800 part-time employees. The overall annual budget for the league is fifty-five million dollars, and they estimate the economic impact to Canada as two hundred million dollars annually. Between 1989 and 1998, the league added twelve new franchises.

Houston quotes hockey great Howie Meeker as saying, "The system is totally wrong. You have a fifteen- or sixteen-year-old who has to leave home and he has no say in where he's going to go. And in his own community, perhaps there's a junior team. It's slavery, absolute slavery."

The CHL will continue to deal in the trade of young men, and make plenty of money doing it. They have a near monopoly over the way in which young men get into the NHL, making hockey unlike any other sport. Kirke writes that, "the draft systems are a reality of competitive hockey, and competitive sport generally." This is simply not true. Young athletes at the elite level in any other sport – track and field, baseball, rowing, speed skating, basketball, soccer, cycling – can choose where they will live and train. Hockey is the only sport with a draft system. Athletes can choose to stay home, train at high-performance centres, move to wherever the best facilities and coaches are located, try for American scholarships, or leave the country and train in the United States or Europe. They have options, they know the standards set by the Canadian Olympic Association in their sport, and they know what kind of training is necessary to meet them. While there are serious potential problems for these athletes in the form of abusive coaches or others in positions of power, they are not bought, sold, and traded as they are in hockey.

The CHL is not alone in trying to prevent sexual assault from occurring within its ranks. By the end of May 1997, the Canadian Hockey Association had launched its own prevention kit and program, aimed at younger players. The next week, the president of the Flamborough Minor Hockey Association, forty-four-year-old Richard Janes, his forty-year-old wife, Marianne, and a fifteen-year-old were charged with distribution and possession of child pornography after police raided their home and found "nearly 5,000 graphic files as well as approximately 200 pornographic magazines." (Charges against Richard and Marianne Janes were later dropped.) This after a winter of disclosures about coaches and minor-hockey-association board members.

The campaign has come far too late for many victims, but the CHA has allocated a good chunk of its 1997–98 budget to remedy the illness of abuse. The package contains the following:

- A cutout puck telling kids what to look for. "A coach forces you to play when you're hurt – this is a form of abuse," says the puck. "An older person tries to touch you sexually – this is sexual abuse. Another player keeps insulting you because of your skin colour – this is harassment."

- A pamphlet aimed at older kids and parents outlining harassment issues.
- A 1-800 number for the Kids Help Phone so players can talk to trained counsellors.
- Posters and bag tags to be used as part of a public-service campaign to help make kids more aware of the potential dangers.

A review of the issue through the CHA's course for instructing coaches has already commenced. A screening process for all volunteers, paid staff, and other officials of the CHA will also be implemented, and the CHA recommends its member associations do the same. In addition, a handbook for administrators is being developed, and when it is, member associations will be responsible for adopting policies similar to those of the CHA.

While the kit is a vast improvement on the position taken by the CHA on physical and sexual abuse in 1996 – which was no position at all – there are still areas that are lacking.

Sexual harassment and assault are much more prevalent problems for women athletes than they are for men. There are thirty thousand girls and women in the CHA, yet until September 1997, there were no women members of the sexual-assault and harassment committee from within hockey. In March 1997, Jamie McDonald, head of the CHA's coaching development, described the female membership of the committee in this way: "We have a gal by the name of Judy Fairholme from the Red Cross, who has handled these issues for years, and another gal from Concordia, but her name slips my mind at this time." The expert from Concordia was Sally Spilhaus, the university's adviser on rights and responsibilities, who, prior to her arrival in 1991 to the university, was involved in community-based services for women in Montreal. Neither woman was retained as a permanent member of the committee.

The CHA is also responsible for international coaching programs. In June 1996, they hosted an international coaching conference including a special program for the coaches on junior development. Three hundred coaches from around the world attended the conference, held in Toronto at the Hockey Hall of Fame, which covered technical, tactical, psychological, and physiological aspects of high-performance hockey. But before it got started, organizer Rick Morocco, who is also the manager of the Centre for Excellence at the Hockey Hall of Fame, kicked the event off with a bevy of dancing girls in national team jerseys and short shorts.

Morocco defends the chorus line, saying, "We wanted coaches to know this wasn't just going to be a hard-core hockey conference. It's going to be fun and exciting, giving them a bit of the flame of the city. The girls had hockey sticks, then there was music, and dance. It got everyone ready for the weekend. We held it at the Royal York, a high-class hotel. In the past the conference was held at the University of Calgary, and we wanted to show them something different."

Morocco did not see a problem with presenting semi-clad women' as entertainment and then presenting the fully clothed Canadian junior men's team, which had won the world championship that year. There was no introduction of the members of the Canadian women's team, who were also the world champions.

"If two or three people were offended, that's unfortunate," says Morocco. "Ninety-nine per cent were quite pleased."

The CHA has a history of discriminating against women. From 1985 to 1988, the Ontario branch fought Justine Blainey at the Ontario Human Rights Commission and in the courts at every level up to the Supreme Court of Canada to keep the twelve-year-old girl out of boys' hockey. Ten years before that, they had mounted a similar legal fight against Gail Cummings, a twelve-year-old star goalie from Huntsville, Ontario, who wanted to keep playing on a boys' team. The OHA successfully lobbied the Ontario government to have the Ontario Human Rights Code amended so discrimination against women and girls in sport wouldn't contravene the code. Five years after the amendments took place, the Blainey decision found them to be unconstitutional. Despite this victory, girls across the country have had to fight for years to have their positions on boys' teams seen as legitimate.

At the first women's world championship in 1990 in Ottawa, the Canadian team was outfitted in pink uniforms supplied by the CHA. Many women watching felt the CHA wanted to belittle the efforts of the team by putting them in a colour that by convention is for "little girls." The CHA's record of financially supporting girls and women's hockey reflects its discomfort with a female presence. The 1994–95 CHA overall budget (the last one the association released that broke down expenditures for males and females) was $8,860,837. Less than 3 per cent – $210,710 – went to women.

If the CHA has a credibility problem in terms of how they treat women, more credibility problems will arise with its use of NHL players speaking out about harassment and abuse. The players will star in commercials telling kids to report abuse and how to distinguish a bad touch from a good touch from an older person. Yet the kids will be watching those same players fighting on the ice and taking illegal cheap shots at each other. What is a "bad touch" in this context?

There are even those, such as Don Cherry, who will go to great lengths to teach children that bad touch is what hockey is all about. How will kids be able to reconcile the new CHA message with the one they receive weekly from him? Cherry may be a broad caricature of reactionary hockey values, not meant to be taken seriously, but to children there is no higher authority. On one occasion Cherry called Tomas Sandstrom a "Dirty Swede" after Doug Gilmour slashed him, and advocated that someone should break Ulf Samuelsson's arm. He called Pavel Bure a "Little Weasel," and complained in 1993 when the Memorial Cup was also referred to as "Coupe Memorial."

"What's this Coupe Memorial? I don't understand," he said on "Coach's Corner." It was a remark that would raise debate in the House of Commons, with MPs accusing him of racism.

When asked if he approved of women in the dressing room, Cherry didn't think that meant women players or reporters. "I think every NHL team should have one," was his reply.

Cherry has a great influence off-air, too. Even the name of his "Rock 'Em, Sock 'Em" videos reinforces a language of violence. His doctrine of violent intolerance is spread constantly while he's not on "Coach's Corner," through VCRs across the country and in commercials.

The NHL, the CHL, and Don Cherry are still seen by young males as the ultimate expression of masculinity in hockey. At the same CHA annual general meeting at which the new program was introduced, both Ontario and Saskatchewan put forth a motion to include body-checking for children under twelve. The motion wasn't approved, but some time later, the CHA did approve a pilot project for 1998–99 whereby checking was allowed for boys at the atom level (eleven years and younger) within the Ontario Hockey Federation. We will have to see whether boys and young men can reconcile these contradicting messages, and how hockey explains why purposely hurting another person is not a "bad touch."

On the positive side, while the social and psychological problems attached to the game are numerous and complex, the CHA has joined an organization whose aim is to address them. The Anti-Harassment Sport Collective, based in Ottawa, was started by the Canadian Association for Women in Sport and Physical Activity (CAWS), and perhaps the CHA's association with this group is the first step toward heterogeneity in hockey so all athletes can enjoy the national game. A list of the collective's publications can be found in the Bibliography. Parents are well advised to read up on its work.

The collective has a holistic approach. It understands that sexual abuse won't stop when you tell people they should respect one another, or even when you have counsellors available to athletes, though that is certainly a step in the right direction. They see the problem as systemic – something that is so old and accepted that, without anyone setting out to do so, it is ingrained in the system. Not surprisingly, the collective is led by women, who, as psychologist Linda Campbell says, "developed a consciousness on the issue" through talking about and analysing their own experiences. Many of the women come with an understanding of abuse in sport based on first-hand experience and give the collective the kind of knowledge and background the all-male CHA and CHL committees lack.

Since 1993, when the CBC broadcast "Crossing the Line," a documentary on coaches in all sports and sexual abuse, "a massive evaluation of the NCCP [National Coaching Certification Program] has taken place," according to Tom Kinsman, executive director of the Coaching Association of Canada (CAC). "If there is a complaint about a coach, we hope to have a tribunal up and running soon. It would be comprised of a chair from the Ottawa Centre for Sport and Law, and two peers of the coach drawn from a pool of coaches who would make themselves available to sit on such a tribunal. Athletes would help us select the coaches for the tribunal, and the athlete with a complaint would be able to select one of the coaches who would arbitrate.

"Ideally, we wouldn't even have to go that far. By the fall of 1997, there will be harassment officers in sport who will try to mediate the dispute and find solutions without confrontation."

We shall have to see how athletes react to coaches being self-regulated. Like the CHL, the CAC has given its own organization the exclusive right to decide whether athletes have a valid concern about coaches. It is to the CHA's credit that the committee has recommended that its investigators should come from outside hockey.

The work in this area by Dr. Sandra Kirby of the University of Winnipeg, and Dr. Celia Brackenridge of the Cheltenham and Gloucester College of Higher Education in England, draws on a massive study done in the United States that showed that the combination of a code of ethics and self-regulation did not decrease abuse by health-care professionals and clergy.[2]

Kirby and Brackenridge quote the American study, which shows that despite the introduction of what were considered safeguards against abuse, complaints to ethics committees and licensure boards and malpractice actions related to sexual misconduct by therapists increased steadily during the 1970s and 1980s. They found no evidence that studies and discussions, or even the refinements in the ethics codes, changed professional behaviours as long as the professionals were self-regulated.

There have been no detailed studies on the extent of sexual assault of children and young adults in sport, but Kirby, and Lorraine Greaves of the University of Western Ontario, did publish a 1996–97 study of male and female Canadian national-team athletes that showed 22.8 per cent of them "had had sexual intercourse with a person in sport in a position of authority over them. One-quarter of those described also being slapped, hit, kicked or beaten by that person."[3]

If the governing bodies in hockey are *in loco parentis* to the children playing the game (as lawyer Fran Huck argues in Chapter 8), they, too, need to address issues of abuse if they are to protect their charges. Kirby and Brackenridge argue that, "In Canada, even though sport organizations are predominantly volunteer, they do fall under the common law, as well as under numerous statutes, and are, thus, inside the legal framework, though not necessarily the workplace framework, of rights and responsibilities." In their paper, they introduce the concept of "duty of care." Building on the extensive work of Lorraine Street, executive director of the Canadian Association of Volunteer Bureaux and Centres, they quote from *The Screening Handbook: Protecting Clients, Staff, and the Community*, which defines "duty of care" as "the obligation of individuals or organizations to take reasonable measures to care for and to protect their clients to an appropriate level or standard. If the clients are vulnerable, if they cannot protect, defend, or assert themselves, permanently or temporarily, because of age, disability, or circumstances, then that duty becomes more intense and the standard higher."[4]

They add that "the sport community must show its commitment to make sport better, to address the concerns directly and to create programs, tools and evaluation measures to ameliorate the situation. We believe that the duty of care needs to be at the centre of the sport response." They argue that adults responsible for children's sport must assume "an active duty" to provide a healthy experience for children. Those seeking new directions in sport would do well to examine Kirby and Brackenridge's work in greater detail. Despite their international reputation in the field, they were not consulted by Gordon Kirke during the writing of his "Players First" report.

To make arenas safer, we need to bring more people in from the outside, and not just for the games. The mixing of people, the breaking down of hierarchies so prevalent in sport, the openness of the event, and the levelling of the playing field, where both sexes, and all age groups and skills are given equal access, are all hallmarks of heterogeneity. Peggy Reeves Sanday argues that secret acts and the lies that cover them up can't occur as easily in the openness of heterogeneity. There is never going to be a totally rape-free culture, but unless we work toward that goal, predators will simply find new ways to continue taking what they want. We must create a climate that allows children and young adults to live full physical, sexual, emotional, and intellectual lives and that doesn't foster values based on predatory relationships and commodification.

Certain pockets of Canada have already started to change. In one community centre in North York, north of Toronto, there is a hockey rink – nothing unusual about that – but there is also a bocce court, used by the Italian community in the neighbourhood. Because there are plenty of Italians coming into the centre, an espresso bar has been set up. Because there is an espresso bar, the centre has become a place where people drop in simply to visit with one another. Hockey is not the only game in town. In fact, it may be completely ignored by a population that is much more concerned with discussing soccer scores in Italy, or the state of this year's grape harvest, despite their proximity to the rink.

When the building houses more than just an ice rink, the power of those who run the hockey clubs diminishes. This setup also gives children access to more adults with no connection to the hockey power structure, people they can go to with problems they feel wouldn't be addressed by those in the hockey loop. This is the kind of heterogeneity – one that allows for diversity and ensures that a small group of people doesn't wield too much power in the lives and the environment of children – that Professor Reeves Sanday stresses we need if we want to build a safer environment for young people. These are real family values, she says. The next step is for these other stakeholders to have a real share of the power, and, for instance, sit on the arena's board of directors.

There is another example of heterogeneity in arenas at the Olympic Oval in Calgary. The Oval is designated a National Training Centre by Sport Canada. Its facilities, part of the University of Calgary's campus, are world-class. Hockey rinks make up the infield of the Oval, while the speed-skating track snakes around them and a running track encompasses everything. There are training depots near the track, where athletes work out on stationary bikes and do circuit training. Olympic athletes mingle with each other and with residents of the city. The facilities are open to all, so at lunchtime, Olympic speed-skating silver-medallist Susan Auch may be sharing the ice with a group of secretaries donning speed-skates for the first time, while decathlete Michael Smith does a warm-up on the track and the women's national hockey team does drills on the inner rinks.

The Oval is just steps away from the office of Athletes' Services manager Karen Strong, called "A Room with a View," where athletes can come for confidential talks and to be referred to psychologists or counsellors if need be. "One benefit of the Oval is that people don't feel isolated," says Strong. "Whatever happens to someone can be talked about here. We hope to provide links and peer support for athletes who have been harassed, assaulted, or have eating disorders. Obviously, people come in with different emotional levels on these things. We can set up appointments with the Calgary Sexual Assault Centre, and pay for a minimum of five professional counselling sessions. We're here for the athlete, but we're part of the community."

Even though the program hasn't been around long, and originally focused on helping develop athletes' careers when they leave their sport, Strong feels emotional issues must be dealt with first before athletes can do their best, both in sports and in the job market. "People are comfortable coming here. Since Ellen [DeGeneres] came out on television, three athletes have told me they're gay," she says, two weeks after the show aired. "The door is open."

In sports other than hockey, Canadian athletes frequently mix freely in a manner similar to the Oval program, also creating a heterogeneous, mixed-sex climate. Cyclists, rowers, runners, triathletes, and canoeists will join skiers in the winter, and in summer, skiers and speed-skaters enter triathlons, runs, and fun rides. There is a very fluid movement amongst many athletes. As William Houston noted in his May 1997 series on hockey in the Globe and Mail, Canadian male hockey players tend not to cross-train in other sports, while players from the United States, Russia, and Sweden play a great deal of soccer and train seriously in their off-season. (Some Canadian male players play lacrosse or soccer, but not to any significant degree. Golf does not enhance fitness or hockey skills, and it is played with other hockey players.) Canadian male hockey players are consequently isolated, especially from women athletes.

The fact that there are many women on staff at the Oval makes the facility far safer. Psychologist Dr. Fred Mathews notes that women commit only 15 per cent of sexual assaults, so the chances of a child being abused drops considerably as soon as there are also women in charge of sports. Other experts put the percentage even lower.

Bill Lang, Sr., who pressed charges against the Markham Waxers in the 1987 initiation of his son, coaches an Ontario Minor Hockey League minor novice team. "We have a woman, who is also a probation officer, as manager," says Lang, "and the co-manager is female, too. We want to do everything possible to show parents we're serious about safety." The very obvious solution of putting women in coaching positions to reduce the risk of sexual assault was not mentioned in either the CHL's or CHA's programs or policies that tried to address this issue.

Women also bring children to sport. As women athletes from the 1970s and 1980s become mothers and caregivers, they have had to build childcare into their plans. Childcare facilities in arenas and other venues are needed so women will have better access to coaching jobs. Knowing how to care for children is not a genetic female trait. They are not naturally more nurturing than men, but they have learned since early childhood that taking care of people is part of being human. Not surprisingly, they have designed their sports system with this in mind. It is time for men to adopt this model, because if women adopt the male model of sport, they will soon take on the characteristics of their male peers.

"Because women are not genetically morally superior to men," says Peggy Reeves Sanday, "they have just as much potential to become abusers as men do. We are already beginning to see, in areas where women have gained considerable power similar to that of men and have not adopted an egalitarian approach, that they too can be sexually abusive. We're seeing it in female-female abuse, as opposed to female-male, and it's very troublesome. The point of the women's movement is not to mimic men, but to find new models to eradicate, rather than replicate, violence and abuse."

In the pursuit of winning at all costs, in the drive to profit from young people's bodies, and in the need to live vicariously through the physicality and success of others, sport has lost much of what gives it balance. Just as elite sport needs to become an athlete-centred activity (as opposed to owner/coach/bureaucrat-centred), sport, physical activity, play, and the society in which these activities happen, need to care much more about children. Communities, parents, extended families, and all levels of government need to provide a loving and safe environment before a child even picks up a hockey stick. People in hockey tend to live in a protective bubble, as if the real world were of no concern and life begins at centre ice. But children, and the adults responsible for them, are the product of an entire culture, so how does hockey and our society tell children they are protected and loved? The word "love," here, is not used in the way Graham James used it so frequently to describe his feelings for Sheldon Kennedy.

Graham James is not alone among coaches when he believes love is about control. York University sports psychologist Sue Wilson was giving a seminar to coaches on sexual abuse when one coach countered, "They're going to get their sexual experience somewhere. We care about them, so they may as well get it from us."

James and the thousands of others like him who physically and sexually assault children don't know what love means. Love for children means providing them with protection, care, and a great appreciation for their potential. Love seeks ways to let children flourish.

Walk into an arena. Is there love for children here? If you've spent any time in the variety of schools or sports or community centres in Canada, you will know you can tell a lot about an institution just by the way it *feels*. Children assess a new environment on this intuitive level. Arenas are also places where children go to learn, but are they conducive to positive learning? Are they places where children will learn the values of playfulness, honesty, integrity, self-discipline, excellence, respect for oneself and for others? More important, will a child feel loved here? Or is it more like a factory, where the bosses are trying to convince themselves they have a future NHL star among the workers? Is it a place where children are allowed to discover a great ambition or just daydream, depending on how they feel that day? Or are children there because someone else's dream was never realized.

The ways in which our culture neglects its duty to children is a subject far beyond the scope of this book, but the fact that millions of children in North America alone live in poverty while a relatively small number of adults become exceedingly wealthy, and bank profits skyrocket, tells us about priorities. That governments have slashed the social safety net that once saved so many children from a slide into lifelong poverty, and instead preach a *laissez-faire* approach to survival, tells us about priorities. That the automobile is arguably the number-one love object of North Americans, and the number-one cause of death of their children, tells us about priorities. Hockey arenas are built way beyond walking distance for most children, so they have to be driven to or from a game. Yet who decided to place hockey rinks inside, away from fresh air and out of the reach of most children? What happened to free, accessible, outdoor rinks right in the middle of the community?

Most of the experts on young sexual offenders and victims mentioned in this book have worked at one time or another with the First Nations community. "Native people have recognized that there is a tremendous problem in their community in terms of physical and sexual abuse, because of loss of culture and identity, their horrific experiences in residential schools, and the generations who survived it and replicated it," says Dr. Fred Mathews, director of Central Toronto Youth Services. "Naming the problem is the first step in healing. With native youths committing suicide at a rate six times greater than non-native youths, First Nations people have said, 'We have a problem that is killing our children, and we want to stop it.'"

Because of the way in which their culture, self-esteem, and right to determine their own future have been taken away over countless generations, for most native people, sexual abuse and the litany of problems that accompany it are a fact of life. Some communities have alcoholism, unemployment, and sexual-abuse rates that have hit 80 per cent. But unlike the CHL, who are unable to face systemic sexual abuse and alcohol problems, these communities started to confront the issue in a comprehensive way approximately fifteen years ago.

The town of La Ronge is situated in northern Saskatchewan near the fifty-fifth parallel. As the airplane this century became so central to Northern life and commerce, over the years La Ronge's airport became a little village in itself, known as Air Ronge. Ron Ratte is the school and home guidance counsellor at Gordon Dennie Elementary School in Air Ronge, where 80 per cent of the students are, like Ratte, First Nations. On an early-December evening, he skates across the perfect surface of an outdoor rink brightened by overhead lights. At least a dozen kids, all with hockey sticks, are out there skating with him. Because Ratte is a school *and home* counsellor, and because "home," in the native community, is as much outdoors as it is in, Ratte believes his job extends to any place children choose to pursue dreams and pucks.

"Kids phone me and say they want to play," says Ratte from his home in Air Ronge. "I pick up the puck, and we play. There may be kids in grades Two, Three, and Four, and there may be Grade Six and bigger kids who have a hockey background. It's up to me to establish the rules so none of the little ones feel they have to leave. Some kids may feel they want to portray the NHL, but they can't do that in this rink. There's no body contact, only good sports. I want the kids to recognize when they are making mistakes, and work to not repeat them. But the first reason we are there is to have fun."

Ratte's philosophy stems from his spiritual belief that he has a responsibility to respect others, from his professional training as a youth care-worker, and from his own experience in hockey at Ile-à-la-Crosse Residential School, north of La Ronge. "The priests told us, 'Let's put together this hockey team,'" says Ratte. "But we had no skates, no padding – how could we play? We used skates with a soft toe and no padding. But it was always against the boys from town, who had the good equipment. If we didn't play, they sent us to our room with no food. It was quite rough.

"This was a form of abuse, physical and psychological. I remember being forced and not having anyone there to speak up for me, like my parents. We had to stick together to survive, but today many of those friends are abusing drugs and alcohol. They are not dealing with the problems from residential school."

Ratte says he's come a long way since those days, but he simply won't tolerate any kind of abuse in any sport he's involved in. "Understanding these issues of abuse is difficult, but for sexually abused people, what better place [to go] than hockey? They see the aggressiveness of it and think it's a good place to get rid of anger. When I go to prisons, I see all the inmates always playing contact hockey. They don't want to curl, they don't want to skate recreationally. The majority want to go where there is violence. They think this is a way to deal with their anger over what has happened in their lives, but it isn't. No one heals without acknowledging their pain."

By having strict rules against violence, and replacing it with understanding and compassion, Ratte hopes the kids he's responsible for don't end up in one of Saskatchewan's many prisons. He's changed hockey in specific ways to achieve those goals. "The first thing I did is take all the hard pucks away," he continues. "I went to the village and I said, 'Lookit, the little kids are being shoved around by these big guys with hard pucks. This is a form of violence, making the rink too intimidating for young ones.' The village agreed, and now there is a sign up at the rink: NO HARD PUCKS. The first priority was a sponge puck. It teaches more finesse and control, and automatically takes power away from aggressive players.

"We don't have any goal posts. Maybe we use two shoes; no one can hurt themselves on a hard object that way. The kids keep changing positions. Someone will be a referee one game and a forward the next.

"If the kids score, then they get a pat on the back. I try to give a person positive reinforcement, build self-esteem – little things a lot of kids don't get at home."

The rink belongs to the community, not a conglomerate of businessmen. Anyone driving by can clearly see all the action on and around the ice. From their brightly lit kitchen windows, parents can watch children, and children can see parents. There are no boards, no change rooms, no offices where an adult can draw a child away from his or her friends. This is a safe place to be, and the addition of a trained professional from the children's own community makes it even safer. "At the same time I'm teaching the kids hockey and social skills, I'm watching them. I'm observing. Who is isolating themselves? Who looks to be having problems? Hockey becomes both therapy and assessment."

Ratte says non-natives should ask themselves why native kids keep to themselves so much in a white arena. "You go into the arena in Prince Albert [where there is a junior team], and it's all white, but so many native people live there. Why is that? What gaps exist racially and through poverty that keep us out? It's hard to explain in the NHL, too. There's not many blacks, either.

"Perhaps," he concludes, "white people haven't had enough time to learn from the First Nations people."

No one group has a monopoly on virtue. Women and First Nations people have developed egalitarian models of sport compared to those developed by the white men who run hockey only because they have learned values that reflect that philosophy. Judging from recent Olympic and world championship results, the Canadian system can no longer be relied upon to produce champions, though this is a goal most Canadians still seem to believe is worth aiming for. What needs to change, then, is the route taken to reach that goal. So let's keep the goal, add to it so more children can play, even if they're not going to be champions, and abandon the present path.

It is up to the community to take back hockey so children and young people can have holistic, healthy experiences in the game. The arena is the place to start. If players are to understand that there is no relationship between becoming a good hockey player and being a good person, we need to teach them that they are no better than anyone else. This should start when they are young, in an arena that reflects these values.

While there is nothing wrong with honouring excellence in hockey from the past, arena hallways and trophy cases showcase only white male stars. Canadian women have played hockey for more than one hundred years and excelled at it, but you would never know from the photos, tributes, and trophies. They barnstormed American arenas in the forties, and most recently have been almost unstoppable world-wide. Their story is not told.

First Nations people like Ron Ratte, and plenty of others like him, have the disturbing stories of residential school and hockey to tell. One Ojibwa elder says he played on the school's team because athletes got more food, and the kids were always hungry. There were people like Freddie Sasakamoose, who, as sportswriter Brenda Zeman reports in her book *To Run with Longboat*, "walked out on the Chicago Blackhawks" in the 1950s.[5] He was born on the Whitefish Reserve in Saskatchewan, learned to skate on a slough, and used rocks or frozen apples for pucks. He made it into the NHL, but came home to his wife and community when she wouldn't move to the big city. Where are these fascinating stories?

Then there are the Carnegie brothers of Toronto, Herbert and Ozzie, and their friend Mannie McIntyre of Montreal. They were three of the top hockey players in the 1940s, but they were also black, and weren't allowed to try out for the NHL. They have plenty of stories to tell, and what better place than in those halls that once shut them out?

Arenas tell only a small part of the Canadian story. Why not make some room among the trophies and plaques and tell some other chapters in the story?

What happens on the ice also needs to change. There should be far more recreational ice-time, allowing children the opportunity to work on their skating and socialize with members of their family on the ice. This is an area in which CHA players are lagging behind the Europeans, who have a much higher practise-to-play ratio. William Houston's series in the *Globe* showed that we will produce far better players if they practise more often and play fewer games. There should also be more non-checking recreational hockey, where everyone gets the chance to play and not just sit on the bench.

Girls and boys should play hockey together, because it is the most natural thing for them to do. The ways in which our culture divides children simply because they are of two sexes is unnatural and utterly wrong. How do boys, especially those in the male-only world of hockey, learn about girls' and women's bodies? Usually at school in uncomfortable health classes, on the playground, and through porn and talk in the locker room.

Playing sports with girls allows boys to witness strong, alive, assertive female bodies that thrive equally in the heat of competition or in the intimacy of love. After years of colliding on the ice rink with girls who sweat, spit, and skate hard, boys will not only learn about female bodies and their strength, they will also learn, without booklets and pamphlets, to respect girls and women, because they share in the game that boys most love. They need to learn that it is also perfectly natural for girls and women to like sex, but only if it is consensual. The way in which the girls in this book were humiliated and degraded effectively by entire towns is a terrible crime, whether the sex was consensual or not.

In order to achieve an egalitarian environment in hockey, we first need to create more opportunities for girls to play in a nurturing place that encourages them to return to sport and build skills – and that means all-girl programs and teams until girls have the skills and confidence to play with boys. Ultimately, our goal should be a sporting culture that welcomes all comers and selects its teams from among them using ability as the only criterion. When girls are given equal access to ice time and coaching, and adults believe they have an equal right to dream big dreams, they will develop strength and skills to their full potential. Right now it is easier for a girl to be a "puck bunny" than it is for her to play hockey.

The Don Rowing Club in Mississauga, Ontario, figured out years ago how to share the ice. The club has been home to some of the most successful women rowers in the world, including Olympic medallists Kay Worthington and Silken and Daniele Laumann, as well as world lightweight rowing champion Heather Hatten. Each year on New Year's Eve, the club rented ice at a Mississauga arena and put together two hockey teams. But even though they had world-class women athletes, the men in the club, who had grown up playing the game, were dominating the puck. The solution was to make up new rules. The club simply decided that men were not allowed to skate beyond the blueline with the puck; they would be obligated to give it to a woman. Men did the backroom work, and women did all the scoring – a nice reversal of roles.

Competitive hockey is unlikely to adopt such a creative solution, but it is worth remembering that, as Ron Ratte says, we construct sport, therefore we can change any rule we want. At the tyke level, hockey has already been made more welcoming to little ones by cutting the ice area in half, so is it so outrageous to suggest we change the rules so both sexes can play hockey together at *all* levels?

And what if the whole family wants to play? Norway and Sweden have a program called "Mom and Dad Are the Team," which encourages whole families to come to the sports centre together. Childcare is provided.

There are many other sports that have found ways to recognize everyone's right to play. Watch a marathon or canoe race, a Nordic ski loppet, a triathlon, or a mass-start mountain-bike race. Men and women compete in these sports together, and the top women beat a good 95 per cent of the men's field. Men can't feel superior in these circumstances. At some ten-kilometre runs, there are enough men running with baby strollers to have their own category.

Three-on-three street tournaments in basketball have the same kind of community feel to them. All age levels, all abilities, and both single-sex and mixed teams are invited to compete. Roads are closed to traffic while young people take over the streets, and entire families come to cheer them on. Mothers mix with teachers, who mix with sponsors, who mix with neighbours, who mix with little brothers and sisters still at the toddler stage. Kids love being there because it's very cool – with street fashion, music, and a sense of spontaneity and creativity – but it's also clean, healthy fun.

Hockey should take note of these egalitarian, heterogeneous sports, and if it doesn't voluntarily make changes, all levels of government funding should be withheld until resources are equitably distributed. This won't work for the CHL, since it is a privately owned organization, but if any CHA money is allocated to the CHL, female hockey players and their parents must make sure that an equal amount goes to girls. When public money is spent on arenas, as it was in the Sault, then parents must fight for their daughters' right to equal access. Public money is also spent on the national junior men's team to prepare for and participate at the World Junior Championships. An equal amount needs to be spent on development programs for girls of the same age. If parents of girls in major-junior towns feel the right of their daughters to equal ice time is not being respected, they need to challenge the arena management. Many junior teams have arrangements with municipalities that give them favourable status in exchange for representation on the board, or a cut of the profits.

Female hockey players need advocates. Imagine what could happen if girls walked into arenas, and instead of watching teams of boys and young men, they were there to play their own game, and watch a major-junior women's team afterwards. What if players weren't owned by conglomerates, but had contracts with their communities emphasizing rights and responsibilities, like those between national-team athletes and Sport Canada? How many girls would still choose to live the national dream vicariously through boys when instead they could achieve it for themselves, through their own strength, talent, and heart?

Women in hockey aren't as political as female athletes in other sports. Those who point out the inequities risk being shut out of hockey altogether. But rocking the boat does work. Rowing and cycling have a history of outspoken feminist advocates who worked over several years to ensure funding and programs were allocated equitably. Today, the women on the national teams of both sports are among the best in the world. While our national women's hockey teams have been the perennial world champions, they all must hold down day jobs in order to make ends meet. The rowers and cyclists are professional athletes who benefit from substantial sponsorship contracts. What's more, because rowing and cycling events for men and women occur at the same time in the same location, the media has equal access to the women's team. Contrast this to the double standards in competitive hockey, when only the final game of the 1997 Women's World Hockey Championship was aired on television.

In Scandinavia, sport governing bodies were given set periods within which they were to implement equity plans. Like all government boards and committees, sports had to show that neither sex accounted for fewer than 40 per cent of all decision-makers or government funding would be cut off. While women's hockey has yet to take off in Scandinavia the way it has in Canada (despite the women's limited ice time here), after men's soccer, men's ice hockey, and men's handball, women's soccer is Sweden's fourth most popular sport.

Sport and physical activity are marketed by Sport Canada to children and their parents in a holistic "healthy body, healthy mind" framework. One only has to look at an ad for the "Initiation Program" run by the CHA, intended to bring a higher level of coaching to beginner levels, to see how fundamental this approach is to the marketing of amateur sport. But while sport can be a wonderful and positive aspect of a person's life, while it can encompass the physical, spiritual, cultural, and intellectual, and contribute to the whole person, it also remains a nightmare for thousands of children. Not only are they at risk of being sexually abused, many also face physical and emotional abuse, as well as racism and sexism.

If we believe children should have the right to dream, whether the dream be large or small, then we can't just change a few policies and procedures in hockey and expect that the lives of children will change for the better. To ensure a safe environment where these dreams can be fulfilled, the culture needs to change. There is nothing in the world quite like challenging oneself by trying to kindle something felt in the heart, and nothing worse than having that flame snuffed out.

# Appendix A: Criminal Convictions and Sanctions

While both the CHL and the CHA have implemented police checks on prospective employees and volunteers, neither organization has compiled a list of sex offenders, or of those who may represent a high risk of violent offences of a non-sexual nature. The following is a very partial list of criminal convictions following incidents of physical and sexual violence in minor and junior hockey, and of sanctions leveled by hockey organizations after extraordinary amounts of violence on the ice.

- Brampton, Ontario: On April 16, 1974, a brawl occurred between a Bramalea Junior B team and their Hamilton counterparts. Several vicious fights broke out, including three where players were awarded no penalty minutes. One player left the penalty box to resume fighting, and two more continued the fight in the hallway to the locker room. Soon rival fans also participated in violent acts, and fourteen police officers were needed to control the melee. In response, the OHA commissioned the report "An Investigation into Violence in Amateur Hockey," written by Bill McMurtry.

- Markham, Ontario: In January 1987, Bill Lang Jr. was assaulted while senior players on the Markham Waxers Junior B team tried to make him strip and masturbate on the bus

233

234 CROSSING THE LINE

during a rookie initiation. In September 1988, Art West and Pat Mazzoli were found guilty of assault and given an absolute discharge. Lang and his parents say they alerted the OHA to the issue of initiations, but no action was taken.

- Czechoslovakia: In January 1987, a bench-clearing brawl instigated by the Canadian National Junior Team at the World Championships made headlines around the world, and re-enforced the perception that Canadians are consumed with violence in hockey. Coaches Pat Burns and Bert Templeton were suspended by the CHA, but both continue to flourish in other hockey organizations.

- Montreal, Quebec: In 1989, minor hockey coach Stephane Valois was charged with sexual assault. In April 1990 he was convicted and sentenced to five months in jail.

- Toronto, Ontario: In December 1990, Ed Palacios, a long-time coach in the Metropolitan Toronto Hockey League, who coached for Leaside, was convicted after over one hundred charges of sexual assault were laid. Players on the team said he always chose the nicest-looking boys, and gave them special favours.

- Hamilton, Ontario: In May 1991, minor hockey coach James Hutchison was charged and convicted on several counts of sexual assault when a player came forward about abuse that occurred from 1985 to 1990. The player had approached police in 1985, and no charges were laid, though Hutchison was warned that they were watching him. Several more players came forward, and a civil suit by the families of players followed in December 1993.

- Drummondville, Quebec: In 1991, Jean Begin, coach of the major junior Drummondville Voltigeurs, was sentenced to six months in jail for sexually assaulting young boys who frequented the arena in which he coached. He was married and had two children. Upon release from prison, he committed suicide.

- Sault Ste. Marie, Ontario: On January 17, 1993, Jarret Reid, assistant captain of the Sault Greyhounds, was charged with sexual assault after his former girlfriend went to the police. In June 1993, twenty-one additional charges were laid, including five sexual assaults, nine assaults causing bodily harm, two break and enters, one uttering a death threat, and two breaches of bail after police interviewed another girlfriend. In July 1995, Reid was acquitted on the first charge, and in September 1995 pleaded guilty to sexual assault, assault, assault causing bodily harm, and break and enter. He was sentenced to nine months in jail, and served three. In April 1997, Reid knowingly broke American law by crossing the border illegally to play on the CIAU All-Star hockey team as a member of the St. Francis Xavier Xmen. That same month, Reid was charged with three counts of assault and one count of breach of recognizance. In October 1997, Reid pleaded guilty to one count of assault, then two weeks later reversed his plea. In February 1998, Reid was sentenced to five months in Pictou County Correctional Centre.

- Chatham, Ontario: In October 1993, an initiation party was held for the Tilbury Hawks Jr. team. In January 1994, 135 sex-crime charges were laid against senior players, owners, managers, coaches, and trainers. In June 1994, Ed Fiala, the captain of the team, and Paul Everaert, the trainer, were convicted of performing an indecent act and fined $6,000 in total, sentenced to two years' probation, and were not allowed to be in an arena, or work as a coach, manager, trainer, or owner for three years.

- London, Ontario: On December 18, 1995, a thirteen-year-old Kemptville minor was charged with assault and assault causing bodily harm after an on-ice brawl. He broke another player's jaw and a tooth. The minor was sentenced to one years' probation, put in custody of a half-way house, and banned from organized hockey for one year.

- Milton, Ontario: On January 14, 1996, David Aussem of the Tier 2 Junior Milton Merchants used his hockey stick to attack Chris Heron of the Bramalea Blues during a warm-up before their game. Aussem had to skate across the ice to cross-check Heron, who was knocked unconscious. Aussem was convicted of assault with a weapon and common assault (he also punched the Blues' general manager while off the ice), and received eighteen months' probation and one hundred hours of community work in amateur hockey involving speaking out about "undue violence."

- Calgary, Alberta: On August 23, 1996, Sheldon Kennedy gave a statement of fact to Calgary City Police, alleging several sexual assaults by former Swift Current Bronco coach Graham James. On January 2, 1997, James pleaded guilty to over three hundred counts involving Kennedy, and another fifty with a second complainant. On October 2, 1997, two more sexual-assault charges were laid against James after a former player came forward, from the days when James coached minor hockey in Winnipeg. The player was fourteen at the time. On January 14, 1997, former Broncos player Darren McLean alleged that James had paid players to have sex with girls and videotaped them. No investigation followed.

- Calgary, Alberta: In January, 1997, minor hockey coach Rob Allabee was charged with two counts of sexual assault, one count of sexual exploitation, and one count of forcible confinement after two boys (one of them a hockey player) came forward. Allabee also sat on the board of directors for the Calgary Minor Hockey Association. On May 27, 1998, Allabee was sentenced, after being convicted on the sexual-exploitation charge, to two and a half years in jail. He awaits trial on one of the sexual assault charges and the forcible confinement charge.

• Prince Rupert, British Columbia: On March 16, 1997, Arnold Douglas White, coach of the local minor hockey team committed suicide after he was charged with sexually abusing five players.

• Cold Lake, Alberta: In August, 1997, Barclay MacFie, a former junior player with the St. Albert Saints, the Red Deer Rustlers, and the Hobema Hawks, was charged with first-degree murder, kidnapping, sexual assault, and assault causing bodily harm, after his wife, Carol Meredith, was dragged kicking and screaming from her relative's home. Later that week, her body was found in MacFie's truck. MacFie frequently instigated fights on ice, and was violent in the dressing room after games, earning record penalty minutes during his junior career. In May 1998, MacFie was convicted of first-degree murder.

• Winnipeg, Manitoba: On October 2, 1997, two more charges of sexual abuse were laid against convicted sex abuser Graham James, after players who played for James in the 1970s when he coached minor hockey came forward to police. In February 1998, James pleaded guilty, his new sentence to be served concurrently with his existing sentence.

• Kitchener, Ontario: In October 1997, major junior general manager of the Kitchener Rangers, Ken Ahara, was fired as director of operations for the national under-seventeen hockey team by CHA president Murray Costello. He was relieved of his duties with the Rangers later in the same week and barred from the OHL. Ahara was alleged to have taken three prospective players into a hotel room one at a time in May 1997 and told them to strip to the waist. He told them he wanted to feel their muscles and see how strong they were.

The players alleged he touched their upper bodies in an improper manner.

• Toronto, Ontario: On November 13, 1997, an assistant coach with the East Enders, a MTHL AA atom team, told the team they were "fucking little cunts" after they lost a game. He was suspended for one week, and apologized to the team. On December 28, other coaches with the team told the players they were "fucking losers" who couldn't make a "fucking house league team," adding they had wasted their "fucking gas money." These coaches received no sanctions and apologized, saying they would exercise a zero-tolerance plan on swearing.

• Lindsay, Ontario: In November 1997, Bryan Jacksie, coach of the Double-A major peewee Central Ontario Wolves, resigned from his post when the Ontario Hockey Federation launched an investigation into Jacksie's thirty-seven convictions, which included charges for drunk driving, assault, and two assaults causing bodily harm. Earlier the Ontario Minor Hockey Association was alerted to his record but did not do a criminal record check. In December, the OHF cleared him to coach, but the Wolves did not renew his contract.

• Cobourg, Ontario: On December 22, 1997, during a pre-game warm-up, a fight broke out between the Ajax Axemen and Cobourg Cougars, a Tier 2 Junior team. Marcus Quinn of the Axemen suffered a fractured skull after, he said, an opposing player knocked him to the ice with a punch, and his coach had a tendon and nerves severed in his ankle during the melee. Police are investigating. No officials were on the ice, though they were nearby when the fight broke out. The OHA has implemented a rule that states OHA officials must be on the ice during all warm-ups.

• Toronto, Ontario: In May, 1998, the Ontario Hockey League suspended Jesse Boulerice of the Plymouth Whalers for the

1998-99 season after he attacked Guelph Storm player Andrew Long. Long sustained a concussion, broken nose, two other broken facial bones, cuts requiring twenty stitches, and two black eyes after Boulerice delivered a two-handed slash to the face during a play-off game. Long was unable to join his team at the Memorial Cup, but since Boulerice was in his last year of junior play, the suspension will have little or no consequence to his playing time next year.

• Moncton, New Brunswick: On May 22, 1998, Tom Keswick, a former minor hockey coach, was sentenced to fourteen months in jail for sexually assaulting three players. He pleaded guilty to charges of sexual indecency and gross indecency. The offences occurred in the 1970s, when the victims were thirteen years old.

# Appendix B: List of Incidents Compiled by the CHA's Director of Rules and Regulations

The list below contains only some of the many incidents compiled by Mike McGraw of the CHA during the first year of the Speak Out! program (1997-1998 season).

- A team personnel member asked teenage boys to remove their shirts and pants during recruiting interviews so that he could check their muscle tone.

- A black player appealed to move from one association to another due to relentless racial harassment.

- A pre-novice player was grabbed and thrown to the ground beside the bench after a "bad shift." The player is still in counselling for post-traumatic-stress disorder, his work at school has suffered, and his parents are pressing assault charges. The coach was permitted to remain with the team and the player moved to a lower team.

- A concerned parent observed a coach slash a player across the back of his pants during a practice.

- A novice player was told to "quit slamming your stick on the ice while I'm talking or I'll break it over your fucking head."

- A goaltender with a history of seizures was kneed in the head while leaving his net to freeze the puck during the game. The trainer suspected a concussion, but on escorting the player to the bench was met by the coach who would not let the player leave the game and told him not to "pull this shit on me – get your equipment back on and get back in net." The player was forced to finish the game.

- A minor hockey association sought a counsellor for a number of male players who had been victims of sexual assault at the hands of their coach. One of the players, now an adult, would not let his son play minor hockey, as he could not bring himself to enter, or even drive past, an arena.

- Players inserted toothpaste in another player's rectum as part of an initiation ritual.

- A player who had a "bad shift" was confronted by his coach, who verbally abused the player. The player responded by swearing back at his coach, at which point the coach grabbed him by the throat and threw him into the boards. Although there were over two hundred adults watching this event, including two police officers, no police report was made until the Kids Help Phone and the CHA were contacted.

- The parents of a young black player removed him from hockey due to the ongoing use of the "N-word" on the ice.

- A volunteer walked into an arena and was confronted by a woman who wondered why her ex-husband was coaching an atom team. When the volunteer asked why this was a problem, the woman informed him that her husband was a convicted pedophile. This was later confirmed to be correct.

- A player who had taken a questionable penalty returned to the bench where he was shoved in the back to the middle of the bench, yelled at for being "stupid," and then grabbed by the collar and thrown further down the bench.

• A coach of an atom team used the word "cunt" to refer to girls on the opposing, integrated team.

• A coach, frustrated at his team's "lack of toughness," told one player, in front of the entire team, to "go home and suck your mother's tit."

• A player had a run-in with an opponent on the ice. After the game, he was confronted by the opponent in the parking lot, and the opponent threw a punch. The players began to fight. The opponent's father showed up, grabbed the other boy, and began to punch him. The opponent's sister also showed up and began to punch him. Parents broke up the fight, the police were called, and the player visited the hospital for treatment of bruises to his eye, orbital bone, head, and cuts to his lip and mouth. An insurance claim was made to the CHA.

• The verbal abuse which a minor hockey coach heaped upon an official was dismissed as "nothing worse than you would hear sitting behind the bench during a Junior A game." The official had to take a leave of absence.

• Over 40 per cent of the officials in a region quit, due largely to the verbal abuse they were subjected to by parents and coaches.

• The coach of a minor team showed up at the home of a novice-level player who had requested his release, and when the boy's father answered the door, he threw the player's registration certificate at the father, with the boy watching, and screamed, "good riddance, we don't need you!" The boy was subsequently treated by a physician for stomach problems due to stress.

• A player who was taking his time getting dressed after a game was locked in the dressing room by his coach. The coach walked to the lobby, gave the key to the boy's father, and told him to go get his son when he was ready. The boy's father arrived just as his son was climbing through a heating vent to escape.

• An official, during a game involving a bilingual girls' team, told the players on the bench "not to speak French, I hate it."

• After a brawl broke out following a midget-level game, and players sat in the dressing room, nursing black eyes and cuts while the police arrived to maintain order, the coaches of both teams engaged in a furious fight that had to be broken up by volunteers.

• A team of adolescents was shown pornographic magazines as an incentive to win hockey games. More wins, more porn.

• A scout was charged with sexual assault after adolescent players spent the night at his house and were forced to shower and sleep with him.

• A group of midget-level players were forced, by their coaches, to consume beer on a bus trip home from a tournament as part of an initiation rite for the new players. Players who refused to participate were ridiculed and ostracized by players and coaches and eventually quit the team.

• A minor hockey executive, upon receiving a telephone call from a concerned parent who inquired as to what the association was doing to prevent abuse and harassment responded, "You have nothing to worry about – we don't have any faggots here."

• A novice-level coach was removed from his duties for verbally abusing seven- to nine-year-old boys, including swearing,

making sexist remarks, intimidation, ridiculing, and screaming. Two months later, one of the parents who was instru-
mental in having the coach removed discovered that he was
coaching young boys again in the same city.

- A player who talked back to his coach on the bench was
  grabbed by the back of his head. The coach slammed his head
  into the screen attached to the boards.

- A player tried out for a team and was one of the last cuts.
  Parents of some of the players who made the team encouraged the player's mother to appeal his cut from the team, as
  he was one of the best players during the tryouts. The player's
  mother appealed, and, as the coaching staff had not docu-
  mented any evaluations, or provided any rationale, the player
  was subsequently put on the team. The coaches ostracized
  the player and organized parents on the team in a letter-
  writing and telephone-call campaign aimed at the minor
  hockey president. The tone of hatred in the letters to the
  president were such that he told the mother he "feared for
  her and her son's lives."

- A coach presented a young male player with a Barbie doll at
  a team Christmas party. The humiliated player left the party
  in tears.

- The manager of a pee-wee team was charged with invitation
  to sexual touching.

- A black referee was subjected to racial abuse, including being
  called "nigger" by parents and players and being physically
  threatened by a player.

- A coach permitted both boys and girls on an integrated team
  to shower at the same time, and another forced adolescent
  players to shower at the rink, even if they didn't want to.

- A former team trainer and long-time hockey volunteer and teaching assistant was convicted of sexual assault of minors. One victim committed suicide, and it is alleged that several other individuals who had been on the man's teams and committed suicide were also his victims.

- A coach stepped on the hands of a player who was stretching on the dressing room floor, then knocked down a row of sticks and ordered the player to pick them up. When the player refused, the coach grabbed him and lifted him off the ground and up against the wall.

- Young players were investigated for a ritual in which they held down other players and slapped their genitals in the other players' faces.

- A team official, in refusing to release a player, commented, "He's my player. I own him. He's mine. He goes where I say he does."

- A team official received a letter from a long-time volunteer who he had met several times at an out-of-town tournament. The letter requested a picture of his family for his photo album as a souvenir of past times. The volunteer proceeded to explain in the letter that he was incarcerated while awaiting sentencing on over fifteen charges of sexual assault.

- A middle aged coach befriended a child on his team who was new in town. The coach spent time with the boy on weekends, taking him and other players to movies, etc. On a road trip, the coach purchased over $400 in gifts and equipment for the player, and shared a room alone with him. The coach also had extended telephone conversations with the boy on the phone at nights. When the boy threatened to run away from home and live with his coach, his parents monitored his phone calls, and taped the coach describing his genitals to the player. The player's parents also caught the coach waiting for the boy behind their house. There was not enough evidence for the police to proceed.

- A coach made his young players skate around the face-off circles, in the middle of which he had placed buckets. The players were not permitted to stop skating until they vomited into the buckets.

- Parents calling in to express concern over physical and emotional abuse commented on many occasions that they would have reported their concerns to the police, child protection agencies, or the local minor hockey association "if it wasn't hockey." Several proceed to add that, "If this had happened at school, at the mall, or in another sport, I would have reported it immediately. But it's hockey, and I don't want my kid to get blackballed and never play again."

# Notes

INTRODUCTION

1. Gordon Kirke, *Players First* (Toronto: Canadian Hockey League, 1997), p. 3.
2. Peggy Reeves Sanday, *A Woman Scorned: Acquaintance Rape on Trial* (New York: Doubleday, 1996), pp. 25-26.
3. Linda Campbell et al., *The Marymound Model: A Sequential Approach to the Treatment of Male Adolescent Sex Offenders and Sex Abuse Victims* (Winnipeg: Marymound Inc. Family Resource Centre, 1992), pp. 71-100.
4. Frederick Mathews, *The Invisible Boy: Revisioning the Victimization of Male Children and Teens* (Ottawa: Health Canada, 1997), pp. 27-38.

CHAPTER 1: Memorial Cup Celebrations

1. The author's description of the following events, and the direct quotes from the parties involved, are taken from court records.

CHAPTER 2: Young Gods

1. Campbell et al., *The Marymound Model: A Sequential Approach to the Treatment of Male Adolescent Sex Offenders and Sex Abuse Victims*, pp. 71-100.

2. Steven M. Ortiz, "Traveling with the Ball Club: A Code of Conduct for Wives Only," *Symbolic Interaction*, vol. 20, no.3 (1997), and Erving Goffman, *On the Characteristics of Total Institutions* (Garden City, N.Y.: Anchor/Doubleday, 1961), pp. 1-124.

CHAPTER 3: Analysing the Game

1. Leola Johnston, "Hertz Don't It? Corporate Ideas About Race in the Making of O.J. Simpson" (paper presented at the North American Society of the Sociology of Sport conference, Birmingham, Alabama, November 1996).
2. Garland F. White, Janet Katz, Kathryn Scarborough, "The Impact of Professional Football Games upon Violent Assaults on Women," *Violence and Victims*, vol. 7, no. 2 (1992), pp. 157-71.

CHAPTER 4: Baptized a Hawk

1. Ontario Hockey Association, *Constitution Regulations and Rules of Competition Manual* (Cambridge: updated annually), J23.
2. Mark C. Carnes, *Secret Ritual and Manhood in Victorian America* (New Haven: Yale University Press, 1989), pp. 67-150.
3. Alan Klein, "Of Muscles and Men," *The Sciences*, vol. 33, no. 6 (November/December 1993).
4. Susan Faludi, "The Naked Citadel," *The New Yorker* (September 1994).
5. Brian Pronger, *The Arena of Masculinity: Sports, Homosexuality, and the Meaning of Sex* (Toronto: Summerhill Press, 1990).
6. Mathews, *Youth Gangs on Youth Gangs* (Ottawa: Solicitor General Canada, 1993).

CHAPTER 5: When You Know You Just Have To Score

1. The author's description of the following events, and the direct quotes from the parties involved, are taken from court records.
2. See note above.
3. Reeves Sanday, *A Woman Scorned: Acquaintance Rape on Trial*, pp. 25-26.

4. Todd W. Crosset, Jeffrey R. Benedict, Mark A. McDonald, "Male Student-Athletes Reported for Sexual Assault: A Survey of Campus Police Departments and Judicial Affairs Offices," *Journal of Sport and Social Issues* (May 1995).
5. Jeffrey R. Benedict and Alan Klein, "Arrest and Conviction Rates for Athletes Accused of Sexual Assault," *Sociology of Sport Journal*, vol. 14, no.1 (1997).

CHAPTER 6: The Empty Net, Part One

1. The author's description of the following events, and the direct quotes from the parties involved, are taken from court records.
2. Reeves Sanday, *Fraternity Gang Rape: Sex, Brotherhood, and Privilege on Campus* (New York: New York University Press, 1990).
3. Reeves Sanday, *A Woman Scorned: Acquaintance Rape on Trial*, pp. 189-93.
4. Ibid.
5. Steven M. Ortiz, "Control Games: The Dynamics of Marital Power in Sport Families" (paper presented at the annual meeting of the American Sociological Association, Toronto, August 1997).

CHAPTER 9: Changing the Line-Up

1. Peter Donnelly, "Child Labour, Sport Labour: Applying Child Labour Laws to Sport" (paper presented at the North American Society of the Sociology of Sport conference, Birmingham, Alabama, November 1996).
2. Sandra Kirby, Celia Brackenridge, "Coming to Terms: Sexual Abuse in Sport" (unpublished manuscript), pp. 5-10.
3. Lorraine Greaves, Sandra Kirby, "Le Jeu Indit: Harcelment Axuel dans le Sport," *Reserche Feminist*, vol. 10, no. 1 (1997).
4. Lorraine Street, *The Screening Handbook: Protecting Clients, Staff, and the Community* (Ottawa: 1996).
5. Brenda Zeman, *To Run with Longboat: Twelve Stories of Indian Athletes in Canada* (Edmonton: GMS2 Ventures, 1988).

# Bibliography

Ayres, Boswell A. and Joan Spade. "Fraternities and Collegiate Rape Culture: Why Are Some Fraternities More Dangerous Places for Women?" *Gender & Society.* Vol. 10, no. 2. April 1996, pp. 133-147.

Barnard, Sandie. *Good Sports Don't Hurt – Sexual Harassment Does.* Toronto: Ministry of Culture, Citizenship and Recreation, 1996.

Benedict, Jeffrey R. *Public Heroes, Private Felons: Athletes and Crimes Against Women.* Boston: Northwestern University Press, 1997.

Benedict, Jeffrey R. and Alan Klein. "Arrest and Conviction Rates for Athletes Accused of Sexual Assault." *Sociology of Sport Journal.* Vol. 14, no. 1, 1997.

Berke, Phyllis and Sue Vail. *Walking the Talk.* Toronto: Ministry of Culture and Recreation, 1995.

Bloom, Gordon A. and Michael Smith. "Hockey Violence: A Test of Cultural Spillover Theory." *Sport Sociology Journal.* Vol. 13, no. 1, 1996, pp. 65-77.

Bolton, Sue, et al. "Queen's Football Makes 'Choices.'" *Action Bulletin.* The Canadian Association for Women and Physical Activity. Winter 1997, pp. 9-10.

Brackenridge, Celia. "Dangerous Relations: Men, Women, and Sexual Abuse in Sport." Inaugural Lecture, Department of Leisure Management, Cheltenham and Gloucester College of Higher Education, 17 March 1997.

Burton Nelson, Mariah. *The Stronger Women Get, The More Men Love Football: Sexism and the American Culture of Sports*. New York: Harcourt Brace, 1994.

CAAWS Collective Action to Address Harassment. *Harassment in Sport: A Guide to Policies, Procedures, and Resources*. Ottawa: Canadian Association for Women, Sport and Physical Activity, 1994.

Campbell, Linda, et al. *The Marymound Model: A Sequential Approach to the Treatment of Male Adolescent Sexual Offenders and Sexual Abuse Victims*. Winnipeg: Marymound, Inc. Family Resource Centre, 1992.

Carnes, Mark C. *Secret Ritual and Manhood in Victorian America*. New Haven: Yale University Press, 1989.

Crosset, Todd W., Jeffrey R. Benedict, Mark A. McDonald. "Male Student-Athletes Reported for Sexual Assault: A Survey of Campus Police Departments and Judicial Affairs Offices." *Journal of Sport and Social Issues*. May 1995.

Donnelly, Peter. "Child Labour, Sport Labour: Applying Child Labour Laws to Sport." Paper presented at the North American Society of the Sociology of Sport Conference, Birmingham, Alabama, November 1996.

Donnelly, Peter and Robert Sparks. "Child Sexual Abuse in Sport." Hamilton: McMaster University, Departments of Kinesiology and Sociology, 1997.

Donnelly, Peter and Kevin Young. "The Construction and Confirmation of Identity in Sport Subcultures." *Sociology of Sport Journal*. 1988, pp. 223-240.

Faludi, Susan. "The Naked Citadel." *The New Yorker*. September 1994.

Frintner, Mary Pat and Laurna Rubinson. "Acquaintance Rape: The Influence of Alcohol, Fraternity Membership, and Sports Team Membership." *Journal of Sex Education and Theory*. Vol. 19, no. 4, 1993, pp. 272-284.

Goffman, Erving. *On the Characteristics of Total Institutions*. Garden City, N.Y.: Anchor/Doubleday, 1961.

Government of British Columbia. Sport B.C., Coach's Association of B.C., Promotions Plus. "What Parents Can Do About

Harassment in Sport." Available through Sport Safe Program, Vancouver office of Sport B.C.

Gruneau, Richard and David Whitson. *Hockey Night in Canada: Sport, Identity, and Cultural Politics.* Toronto: Garamond Press, 1993.

Hall, Darlene and Fred Mathews. *The Development of Sexual Behaviour Problems in Children and Youth.* Toronto: Central Toronto Youth Services, The Creche Child and Family Centre, 1996.

Harassment and Abuse in Sport Collective, the Canadian Association for the Advancement of Women and Sport and Physical Activity, and the Canadian Hockey Association. *Speak Out! . . . Act Now!: A Guide to Preventing and Responding to Abuse and Harassment for Sport Clubs and Associations.* Ottawa, 1998.

Johnston, Leola. "Hertz Don't It? Corporate Ideas About Race in the Making of O. J. Simpson." Paper presented at the North American Society of the Sociology of Sport conference, Birmingham, Alabama, November 1996.

Kirby, Sandra and Celia Brackenridge. "Coming to Terms: Sexual Abuse in Sport." Unpublished manuscript.

Kirke, Gordon. *Players First.* Toronto: Canadian Hockey League, 1997.

Klein, Alan. "Of Muscles and Men," *The Sciences.* Vol. 33, no. 6. November/December 1993.

Lanchberry Sheldon, et al. *Fair Play Means Safety for All: A Guide to Understanding Abuse and Harassment for Parents and Guardians.* Calgary: Canadian Hockey Association, 1997.

Malszecki, Gregory. "He Shoots! He Scores! Metaphors of War in Sport and the Political Linguistics of Virility." Ph.D. dissertation, York University, Graduate Program in Social and Political Thought, 1995.

Mathews, Frederick. *The Invisible Boy: Revisioning the Victimization of Male Children and Teens.* Ottawa: Health Canada, 1997.

Mathews, Frederick. *Youth Gangs on Youth Gangs.* Toronto and Ottawa: Central Toronto Youth Services and the Solicitor General of Canada, 1993.

McGregor, Marg, et al. "Collective Action to Address Harassment in Sport." Ottawa: Canadian Association for Women, Sport, and Physical Activity, 1997. (Quarterly updates available).

Messner, Michael. "Studying Up on Sex." *Sociology of Sport Journal.* Vol. 13, no. 1, 1996, pp. 221-237.

Miedzian, Myriam. *Boys Will Be Boys: Breaking the Links Between Masculinity and Violence.* New York: Doubleday, 1991.

Ontario Hockey Association. *Constitution Regulations and Rules of Competition Manual.* Cambridge, updated annually.

Ortiz, Steven M. "Control Games: The Dynamics of Marital Power in Sport Families." Paper presented at the annual general meeting of the American Sociological Association, Toronto, August 1997.

Ortiz, Steven M. "Traveling with the Ball Club: A Code of Conduct for Wives Only." *Symbolic Interaction.* Vol. 20, no.3.

Ortiz, Steven M. "When Happiness Ends and Coping Begins: The Private Pain of the Professional Athlete's Wife." Ph.D. dissertation, University of California, Berkeley, Faculty of Sociology, 1993.

Parrot, Andrea, et al. "A Rape Awareness and Prevention Model for Male Athletes." *Journal of American College Health.* January 1994, pp. 179-184.

Pronger, Brian. *The Arena of Masculinity: Sport, Homosexuality, and the Meaning of Sex.* Toronto: Summerhill Press, 1990.

Reeves Sanday, Peggy. *A Woman Scorned: Acquaintance Rape on Trial.* New York: Doubleday, 1996.

Reeves Sanday, Peggy. *Fraternity Gang Rape: Sex, Brotherhood, and Privilege on Campus.* New York: New York University Press, 1990

Robertson, Sheila. "Coaching, Trust, and Sex." *Coaches Report.* Vol. 3, no. 3, 1997, pp. 4-7.

Strachan, Dorothy and Paul Thomlinson. *Power and Ethics.* Ottawa: National Coaching Certification Program, 1997.

White, Garland F., Janet Katz, and Kathryn Scarborough. "The Impact of Professional Football Games upon Violent Assaults on Women." *Violence and Victims.* Vol. 7, no. 2, 1992, pp. 157-71.

Young, Kevin and Michael Smith. "Mass Media Treatment of Violence in Sports and Its Effects." *Current Psychology: Research & Reviews.* Vol. 7, no. 4. Winter 1988-89, pp. 298-311.

Young, Kevin. "Sport and Collective Violence." *Exercise and Sport Sciences Reviews.* Vol. 19, 1991, pp. 539-587.

Zeman, Brenda. *To Run with Longboat: Twelve Stories of Indian Athletes in Canada*. Edited by David Williams. Edmonton: GMS2 Ventures, 1988.